VIDEO PEDAGOGY IN ACTION

Combining video analysis with the well-known Gradual Release of Responsibility (GRR) model, this book offers teacher educators a fresh perspective and a new tool for supporting teachers' learning and reflection. The clearly articulated and useful framework shifts the focus away from children and toward teachers' thinking about their own teaching practice. Interwoven with practical examples of the framework in use, this book identifies ways that teachers and teacher educators can foster more productive kinds of reflection about video-recorded classroom interactions and support preservice and inservice teachers. Offering key tools such as templates for reflection, video viewing guides, self-analysis checklists, and activities, this book moves the field forward and establishes video reflection and the GRR process as critical tools for teacher reflection, professional development, and effective teaching and learning.

Mary B. McVee is Professor of Literacy Education and Director of the Center for Literacy & Reading Instruction (CLaRI) at the University at Buffalo, SUNY, USA.

Lynn E. Shanahan is Associate Professor of Literacy Education at University at Buffalo, SUNY, USA.

H. Emily Hayden is Assistant Professor of Literacy Education at Iowa State University, Ames, USA.

Fenice B. Boyd is Professor and Chair of the Instruction and Teacher Education Department at University of South Carolina, USA.

P. David Pearson is former Dean and Professor in Language and Literacy and Human Development at the University of California Berkeley, USA.

VIDEO PEDAGOGY IN ACTION

Critical Reflective Inquiry
Using the Gradual Release
of Responsibility Model

*Mary B. McVee, Lynn E. Shanahan,
H. Emily Hayden, Fenice B. Boyd,
and P. David Pearson with
Jennifer Reichenberg*

Routledge
Taylor & Francis Group

NEW YORK AND LONDON

First published 2018
by Routledge
711 Third Avenue, New York, NY 10017

and by Routledge
2 Park Square, Milton Park, Abingdon, Oxon, OX14 4RN

Routledge is an imprint of the Taylor & Francis Group, an informa business

© 2018 Taylor & Francis

The right of Mary B. McVee, Lynn E. Shanahan, H. Emily Hayden, Fenice B. Boyd, and P. David Pearson to be identified as authors of this work has been asserted by them in accordance with sections 77 and 78 of the Copyright, Designs and Patents Act 1988.

Library of Congress Cataloging-in-Publication Data
Names: McVee, Mary B., author.
Title: Video pedagogy in action: critical reflective inquiry using the gradual release of responsibility model / by Mary B. McVee, Lynn E. Shanahan, H. Emily Hayden, Fenice B. Boyd, P. David Pearson; with Jennifer Sharples Reichenberg.
Description: New York, NY: Routledge, 2018. | Includes bibliographical references and index.
Identifiers: LCCN 2017034992 | ISBN 9781138039797 (hardback) | ISBN 9781138039803 (pbk.) | ISBN 9781315175638 (ebook)
Subjects: LCSH: Reflective teaching. | Interaction analysis in education. | Teachers—In-service training—Audio-visual aids. | Video tapes in education.
Classification: LCC LB1025.3 .M398 2018 | DDC 371.102—dc23
LC record available at https://lccn.loc.gov/2017034992

ISBN: 978-1-138-03979-7 (hbk)
ISBN: 978-1-138-03980-3 (pbk)
ISBN: 978-1-315-17563-8 (ebk)

Typeset in Bembo
by codeMantra

Tell me, what is it you plan to do with your one wild and precious life?

~Mary Oliver

This book is dedicated to the memory and continuing legacy of Mary Alyce Pearson whose vibrant spirit personified the principles written upon these pages: to live and work in community and for community, to strive to become a better teacher and a better person, to develop quiet reflection and introspection, to stand for and work for justice, and to care for others and listen to their cares.

CONTENTS

FIGURES AND TABLES

Figures

Tables

PREFACE

Even though there is long-standing use of video in education to develop pre-service and inservice teachers' reflective practices, teachers and those requiring teachers to reflect on video (e.g., teacher educators, state departments of education, or school administrators) must be mindful that it is not the video that makes the difference. It is the practice of reflective inquiry and engagement with video by the teacher that makes the difference. We, like many other teacher educators, have realized that at times our preservice and inservice teachers were reflecting at superficial levels—revisiting events but without the deeper perplexity and pondering that Dewey, Schon, and others have long called for teachers to engage in.

Our goal in writing *Video Pedagogy in Action: Critical Reflective Inquiry Using the Gradual Release of Responsibility Model* was to define a specific structural framework for using video with individuals and groups across educational settings, through the application of the Gradual Release of Responsibility (GRR) Model as originally developed by Pearson and Gallagher (1985). In the book, we include interwoven examples and chapters that establish a well-articulated framework for video reflection that draws upon the GRR. We hope that the book will provide direction in using video to mediate teacher reflection.

Such a goal is extremely relevant, given that many scholars have posited that a guiding framework for targeted reflection is not only necessary but essential if preservice and inservice teachers are to move beyond technical description of their teaching actions toward critical reflective analysis of student responses and teaching interactions. We posit that the GRR is an effective structure to help scaffold teachers' reflections, so they can consider alternative perspectives, modifications, and actions in teaching. The GRR has the added advantage of being familiar to many preservice and inservice teachers because it is so often used in textbooks, district guidelines, journal articles, and professional development to help explain literacy learning, teaching, and growth over time.

Examining the use of video in the reflective process is timely due to the increased attention video reflection is receiving for some state certification requirements (e.g., Education Teaching Performance Assessment, edTPA). Improvement initiatives for practicing teachers, such as National Board Certification, have long had similar requirements for video recording and reflecting. The reflective analysis mandated by such high-stakes initiatives requires teachers to do more than simply describe events in a teaching interaction. Detailed analysis demands teachers to develop inquiry habits of mind, notice evidence of student learning, and then apply what is learned from these inquiries to develop responsive teaching actions. This type of reflection, which we call critical reflective inquiry, results in "more responsive and dynamic teaching, or adaptive expertise" (Hayden, Rundell, & Smyntek-Gworek, 2013, p. 4) because it signifies a teacher who can deliver instruction, notice student responses and evidence or lack of evidence of learning (both formal and informal), and adapt teaching actions based on evidence. Teacher educators and professional development initiatives in school settings have struggled to keep pace with the increases in mandated video records of teaching and the desired outcome of producing reflective practitioners. This book helps to fill that gap.

Several features of this book make it especially useful for preservice and inservice teachers who are learning to reflect on video. These features are:

- A focus on Gradual Release of Responsibility, a framework many teachers are familiar with in their work with children. We shift this focus away from children toward teachers' thinking about their own teaching practice.
- Practical examples and illustrations of video analysis of teaching. These examples and illustrations are deeply grounded in theories of reflection introduced in the text and supported by research studies carried out by the authors.
- Stop and Think sections in each chapter. These segments serve as a useful pedagogical tool for instructors who use this book in their courses, and questions help to guide or prompt reflection from the readers, but with reference to theory and research to support effective practices.
- Reflection templates, video viewing guides, self-analysis checklists, activities, and other practical guides are included in the Appendices

In Chapter 1, Pearson traces the historical origins of the GRR and its influence on the field situating the GRR in larger literacy traditions and giving a "behind the scenes look" at the development and various iterations of the GRR Model. Chapter 2 introduces readers to the GRR Model in the context of teacher reflective inquiry, particularly video reflection. We then elaborate our model of reflective video pedagogy, delineating critical reflective inquiry as the foundation of adaptive expertise. Chapter 3 explores how the GRR works within a Community of Practice (Lave & Wenger, 1991) that functions as a safe place for risk-taking related to sharing one's own teaching practice publicly. Chapter 4 introduces a comprehensive definition of critical reflective inquiry, including a review of the major contributors to the construct (Dewey, 1933; Schon, 1983) and those who have built on their work (Rodgers, 2002a, b; Korthagen & Kessels, 1999). Once these foundational constructs have been introduced, we present chapters illustrating reflective video pedagogy in action.

In Chapters 5–7 the GRR Model is used with preservice and inservice teachers across settings of clinical practicums in university teacher education, school-based practicums, and professional development contexts in school settings including work with struggling readers and writers and students who speak multiple languages. In Chapter 5, we tackle the complexities of teaching that become visible through video reflection with examples of teachers using the four parts of reflective inquiry: Presence, Description, Analysis, and Experimentation. Chapter 6 addresses the shift in teacher education that calls for the use of video to serve as an artifact of teaching competence, and we challenge teacher educators to reflect on how they build a culture of reflection across their teacher education programs. In Chapter 7, we offer specifics about how a literacy coach strategically provides a variety of scaffolding techniques as she uses the GRR Model to coach an inservice teacher who works with diverse multilingual learners.

In Chapter 8 we issue a special challenge for teachers and teacher educators—to examine how positions and positioning play a role in viewing and interpreting video and classroom events, particularly when teaching raises positions and ideologies that rest on assumptions of race, class, gender, ethnicity, or language use.

We conclude in Chapter 9 with an invitation to consider the many models of the GRR presented in the book, and we revisit the most critical elements of the GRR Model and critical principles in reflective video pedagogy.

ACKNOWLEDGMENTS

We would like to acknowledge the Center for Literacy and Reading Instruction (CLaRI) at the University at Buffalo, SUNY for research and technical support related to the development of this book. In particular, thank you to all of the teachers, clinicians, and literacy specialists who participated in research studies, video study groups, and classroom discussions that helped to provide examples, anecdotes, activities, and models. You inspire us to continue reflecting upon our own teaching and working toward improvement.

Thank you to Katarina Silvestri, Chris Jarmark, and Marissa Pytlak for your editing prowess; the book is stronger from all those margin comments and Katarina's work with figures. Thank you to fellow Positioning Theory nerds: Nichole Barrett, Kate Haq, and Katarina Silvestri who read the never-ending chapter and provided feedback and support throughout.

A special thank you to Naomi Silverman at Routledge, who as editor extraordinaire, was instrumental in getting this book off the ground and helping to shape it in so many ways. For our finishing editor Karen Adler and editorial assistant Emma Ortega who were left to carry on the torch, we appreciate your patience and perseverance in helping us see this through until the end.

Jan Zhang was instrumental in formatting and assisting with artwork. Lillianna Zhang created awesome original artwork. We appreciate you both for lending your artistic talents.

We are profoundly grateful to our families, friends, and colleagues who helped us out along the way with support, encouragement, and, of course, a good meal now and again. No one writes a book on an empty stomach!

1

THE GENESIS OF THE GRADUAL RELEASE OF RESPONSIBILITY MODEL

The **Gradual Release of Responsibility (GRR)** Model is a cornerstone of this book. It is the pedagogical model we use to conceptualize, unpack, deliver, and synthesize our approach to teacher professional learning and reflection. Interestingly the model was developed not for adult learners but for K–12 students. It was the outgrowth of the work of a group of researchers at the Center for the Study of Reading in the late 1970s and early 1980s. We will share that genesis story shortly.

Since its publication by Pearson and Gallagher (1983a, 1983b) the GRR Model has been a significant and influential model in the literacy field (Pearson, 2013). It has demonstrated remarkable staying power, and if anything, only increased in use and application. An Ngram graph (See Figure 1.1) provides a visual of the increasing frequency of the term from 1983 to 2008 (the last date for which we have Ngram data).

To bring GRR up to date, a Google Scholar search conducted in mid-2017 turned up 164,000 hits for the term "gradual release of responsibility" in titles, articles, abstracts, books, chapters, and papers. The more restrictive term "gradual release of responsibility model" still yielded over 32,800 hits, indicating that the visual representation is also quite widely used.

A Brief History of the GRR

The Motivation for the Model

For Pearson and several of his colleagues (all but David were doctoral students when this quest began), including Jane Hansen (Hansen, 1981; Hansen & Pearson, 1983), Christine Gordon (Gordon, 1985; Gordon & Pearson, 1983), Taffy Raphael (Raphael & McKinney, 1983; Raphael & Pearson, 1985;

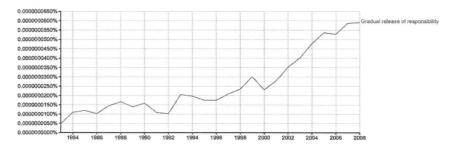

FIGURE 1.1   Ngram of "gradual release of responsibility" from 1983 to 2008.

Raphael & Wonnacut, 1985), and Meg Gallagher (Pearson & Gallagher, 1983a, 1983b), the GRR Model emerged gradually (fittingly!) from a search for some reasonable way to think about how explicit reading comprehension pedagogy could be used to respond to the startling revelations of Dolores Durkin's (1978–1979) classic finding that in the 1970s what was going on in our schools in the name of reading comprehension was neither effective nor instructive.

Basically, what Durkin found in her examination of over 17,997 minutes of instruction in the intermediate grades was that rather than teaching students *how* to understand, teachers were simply requiring students to answer questions. Comprehension instruction consisted of assessments and assignments: Teachers asked questions, and students answered them. The assumptions in this widespread default approach are (a) that students can answer the questions we ask them about the texts they read, and (b) if they cannot, they will improve their question-answering abilities if teachers just increase the amount of question-answering practice they get. The irony, of course, is that this approach simply perpetuates, perhaps even exacerbates, the gap between those who can and those who cannot answer questions successfully in the first place. Why? Because more practice allows those who **can** to refine their good practices and those who **cannot** to refine their maladaptive practices. Pearson and his colleagues were looking for an alternative to the "practice makes perfect (or imperfect)" model of pedagogy.

The Collegial Scaffolding

Fortunately for Pearson and his colleagues, others at the Center for the Study of Reading at the University of Illinois in the early 1980s shared their concern and their quest for more effective pedagogy. Most important, they encountered the work of Ann Brown and Joe Campione, who were using a Vygotskian (1978) perspective to conceptualize instruction; for them, learning occurred in the *zone of proximal development (ZPD)*—that magical space in which students encounter the helpful support of "more knowledgeable others," who can assist them in progressing from what they can accomplish *on their own* to what they can accomplish *with a little boost* from their friends. Ann and Joe introduced the group to another student, Annemarie Palincsar, who was conceptualizing a dissertation (which led to the now famous pedagogical routine known as reciprocal teaching) dealing with these very issues (e.g., Palincsar & Brown, 1984; Palincsar, Brown, & Martin, 1987).

Equally as important, Ann and Joe introduced the group to the recently coined construct of scaffolding from the work of Wood, Bruner, and Ross (1976) and the dynamic assessment practices of Reuven Feuerstein (Feuerstein, Rand, & Hoffman, 1979). Along with Brown and Campione's pedagogical research, the constructs of scaffolding and dynamic assessment were driven by the recently rediscovered Vygotskian socio-cognitive views of learning and development (Vygotsky, 1978), especially the ZPD. Scaffolding provided a powerful label for what it is that the more knowledgeable others could and should do when working in the ZPD. And dynamic assessment turned out to be a prescient way of thinking about what has evolved into formative assessment (Black & William, 1998). The key element in dynamic assessment is changing the question we ask about assessment. No longer do we view assessment as a measurement of how a child performs in comparison to the norm of similar children. Instead, in a dynamic assessment frame, we view assessment as an index of what a child can do when provided with different levels of "scaffolding." So, the question isn't, "Can a child can do X?" Instead, it is, "Under what conditions of scaffolding can a child do X?" This question is soon followed by, "How can I fade the scaffolds over time to lead to completely independent performance?"

The Visual Model

The visual model evolved over time in conversations with Meg, Taffy, Annemarie, Joe, and Ann. Joe actually had a precursor visual representation that somehow displayed something like the distribution of volume of task responsibility—what proportion of the responsibility pie is each taking. And one day, the idea came to David in a noontime conversation. It was just like the classic guns and butter production function curve he had learned about in Econ 1-A at Berkeley in the early 1960s. If we can conceptualize society's priorities as reflecting various combinations of producing food (butter) versus arms (guns), we can conceptualize comprehension task completion as requiring various combinations of student versus teacher responsibility: The more teachers do, the less students do and vice versa. So that's how the idea of plotting teacher responsibility on the Y-axis and student responsibility on the X-axis originated. As soon as we drew a picture of it (see Figure 1.2), it all made sense to us.

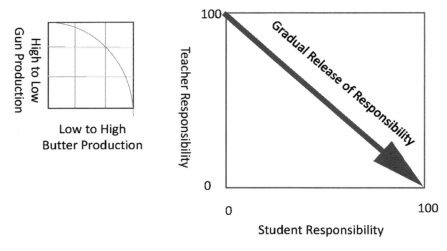

FIGURE 1.2 How guns and butter inspired the "Gradual Release of Responsibility."

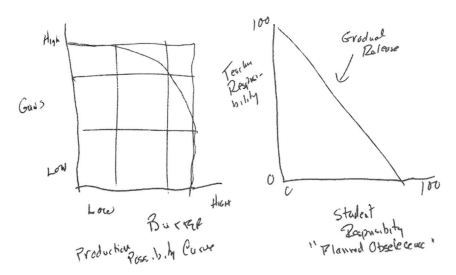

FIGURE 1.3 Facsimile of the original visual depiction of the Gradual Release of Responsibility (circa 1981 by P. David Pearson).

Of course, in those pre-PowerPoint days of the early 1980s, it did not look so polished; the original, literally drawn by David on a lunch napkin, resembled the depiction in Figure 1.3.

Another step forward for the GRR occurred in 1983 when David and Meg Gallagher wrote a piece for *Contemporary Educational Psychology*, entitled "The Instruction of Reading Comprehension."[1] Most important for GRR is that the

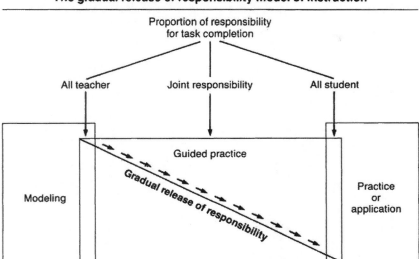

The gradual release of responsibility model of instruction

Proportion of responsibility
for task completion

All teacher   Joint responsibility   All student

Guided practice

Gradual release of responsibility

Modeling

Practice
or
application

From Pearson and Gallagher, 1983, after Campione, 1981.

FIGURE 1.4   The original published version of the GRR Model in *Contemporary Educational Psychology* in 1983.

1983 piece included the original published version of the model, complete with an acknowledgment to Joe Campione for inspiring its creation (see Figure 1.4).

In 1985 David wrote the first of many synthesis pieces on this body of research, this one for *The Reading Teacher*. Entitled "Changing the Face of Reading Comprehension," in it he unpacked the GRR more fully by illustrating the specific roles played by teachers and students in the work of Christine Gordon (Gordon, 1985; Gordon & Pearson, 1983) on drawing inferences and Taffy Raphael (Raphael & McKinney, 1983; Raphael & Pearson, 1985; Raphael & Wonnacott, 1985) on question–answer relationships (QARs). As Hansen, Gordon, and Raphael instantiated the GRR in pedagogical experiments with teachers and students, they became more specific about who did what. Table 1.1 illustrates just how the gradual release was accomplished in the work of Gordon and Raphael.

Over the years, the model has evolved and adapted to new players and new uses. But some of the key concepts from the model have survived throughout its thirty-four-year history. Among them are *Modeling* (a step in which the teacher—or another student—demonstrates how to do the task), *Guided Practice* (where the teacher and the student are sometimes jointly and sometimes separately responsible for enacting different steps in completing the task), and *Independent Practice* (where the teacher has, at least for the moment, completely

TABLE 1.1 Distributing Task Completion Responsibility in the Gradual Release Model

	Stages of Task Responsibility in Gordon's[a] Inference Task			
	Ask Question	Answer Question	Find Clues	Share Reasoning
Modeling	T	T	T	T
Guided practice	T	T	S	S
Guided practice	T	S	T	S
Independent application	T	S	S	S

	Stages of Task Responsibility in Raphael's[b] QAR Task			
	Ask Question	Answer Question	Assign QAR	Justify QAR
Modeling	T	T	T	T
Guided practice	T	T	T	S
Guided practice	T	T	S	S
Independent application	T	S	S	S
True ownership	S	S	S	S

T = Teacher responsibility, S = Student responsibility

a   After Gordon and Pearson (1983).
b   After Raphael (1981), Raphael and Pearson (1985).

released responsibility to the student(s)). We added a stage of *True Ownership* to Raphael's QAR work because the goal was ultimately to have students generate questions. Think of true ownership as a kind of "hyper-independence."

Enhancements in the Model

The model trudged along, pretty much in its classic 1983 form, for a couple of decades, but it was rendered more precise and detailed by a variety of research efforts. Two stand out in particular: *reciprocal teaching* (Palincsar & Brown, 1984) and *transactional strategies instruction* (Pressley, Almasi, et al., 1994; Pressley, El-Dinary, et al., 1992). Like Pearson and his colleagues, both Palincsar and Pressley were interested in responding to Durkin's classic discovery of nothing instructive about comprehension; so, they focused on developing either a routine (the four strategic activities of summarizing, questioning, clarifying, and predicting in reciprocal teaching) or a menu (the list of monitoring and fix-up strategies in transactional strategies instruction). And in the process of demonstrating the efficacy of their approaches, they helped us learn even more about the key characteristics of the GRR—explicit instruction, modeling, guided practice, scaffolding, independent practice (i.e., both application and use), collaborative efforts among students, and opportunities applying the repertoire to authentic texts and reading tasks.

As a consequence of this work and the work of many other scholars, in 2002, when Duke and Pearson, in a chapter summarizing our knowledge of comprehension instruction for teachers, used GRR as the basic model for teaching comprehension strategies, they were able to incorporate much of what others, most notably the reciprocal teaching and transactional strategies groups, had learned. Figure 1.5 illustrates the greater specificity of these advances in the model.

Almost a decade later, when Duke and Pearson, joined by Strachan and Billman (2011), revised their chapter on comprehension instruction, they offered yet a new version of the model (Figure 1.6) that more directly reflects the nature of the steps in the overall instructional approach they favored and, interestingly, situates most of what a teacher does to gradually release responsibility in the middle step of that approach.

Table 1.2 provides an example of what the scaffolds look like in each step in the original model between classroom teachers and children learning to read.

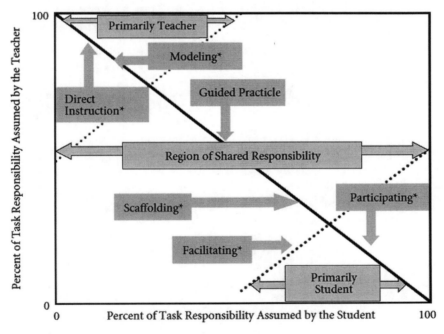

FIGURE 1.5   The model as depicted by Duke and Pearson in 2002. As one moves down the diagonal from upper left to lower right, students assume more, and teachers less, responsibility for task completion. There are three regions of responsibility: primarily teacher in the upper left corner, primarily student in the lower right, and shared responsibility in the center.

Source: This figure is adapted with permission from Pearson and Gallagher (1983); the asterisked terms are borrowed from Raphael and Au (1998).

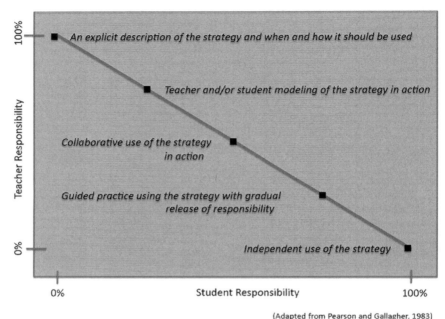

(Adapted from Pearson and Gallagher, 1983)

FIGURE 1.6 The model as depicted by Duke, Pearson, Strachan, Billman in 2011.

The Central Role of Scaffolding in the GRR Model

The scaffolding construct has resided at the core of the GRR Model since its inception. But we doubt that when Wood, Bruner, and Ross (1976) coined the scaffolding metaphor as a way of describing what expert tutors do to promote problem-solving among students, they could have imagined how popular the term would become as a way for educators to describe the pedagogical journey from teacher-dependent to student-independent learning.

The instant David read Wood et al.'s account, he was smitten. It captured exactly what he and his colleagues (Hansen, Raphael, Gordon, and Gallagher) were trying to communicate to teachers about the genius of instruction—that it is a carefully orchestrated dance between teacher and student in which the ultimate and ever-present goal is to render oneself irrelevant and obsolete as a teacher. But just as surely, they wanted to communicate that so much of what was misguided about curriculum and pedagogy in the era that permitted Durkin to assert that the "comprehension" emperor has no clothes (there is *no* instruction) was that teachers frequently began the instructional cycle by rendering themselves irrelevant and obsolete. They soon incorporated the term scaffolding into their lexicon of fundamental teaching moves—along with invoking prior knowledge, employing comprehension strategies, inference, and

TABLE 1.2 An Illustration of the Steps in an Adapted Gradual Release of Responsibility Model[a]

Pedagogical Step	Example of Relevant Teacher Scaffolding Children in the Reading Process
An explicit description of the reading strategy and when and how it should be used	Predicting is making guesses about what will come next in the text you are reading. You should make predictions a lot when you read. For now, you should stop every two pages that you read and make some predictions.
Teacher and/or student modeling of the reading strategy in action	I am going to make predictions while I read this book. I will start with just the cover here. Hmm… I see a picture of an owl. It looks like he—I think it is a he—is wearing pajamas, and he is carrying a candle. I predict that this is going to be a make-believe story because owls don't really wear pajamas and carry candles. I predict it is going to be about this owl, and it is going to take place at nighttime.
Collaborative use of the reading strategy in action	I have made some good predictions so far in the book. From this part on I want you to make predictions with me. Each of us should stop and think about what might happen next… Okay, now let's hear what you think and why…
Guided practice using the reading strategy with gradual release of responsibility	Early on… I have called the three of you together to work on making predictions while you read this and other books. After every few pages, I will ask each of you to stop and make a prediction. We will talk about your predictions and then read on to see if they come true. Later on… Each of you has a chart that lists different pages in your book. When you finish reading a page on the list, stop and make a prediction. Write the prediction in the column that says "Prediction." When you get to the next page on the list, check off whether your prediction "Happened," "Will not happen," or "Still might happen." Then make another prediction and write it down.
Independent use of the reading strategy	It is time for silent reading. As you read today, remember what we have been working on—making predictions while we read. Be sure to make predictions every two or three pages. Ask yourself why you made the prediction you did—what made you think that. Check as you read to see whether your prediction came true. Jamal is passing out Predictions! bookmarks to remind you.

a Adapted, with permission, from Duke et al. (2011).

metacognition—as terms to describe the basics of comprehension instruction. It was the core concept behind GRR when David and Meg coined the term in 1983 to describe the genius of the work that they and other colleagues were engaged in at the Center for the Study of Reading.

What was, and is, so compelling about the scaffolding metaphor is that it captures most of the important insights we have developed about good pedagogy over the last fifty years.[2] A few principles provide important guidance about how to employ scaffolding in robust pedagogy.

Fade Scaffolding Over Time

Other things being equal, we reduce the amount of scaffolding *across* time (and lessons) as students develop greater independent control in applying any strategy, skill, or practice worth acquiring. This is the most common and transparent insight about scaffolding, the very core of the GRR framework. But it does *not* mean, as many infer, that we always begin a sequence with modeling, then move to guided practice, and finally independent practice. We could begin a sequence by asking students to "try it on their own," offering feedback and assistance as students demonstrate the need for it.

James Baumann, an instructional researcher who has made significant contributions to comprehension research, once asked David in a conference session on strategy instruction,

"David, how much explicit instruction should a teacher provide?"

David's response:

"As little as possible."

And David meant it sincerely. There is no inherent virtue in explicit instruction, modeling, or extensive scaffolding. We offer any of them if and when students demonstrate less than completely independent control over an important practice; and we provide just enough scaffolding so that students can perform the activity successfully. It is a "Goldilocks" principle at work—not too much, not too little, but *just the right amount*.

Vary Scaffolding within a Lesson

We vary the amount of scaffolding offered *within* any given lesson as students demonstrate the capacity to control the practice in question. It is extremely powerful for a group of students, within the context of a single lesson, to demonstrate to themselves that they are more self-reliant at the end of the lesson than they were at the beginning.

Vary Scaffolding across Lessons within a Unit, Theme, or Project

Arranging conditions to allow students to gauge their progress over time is very important because it reinforces students' sense of self-efficacy and independence. And working with students to demonstrate to them that they can manage increasingly complex tasks on their own, both as groups and individuals, without teacher support, is an essential component in promoting a "can-do" attitude amongst students. Nothing says that better than reflecting with students at the end of a unit of curriculum on just how far they have come in their independence.

Vary Scaffolding between Students within and across Lessons

Scaffolding demands individualization. We can and should vary scaffolding between students within a single lesson for the very reason that students are inherently different from one another on almost any dimension of consequence. Part of the genius of the GRR Model is that it applies in so many situations. We have already suggested that we can vary the scaffolding provided to students across lessons and across time within a lesson. But we can also differentiate the kind and amount of scaffolding across students within a given lesson. For example, in a discussion about a story or an informational text, one student may need a clue about what page to look at to find relevant information, a second may need the teacher to restate the question in different words, and a third might need some options (turning open-ended question—Why did Henry take Jake's backpack?—into a multiple-choice question—Did Henry take Jake's backpack for revenge or money?).

Scaffolding Will Inevitably Ebb and Flow Over Time, Situations, and Task Demands

This statement serves as a "meta-principle" for the previous four principles. It's all contingent on the degree of competence and independence students reveal to teachers. As teachers, we strive for release, but we are always prepared to revert to greater (or lesser) scaffolding as text, task, and knowledge demands create varying scaffolding needs. This is the most powerful and important insight about scaffolding. If we accept the general notion that reading comprehension represents an interaction between a reader, a text, and a "task" within a socio-cultural context (RAND Reading Study Group, 2002), then we must accept the idea that our comprehension "ability" varies with the text, the task, and the knowledge we bring to the context. Moreover, the path to progress is not always a straight line: Show me a reader who is a master comprehender today, and we'll show you one who isn't tomorrow. All we have to do to transform an abled into a disabled reader is to up the ante on the complexity of the text, the obscurity of its topic, or the cognitive demand of the comprehension task. As teachers, we must always be prepared to revert to greater scaffolding when one of these elements (knowledge, text, topic, or task) creates greater demands on readers. Just as surely, we must be prepared to withdraw that scaffolding when these "stars" of comprehension are more positively aligned. It is this insight that forms the basis of the response to Baumann's query: How much explicit instruction, modeling, and scaffolding—"as little as possible".

Parallel Development

Thus far, we have traced the development of the GRR Model through the lens of a network of researchers who were well-connected professionally, meaning that they were keenly aware of and built upon one another's work over the years from the early 1980s through the early to mid-2000s. This work has been documented in a number of research reviews from the early 1990s (Dole, Duffy, Roehler, & Pearson, 1991; Pearson & Fielding, 1991; Pearson, Roehler, Dole, & Duffy, 1992) through the early 2000s (Duke & Pearson, 2002; Pressley, 2001), and into the early part of the 2010s (Duke, Pearson, Strachan, & Billman, 2011; Wilkinson & Son, 2011).

But there is much more to the story. Beginning in the 1980s and extending all the way into today's world of research and practice, many other scholars and practitioners have adapted the GRR Model to a host of purposes and practices. That was the clear message at the outset of this chapter, where we documented the ever-expanding use of the model, with well over 164,000 hits on the term, *GRR*, over 32,800 hits on the term, *GRR Model*, and about 300 arguably different visual representations of the model.

We could not possibly do justice to all of these variants, but we can highlight a few, just to illustrate the wide range of adaptations.

One of the most widely disseminated adaptations of GRR emanates from the extensive work of Fisher and Frey (2007), in their efforts to engage teachers in both ambitious instruction and authentic learning (see Pearson, 2001). In their model, what is emphasized is who is doing the work, with work responsibility gauged by the relative amount of space allocated to teachers and students in **I do**, **We do**, and **You do** zones. One other significant variation from the original model is the addition of the Collaboration (**You do together**) Zone, which lies in between the Teacher/Student collaboration in the Guided Instruction Phase and the Independent Practice phase. In Vygotskian terms, it implies that the "more knowledgeable other" in the scaffolding relationship need not be a teacher—a perspective with important implications for classroom practice and small group work (Figure 1.7).

A very compelling visualization of the roles teachers play is captured in this cartoon-like version of GRR from the WhatEdSaid website (Sackson, 2011). It is reminiscent of the terminology used by Raphael and Au, 1998, in their version of GRR. The WhatEdSaid (Figure 1.8) terms (Show Me (model), Help Me (share), Watch Me (guide), and Let Me (apply)) map well onto Raphael and Au's teacher roles (Modeling, Scaffolding, Facilitating, and Participating).

These two examples anchor the use of the GRR Model for very different audiences and purposes. As such, they illustrate the wide range of uses to which the model has been put in its original role—to illustrate how teachers can be "instructive" as teachers in their classrooms. We turn now to the role that GRR can play (and has played!) in conceptualizing programs of reflection that lead to teacher learning.

Teacher Responsibility

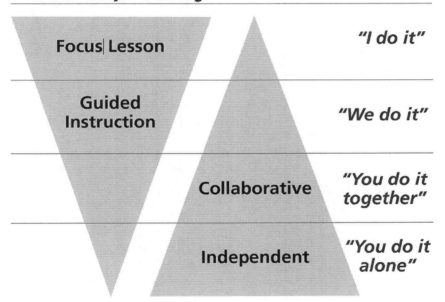

FIGURE 1.7 Fisher and Frey's (2008) version of the GRR Model. Note the emphasis on space as a metaphor for responsibility.

FIGURE 1.8 Visualization of the roles teachers play in the GRR Model.

GRR and Teacher Reflection: The Core of This Volume

Despite the decades-long focus on using the GRR to help teachers think about children's learning, less attention has focused on using the GRR to help preservice and inservice teachers or teacher educators reflect on their own teaching through video (McVee, Shanahan, Pearson, & Rinker, 2015; Shanahan et al., 2013). In one example, Shanahan and Tochelli (2012) describe using the GRR in the context of a professional development for practicing teachers who participated in a video study group. One of the tools used in video analysis was a GRR video analysis framework chart (see Figure 3.5) that supported the teachers as they analyzed and then time stamped video that demonstrated elements of the GRR in their lessons related to reading strategies. These teachers, who had from six to eighteen years of experience, were learning to implement Critical Elements of Strategy Instruction (CESI) (Almasi & Fullerton, 2012) during their guided reading lessons. The components of CESI include "(a) creating a safe and risk-free environment, (b) providing explicit instruction, (c) reducing cognitive processing demands, and (d) creating opportunities for students to verbalize strategy use" (Shanahan et al., 2013, p. 61). Interestingly, these elements used to create a context for successful reading strategy instruction when working with children are similar to what adult learners need in a Community of Practice for video reflection. Optimally, adult learners engaging in video reflection need

- A safe environment where learners feel supported to take risks and analyze videos of their teaching;
- A more knowledgeable other who can provide explicit instruction when needed to help assist learners in reflection on teaching and improvement of teaching;
- An environment and instructional scaffolds that reduce cognitive processing demands during the reflection practice so that adult learners can take incremental steps toward independent reflection;
- Opportunities to engage in reflection about teaching through spoken dialogue, multimodal interactions, and written reflection across a sustained period of time.

Consider Table 1.3. It is the companion to Table 1.2, which focused on illustrating the steps of the GRR Model between children and teachers. Now consider the depiction below, which uses similar steps between adult learners and their teachers.

TABLE 1.3 An Illustration of the Steps in an Adapted Gradual Release of Responsibility Model[a]

Pedagogical Step	Example of Relevant Teacher Scaffolding of Adults during Video-Based Reflection
An explicit description of the reflection strategy and when and how it should be used	With the goal of being able to recognize the components of CESI in an authentic teaching and learning setting, we are going to identify when we see the components of CESI in a lesson using the Video Analysis Framework chart (see Figure 3.5). The use of a framework, like the Video Analysis Chart, helps you to focus when you are engaged in video reflection on the implementation of a new pedagogical practice. When you recognize a component of the CESI model, time stamp and jot down the first few words of the statement so that you can see how you are incorporating the components of the model to meet your students' needs.
Teacher and/or student modeling of the reflection strategy in action	[video begins] I noticed that I am trying to use a concrete anchor [one component of CESI] for the strategy of visualizing at 59 seconds into the lesson. I said, "Alright ladies. I want you to do a little bit of thinking. Why do people wear glasses? What's the reason somebody would wear glasses? What do you think?" The student replied, "To help them see." I continue on and say, "Yeah, so glasses kind of help you see clearer. They help you see things really, really clear. Well guess what? Good readers sometimes use a strategy called visualizing to help them see things clearly when they are reading. What you are doing is you are using your schema and the descriptive words that the author gave you to make some pictures in your mind." By time stamping now I know that I began the lesson trying to anchor the strategy, I am wondering if I continued to circle back to the concrete anchor throughout the lesson. I am going to continue referring to the of CESI Component Video Analysis Framework to determine my proficiency of the implementation of CESI, a new pedagogical strategy.
Collaborative use of the reflection strategy in action	I have used the Video Analysis Framework chart to reflect upon my implementation of CESI. I am going to continue to play the video, and I want you to tell us when you see a CESI component being used in the lesson. When we pause the video, each one of us should use our chart to determine what component is being used.

(Continued)

TABLE 1.3 Continued

Pedagogical Step	Example of Relevant Teacher Scaffolding of Adults during Video-Based Reflection
Guided practice using the reflection strategy with gradual release of responsibility	Today when you work together in triads, you are going to all view the same video on one laptop and share one Video Analysis Framework chart to collaboratively reflect upon. As you reflect in small groups I will join in your group and we will talk about the implementation of CESI. I might ask questions like: What components have you observed? How explicit is the teacher's language when she/he is explaining the strategy? Are the students responding? Is this working, and for whom? For whom is it not working? How do I know? What am I pleased and/or concerned about? Toward the end of our time today, I am going to ask you to reflect on the following: As you are engaged in the use of the Video Analysis Framework chart, ask yourself: How is this tool scaffolding your understanding of the implementation of CESI?
Independent use of the reflection strategy	In preparation of your video study group meeting about CESI tomorrow, watch your own video and one other member of your professional learning community. As you watch, identify the CESI components throughout the lesson using the Video Analysis Framework chart. As you are reflecting on the implementation of the CESI Model think about: Based on what you saw, where should you/the teacher go from here? What are the next steps? If the lesson were to be taught again, what should be kept the same or modified? Later: When we come back together in a whole group, I am going to ask you if you think there should be a modification for the use of the Video Analysis Framework chart. Is it still necessary for you to time stamp for CESI when you reflect on your implementation with the video? If not, describe why you can be gradually released from this scaffolded support.

a Adapted, with permission, from Duke et al. (2011).

This table is only a preliminary illustration of how the GRR Model is just as applicable to teacher reflection as it is to teachers teaching reading comprehension. As such, one goal of this book is to explore how the GRR Model can be applied to teacher education programs, professional development, or in any setting where teachers are viewing video of their own teaching with the goal of reflecting on their own practice in accordance with the principles outlined above. The GRR Model is integral to the process of teacher reflection through video and has the added benefit of being a model that many preservice and inservice teachers may already be familiar with from literacy coursework or even from use in classrooms.

The GRR in a Pedagogy of Video Reflection

Elsewhere we have explored a pedagogy of video reflection (Shanahan et al., 2013) and a comprehensive theoretical model of the GRR in video reflection (McVee et al., 2015).[3] In that previous work, we identified some of the affordances of the GRR in video reflection. The GRR is an apprenticeship model that helps educators scaffold learning and learner development and can be used in a Community of Practice:

- For individual learners/individual learning
- For groups of learners/socially constructed learning in Community of Practice
- For individual action (e.g., reading aloud and using reading strategies to foster comprehension)
- For group action (e.g., discussing and debriefing videos as a group)
- Within a short-term activity (e.g., a mini-lesson on writing)
- Within long-term activities (e.g., multiple video reflections based on teaching in a reading center for 15-week practicum)
- Across time for individuals and groups
- For variable support across individuals and groups
- For variable responsibility across individuals and groups

Many of us have probably had the experience where someone has given us feedback around literacy activities that was well intended but that seemed unhelpful. Comments such as "reflect deeper", "read closely", and "write better" are only useful if we have already built a shared knowledge of the terms "deeper, closely, better" in a specific context. If we are novice writers, reflectors, or readers in a particular domain, these terms are likely not specific enough to help us rethink or change our actions. Constructive feedback needs to be explicit and targeted for different learners with different needs; variable types of support are needed. Furthermore, within education, such feedback is often co-constructed within a Community of Practice such as a professional development group, a literacy practicum class, or a cohort of student teachers.

While it is true that any one of us can engage in video reflection on our own, our contention is that reflection on teaching and learning is more effective when supported by a Community of Practice and by more knowledgeable others. For example, in video reflection a more knowledgeable other (e.g., a teacher educator) often provides variable levels of support to individuals and sub-groups (e.g., dyads, trios, small groups) around reflective processes with the ultimate goal to enable teachers to reflect independently. Every video analysis or reflection task places a cognitive responsibility on the viewer. Within a Community of Practice approach, there are at least two dimensions of support that mediate the viewing task: (1) support provided by others and (2) support

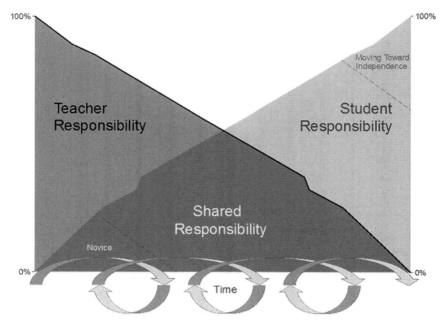

FIGURE 1.9   Teacher and student responsibility in the Gradual Release of Responsibility over time.

through the video analysis task itself (e.g., the type of video, how the task of reflection is framed). The amount of cognitive responsibility placed on the learner during video analysis can be increased or decreased by varying amounts of responsibility placed on other learners. In a best-case scenario, reflection also takes place on an ongoing basis over time. Figure 1.9 represents these ideas through an adapted model of the GRR.

A true novice would begin on the bottom left participating in teacher-directed activities with a maximum support. For example, a teacher educator guiding students in student teaching might introduce a video she has chosen, provide guiding questions for analysis, model her own thinking, and provide multiple scaffolds for novices to enable knowledge construction related to reflection. Over time, the teacher educator will decrease her supports and the responsibility she has taken on while the student teachers would move from novices toward independence in reflection. The process of engaging in reflection and learning is not a straight slide down an even line. It is a process that will include multiple iterations of support and responsibility for instructors and learners. At the bottom of Figure 1.9 the looping arrows represent the iterative nature of learning and of the GRR across time; clearly the more time and the more cycles of reflection, the more that can be learned.

Conclusion

We began this chapter with a look at the historical roots of the GRR Model. One of the reasons for doing this is to make clear the long history, sound research, staying power over the years, and thoughtful genesis that went into the development and elaboration of the first GRR Model (Pearson & Gallagher, 1983a, 1983b). In a digital age teachers, school leaders, and education professionals have an unlimited number of suggestions and resources available, and not all of these resources have been vetted as diligently as the GRR Model. The GRR Model has a history; it is grounded in credible and rigorous work carried out by David and his colleagues, first through the Center for the Study of Reading and then in other settings. The model was applied, elaborated, and adapted by many other scholars and practitioners mentioned throughout this chapter. The model is the keystone in the pedagogy of video reflection presented in the following chapters.

Each chapter in this book will present more examples and further exploration of the GRR in the context of video reflection. Chapter 2 will introduce readers to the GRR Model in the context of teacher reflective inquiry, particularly video reflection. We elaborate our model of reflective video pedagogy, delineating critical reflective inquiry as the foundation of adaptive expertise. Chapter 3 will explore how the GRR works within a Community of Practice (Lave & Wenger, 1991) that functions as a safe place for risk-taking related to sharing one's own teaching practice publicly. Chapter 4 will provide a comprehensive definition of critical reflective inquiry, including a review of the major contributors to the construct (Dewey, 1933; Schön, 1983) and those who have built on their work (Rodgers, 2002a, 2002b; Korthagen & Kessels, 1999).

In Chapters 5–7 we will illustrate reflective video pedagogy in action as the GRR Model is used with preservice and inservice teachers across settings of clinical practicums in university teacher education, school-based practicums, and professional development contexts in school settings including work with struggling readers and writers and students who speak multiple languages. In Chapter 5, we tackle the complexities of teaching that become visible through video reflection with examples of teachers using the four parts of reflective inquiry: Presence, Description, Analysis, and Experimentation. Chapter 6 will address the shift in teacher education that calls for the use of video to serve as an artifact of teaching competence, and we will ask teacher educators to consider how they can build a culture of reflection across their teacher education programs. In Chapter 7, we offer specifics about how a literacy coach strategically provides a variety of scaffolding techniques as she uses the GRR Model to coach an inservice teacher who works with diverse multilingual learners.

In Chapter 8 we will take up a special challenge for teachers and teacher educators—to examine how positions and positioning play a role in viewing and interpreting video and classroom events, particularly when teaching raises positions and ideologies that rest on assumptions of race, class, gender, ethnicity, or language use.

We conclude in Chapter 9 with an invitation to consider the many models of the GRR presented in the book, and we revisit the most critical elements of the GRR Model and critical principles in reflective video pedagogy.

Notes

1 (By the way, a little known fact about the 1983 piece is that a companion entry in that same issue is the classic Paris, Lipson, & Wixson piece, "Becoming a Strategic Reader."
2 This section draws on concepts first produced in a paper by Pearson (2011).
3 This section draws on concepts first produced in a paper by McVee, Shanahan, Pearson, and Rinker (2015).

References

Almasi, J. F., & Fullerton, S. K. (2012). *Teaching strategic processes in reading* (2nd ed.). New York, NY: Guilford Press.

Black, P., & William, D. (1998). Assessment and classroom learning. *Assessment in Education, 5*(1), 7–71.

Dewey, J. (1910/1933). *How we think.* Boston, MA: D. C. Heath and Company.

Dole, J., Duffy, G., Roehler, L., & Pearson, P. D. (1991). Moving from the old to the new: Research on reading comprehension instruction. *Review of Educational Research, 61*(2), 239–264.

Duke, N., & Pearson, P. D. (2002). Effective practices for developing reading comprehension. In A. Farstrup & J. Samuels (Eds.), *What research has to say about reading instruction* (3rd ed.) (pp. 205–242). Newark, DE: International Reading Association.

Duke, N. D., Pearson, P. D., Strachan, S. L., Billman, A. K. (2011). Essential elements of fostering and teaching reading comprehension. In S. J. Samuels & A. Farstrup (Eds.). *What research has to say about reading instruction* (4th ed.) (pp. 51–93). Newark, DE: International Reading Association.

Durkin, D. (1978–1979). What classroom observations reveal about reading comprehension instruction. *Reading Research Quarterly, 14,* 481–533.

Feuerstein, R., Rand, Y., & Hoffman, M. (1979). *The dynamic assessment of retarded performers: The learning potential assessment device (LPAD).* Baltimore, MD: University Park Press.

Fisher, D., & Frey, N. (2008). *Better learning through structured teaching: A framework for the gradual release of responsibility.* Alexandria, VA: Association for Supervision and Curriculum Development.

Gordon, C. J. (1985). Modeling inference awareness across the curriculum. *Journal of Reading, 28,* 444–447.

Gordon, C. J., & Pearson, P. D. (1983). *The effects of instruction in metacomprehension and inferencing on children's comprehension abilities* (Technical Report No. 277). Urbana-Champaign: University of Illinois, Center for the Study of Reading.

Hansen, J. (1981). The effects of inference training and practice on young children's reading comprehension. *Reading Research Quarterly, 16,* 391–417.

Hansen, J., & Pearson, P. D. (1983). An instructional study: Improving the inferential comprehension of good and poor fourth-grade readers. *Journal of Educational Psychology*, *75*, 821–829.

Korthagen, F. A. J., & Kessels, J. P. A. M. (1999). Linking theory and practice: Changing the pedagogy of teacher education. *Educational Researcher*, *28*(4), 4–17.

Lave, J., & Wenger, E. (1991). *Situated learning: Legitimate peripheral participation*. Cambridge, UK: Cambridge University Press.

McVee, M. B., Shanahan, L. E., Pearson, P. D., & Rinker, T. W. (2015). Using the gradual release of responsibility model to support video reflection with preservice and inservice teachers. In E. Ortlieb, M. B. McVee, & L. E. Shanahan (Eds.), *Video reflection in literacy teacher education and development: Lessons from research and practice* (pp. 59–80). Bingley, UK: Emerald Group Publishing.

Palincsar, A. S., & Brown, A. L. (1984). Reciprocal teaching of comprehension fostering and monitoring activities. *Cognition and Instruction*, *1*, 117–175.

Palincsar, A. S., & Brown, A. L. (1986). Interactive teaching to promote independent learning from text. *The Reading Teacher*, *39*, 771–777.

Palincsar, A. S., Brown, A. L., & Martin, S. M. (1987). Peer interaction in reading comprehension instruction. *Educational Psychologist*, *22*, 231–253.

Pearson, P. D. (2011). Toward the next generation of comprehension instruction: A coda. In H. Daniels (Ed.). *Comprehension going forward* (pp. 243–253). Portsmouth, NH: Heinemann.

Pearson, P. D., & Gallagher, M. (1983a). *The instruction of reading comprehension*. (Technical Report No. 297). Urbana-Champaign: University of Illinois, Center for the Study of Reading.

Pearson, P. D., & Gallagher, M. C. (1983b). The instruction of reading comprehension. *Contemporary Educational Psychology*, *8*(3), 317–344.

Pearson, P. D., Roehler, L., Dole, J., & Duffy, G. (1992). Developing expertise in reading comprehension. In S. J. Samuels & A. E. Farstrup (Eds.), *What research says to the teacher* (2nd ed.) (pp. 145–199). Newark, DE: International Reading Association.

Pressley, M., Almasi, J., Schuder, T., Bergman, J., Hite, S., El-Dinary, P. B., & Rachel, B. (1994). Transactional instruction of comprehension strategies: The Montgomery County, Maryland, SAIL Program. *Reading and Writing Quarterly: Overcoming Learning Difficulties*, *10*, 5–19.

Pressley, M., El-Dinary, P.B., Gaskins, I., Schuder, T., Bergman, J. L., Almasi, J., et al. (1992). Beyond direct explanation: Transactional instruction of reading comprehension strategies. *Elementary School Journal*, *92*, 513–555.

Raphael, T. E., & Au, K. H. (Eds.) (1998). *Literature-based instruction: Reshaping the curriculum*. Newton, MA: Christopher Gordon

Raphael, T. E., & McKinney, J. (1983). An examination of 5th and 8th grade children's question\answering behavior: An instructional study in metacognition. *Journal of Reading Behavior*, *15*, 67–86.

Raphael, T. E., & Pearson, P. D. (1985). Increasing students' awareness of sources of information for answering questions. *American Educational Research Journal*, *22*, 217–236.

Raphael, T. E., & Wonnacott, C. A. (1985). Heightening fourth-grade students' sensitivity to sources of information for answering comprehension questions. *Reading Research Quarterly*, *20*, 282–296.

Rodgers, C. (2002a). Defining reflection: Another look at John Dewey and reflective thinking. *Teachers College Record*, *104*(4), 842–866.

Rodgers, C. (2002b). Seeing student learning: Teacher change and the role of reflection. *Harvard Educational Review, 72*(2), 230–253.

Sackson, E. (2011, February 16). Blog from WhatEdSaid: *The power of conversation.* https://whatedsaid.wordpress.com/2011/02/16/the-power-of-conversation/ downloaded on June 12, 2017.

Schön, D. A. (1983). *The reflective practitioner: How professionals think in action.* New York, NY: Basic Books.

Shanahan, L. E., McVee, M. B., Schiller, J. A., Tynan, E. A., D'Abate, R. L., Flury-Kashmanian, C. M., ... Hayden, H. E. (2013). Supporting struggling readers and literacy clinicians through reflective video pedagogy. In E. T. Ortlieb, J. Cheek, & H. Earl (Eds.), *Advanced literacy practices: From the clinic to the classroom literacy* (pp. 303–323). Bingley, UK: Emerald Group Publishing.

Shanahan, L. E., & Tochelli, A. L. (2012). Video-study group: A context to cultivate professional relationships. In P. J. Dunston, S. K. Fullerton, C. C. Bates, K. Headley, & P. M. Stecker (Eds.), *61st Literacy Research Association Conference Yearbook* (pp. 196–211). Oak Creek, WI: Literacy Research Association.

Vygotsky, L. S. (1978). *Mind in society: The development of higher psychological processes.* Cambridge, MA: Harvard University Press.

Wood, D., Bruner, J. S., & Ross, G. (1976). The role of tutoring in problem solving. *Journal of Child Psychology Psychiatry, 17*(2), 89–100.

2

LEARNING THROUGH A PEDAGOGY OF VIDEO REFLECTION AND THE GRADUAL RELEASE OF RESPONSIBILITY MODEL

FIGURE 2.1 Children learning to swim.

Have you ever taught a child to swim? Maybe you have watched a young child who was learning to swim, or even recall how you learned to swim. Typically, children are taught to swim incrementally. Those who are more timid or scared may need to be coaxed into the water holding onto the hand of a parent, sibling, or friend. Some children may be ready to jump into the deep end even before learning to swim, and swim instructors often let children jump in the deep end while also providing safety supports such as floats and adult life guards to assist children and keep them safe. A very common sight in swimming classes is children hugging kickboards to buoy themselves up while kicking across the pool or children being supported by the hands or arms of an adult as the children paddle in place and gain a feel for the sensation of floating. Learning to float, kick, and not to panic are key elements that instructors attend to before children are released to swim on their own. This gradual releasing of responsibility from the instructor to the individual child is preferable to tossing a child off the diving board or dock at the lake and yelling "Sink or swim"—even if surviving such an ordeal makes for an exciting story to share decades later.

Like learning to swim, learning to reflect on one's own teaching can be a somewhat intimidating or even scary experience and support may be needed. Increasingly, teacher candidates in teacher preparation programs (*preservice teachers*) are being asked to reflect on their own teaching through video. In some cases, video recording and analysis are requirements that must be completed for state certification. In other cases, classroom teachers who are already certified (*inservice teachers*) may find themselves being required to video record their teaching for annual performance evaluations, peer-to-peer evaluations, literacy coaching, or professional development initiatives. Previously certified inservice teachers may also find video reflection is required in many graduate level courses. Many teacher educators, mentors, or professional development staff help guide preservice and inservice teachers through video reflection like patient swim instructors helping novice swimmers stay afloat in the difficult currents of reflection. But, increasingly preservice and inservice teachers are required to engage in video reflection with little or no support—rather like being told to jump into the water and learn to swim on their own.

In this volume, we use the **Gradual Release of Responsibility** (GRR) Model (Pearson, 2013; Pearson & Gallagher, 1983) as a means to think about how to approach reflection, and in particular, how to use video as a tool in assisting teacher reflection. Since its introduction in 1983, the model has demonstrated remarkable staying power, despite the fact that the past decades have demonstrated significant shifts in pedagogical approaches, theory, and policy. Even with dramatic changes in education, the model has endured across these varying contexts, demonstrating its adaptability. Teacher educators, teachers, and researchers are likely to be most familiar with the GRR as applied to contexts of teaching and learning for K–12 literacy classrooms where the model has been applied most often to help practitioners think about reading and reading comprehension. Given its adaptability, the model has been used to help practitioners think about writing and genre. In settings of professional development and teacher education, the model has been applied to coaching and teacher reflection.

In previous work we introduced a **pedagogy of video reflection** for literacy preservice and inservice teachers (Shanahan et al., 2013). This was further conceptualized to explore the benefits of using the GRR Model in the context of a pedagogy of video reflection (McVee, Shanahan, Pearson, & Rinker, 2015).

In this current text one purpose is to elaborate upon those ideas and to introduce principles and supports to help preservice and inservice teachers, teacher educators, school leaders, and professional development specialists who wish to guide teachers in using video as a tool for reflecting upon teaching. In particular, we explore how the GRR can help conceptualize the flexible and changeable sharing of responsibility between a more knowledgeable other (e.g., an instructor) and a learner (e.g., a teacher) as an apprenticeship model. An important context for this interchange is a **Community of Practice** (e.g., a video study group, a preservice teacher cohort, a cadre of school administrators). As we will discuss further in Chapter 3, a Community of Practice is comprised of individuals who wish to reflect together on practice under the guidance of an instructor or mentor (Shanahan & Tochelli, 2014). Across various chapters and contexts, we illustrate how a Community of Practice and more knowledgeable others are critical in the development of **reflective inquiry** (Hayden & Chiu, 2015; Hayden, Moore-Russo, & Marino, 2013).

Throughout the book, we explore a theoretical model that considers *Gradual Release of Responsibility for Video Reflection* and how this model can be operationalized through research-based examples of practice. Along the way, we provide video viewing guides, resources, and activities that will be of use to readers. While we will explore reflection and reflective inquiry in depth in Chapter 4, it may be helpful to readers to know that we think of reflection as

> A goal-directed process that moves teachers to identify a situation, process, or experience that is puzzling, interesting, celebratory, or otherwise intriguing and view it through multiple lenses. Developing particular skill sets or dispositions is necessary for reflection, but a particular set of skills or dispositions is not sufficient to become a reflective practitioner. Reflective teachers strive to gain strategic knowledge of a situation in order to develop and explore questions, recognize, or acknowledge complexity of situations, processes or experiences, and make adaptations to their actions, beliefs, positions, and classroom and pedagogical practices. Reflection is interpretive in that individuals bring their knowledge and experiences to the situation. Reflection is self-directed and collaborative in nature.
>
> *(Shanahan et al., 2013, p. 305)*

Principles of Teaching, Learning to Teach, Reflecting, and Learning to Reflect

Complexity in Teaching and Reflecting

Comedian Steve Martin has had a career spanning nearly five decades, appearing on shows such as *Saturday Night Live*, in movies, and performing stand-up comedy for thousands of fans. Martin's comedic routines often look off-the-cuff and easy. Martin is also a skilled, Grammy award-winning musician who, no joke, plays the banjo (www.youtube.com/watch?v=5gNuj8UkyC4). Martin once quipped that he took up the banjo because he wanted to do something that looked complex. Like many professionals who hone a set of specific skills through practice, Martin's flawless comedic performance appears effortless— as if he was born funny and just had to grow into it to make a living—no doubt a reason why one of his comedy albums was titled "Born Standing Up." Martin's comment about doing something that "looked complex" referred to the idea that when a comedian is skilled an audience doesn't think about how a comedian writes and rewrites routines, practices pacing and delivery, and constantly monitors audience reaction while performing. When a skilled co-median is on stage, he appears to be funny without really trying, even though in reality, hours of hard work and reflection (even outright failure) go into perfecting each performance. In contrast, Martin noted that a skilled banjo player's fingers move so inhumanly fast it is difficult not to be impressed and think: "Wow, that looks complicated." Although said for humorous effect, his point was that people will often watch a skilled comedian and think: "That looks so easy."

Like good comedy, good teaching also appears effortless. In the real world, good teachers often make teaching seem as if it were easy. When an effective teacher works with children or youth, the students are attentive. Children engage in learning and are curious about what they are learning; the teacher knows the content matter and has the pedagogical skills to deliver curriculum. Classroom management, organization, and routines are smooth. Classrooms where teachers are not effective may seem out of control because classroom routines have not been set, or learners may be bored and unengaged because a teacher has not mastered the content or the pedagogical skills to deliver content. Some classrooms may even be fun and entertaining, but teachers may be delivering only superficial content and deep learning may be elusive. But whether a teacher is effective or not, there is a stream of thought in broader society that persists in believing that teaching, like good comedy, requires little effort. As the old saying goes, "Teachers are born, not made." However, in this text, we hold firmly to several principles related to teaching. The first of these is

Principle #1

Teaching and reflecting are complex endeavors.

Scaffolding in Teaching and Learning

Any time someone learns something new—whether that new thing is playing the banjo, doing stand-up comedy, teaching, or learning to read, a learner needs some support or scaffolding. The idea of scaffolding (Wood, Bruner, &

FIGURE 2.2 Teaching is a complex endeavor.

Ross, 1978) is a metaphor that has become commonplace in educational circles when describing teaching and learning. Cazden (1983) defines a *scaffold* as "a temporary framework for construction in progress" (p. 6). In the above examples, the point is not merely to show teachers how to reflect or provide a template for reflection. Instead, thoughtful teacher educators make use of video, dialogue, reflection guides, questioning, and many other tools to help create scaffolds upon which teachers can begin constructing new ideas.

Building on the work of Vygotsky (1987), the theory of social constructivism suggests that there is *a zone of proximal development (ZPD)* in learning (Moll, 1990; Rogoff & Wertsch, 1984; Stone, 1993). This idea of a zone, or ZPD, is useful because it can help teachers in all kinds of enterprises be mindful about what learners can do independently and what they can do together or with a more knowledgeable other, such as a teacher, supporting their learning. Most often, parents are the first more knowledgeable others who scaffold a child's literacy development by reading to young children, pointing out images, and engaging in repetitive talk that teaches words and speech patterns. While reading to a child, a parent engages in support both through physical actions, such as gesture, and through verbal interaction. Consider the following example between a father and a child where the father is reading the touch and feel book *Fuzzy Yellow Ducklings* (van Fleet, 1995) (Figure 2.2).

FATHER: [*Reads from the book*]. Fuzzy yellow circle. [*Continues talking to the child*]. Put your fingers there. [*Child puts hand on the circle and rubs the fuzzy fabric*]. Do you feel how fuzzy it is? [*The father rubs his fingers over the fuzzy circle with his child*]. What do you think this is?

CHILD: Duck!

Over time, as the child develops language and cognitive skills, the father can continue to scaffold the child's learning by talking about shapes in the book (e.g., the circle) or textures such as a sticky frog tongue. The father's scaffolding involves multiple modes such as speech and touch. Later, as a child begins formal reading instruction, a teacher might help support a child's learning by intentionally introducing specific scaffolds. Consider the following example summarized from Shanahan and Roof (2013):

Kelly, a second-grade teacher, sat in a chair next to her anchor chart titled *Reading Strategies*. She began the lesson by pointing to the chart and the particular reading strategy, *Making Predictions*. As she pointed, Kelly asked: "What is the strategy we have been working on all week?" She then reminded the students of how they had used information to make predictions, walking them through the elements of the chart. On this particular day, Kelly focused on the reasons why a reader makes predictions: (1) to help the reader focus and (2) to understand. As she explained these reasons for making predictions to the children, Kelly attached an 8 ½ × 11 sheet of paper with a magnet to the top right-hand corner of the anchor chart. This visual aid (Figure 2.3), created by Kelly, had two images—a pair of eyeglasses and a cartoon of a person with a light bulb over his head. These images illustrated two reasons that readers make predictions (i.e., focusing and understanding).

With the previous context in mind, Figure 2.4 provides a brief excerpt of this lesson where Kelly introduced gestures to represent the reasons why readers predict.

Kelly was able to communicate the reasons for predicting (to focus and to understand) while reading in three different ways. She (1) used explicit instructional language, (2) modeled gestures, and (3) then had the students practice the speech and gestures with her. Here we see a multimodal communicative event occurring between Kelly and her students. Kelly used multiple modes of communication: verbal explanation, a print-based chart on reading strategies, an image- and print-based chart on focusing and understanding, and two different types of gestures. All of these provide scaffolds for her students. Note too that this was not her only lesson on the reading strategy of predicting. She had already begun introducing the children to this idea, and she continued to revisit the idea with them. This included using the two gestures to indicate why predictions are made (i.e., to focus and to understand). Shanahan et al. also reported that the children took up these gestures and began using them while they verbalized the names of the strategies. What is particularly impressive is that while Kelly obviously spent a lot of time creating charts, images, and thoughtfully planning co-related gestures ahead of time, the explanation of the lesson around predicting to focus and to understand, and introduction of the chart (Figure 2.3) took only about a minute. It was artfully planned and delivered, and extremely efficient.

In each of the examples above, the parent and the teacher both have goals in mind. For the parent, it might be simple enjoyment of cuddling up with a

FIGURE 2.3 Kelly's visual aid to introduce reasons why readers predict
Source: Shanahan & Roof, 2013.

child to spend time together or taking some time to wind down before nap-time. The end goal for a parent might also include the activity of reading itself because the parent knows that reading aloud will help his child grow into a reader. The teacher may have a general goal in a reading activity such as helping children develop a love of reading, but there are also specific goals such as helping children to use reading strategies such as learning to make predictions while reading to focus and to understand. Both the parent's and the teacher's goals involve looking ahead in the child's development to see an end point where they want the child to go. For literacy teachers, this notion

....There are *two reasons why we make predictions.* | The first one is it helps us stay *focused,* | and helps us to *understand....*

FIGURE 2.4 Kelly uses gestures to help young readers
Source: Shanahan & Roof, 2013.

of an end point is particularly important because a teacher's vocation is framed around helping children achieve growth and progress in reading, writing, and language over time, usually as framed by the beginning and endings of marking periods or grade levels. Taking into account a child's developmental trajectory and age, a teacher's ultimate goal is to enable a child to function fully independently as a reader and writer.

Learning to reflect through video is similar to acquiring other literacy skills like those discussed above because educators must always consider the end goals of learning. For example, a preservice teacher's goal might be to complete video reflection for state certification (e.g., meet requirements of the Educative Teacher Performance Assessment, more commonly known as ed-TPA, or the Praxis Performance Assessment for Teachers, or PPAT). An inservice teacher might engage in video reflection with colleagues in a professional development group to ultimately improve reading strategy instruction in their classrooms. There is always a distant end point in mind.

Part of what makes teaching complex is teachers must simultaneously be thinking ahead to the learning outcomes they want to achieve but at the same time, they must be thinking about the in-the-moment processes that create conditions for what they are trying to teach. Psychologists refer to this as **prolepsis** (see Cole, 1996 for an extended discussion). This means that in teaching children, and in teaching teachers, there is always a sense in which any type of instructional scaffolding is **teleological**. To say that scaffolding is teleological means that the scaffolds are designed intentionally with specific purposes or goals that are linked to a future outcome.

Some readers might be thinking

> Well, yes, I want to use video to document my teaching so I can pass my state certification requirements, but I also want to learn as much as I can in the process, so it's a little narrow-minded to say my only goal is to complete a video for state certification.

A similar statement might be made by inservice teachers who want to improve strategy instruction but who also want to use the process of reflection to become better teachers all around and learn as much as they can from their colleagues in the process. These goals expressed by teachers relate to scaffolding in an important way. *Scaffolding is not about the end goal; it is about the process of reaching the end goal.* This means that teachers and teacher educators must always be mindful of prolepsis—keeping the end learning objectives in mind even in the process and thinking about current and future (teleological) conditions to help foster learning. This is represented by the second principle about teaching and learning:

Principle #2

Learning to teach and learning to reflect are scaffolded processes. Teachers consider what learners need to learn and do in the present and what learners need to learn and do in the future.

FIGURE 2.5   Scaffolding is essential in learning to teach and learning to reflect.

Considering Scaffolding and Complexity through the Gradual Release of Responsibility

 Stop and Think

1. Think about a time when someone tried to teach you a new skill or when you tried to teach someone a new skill. (This could be an active skill such as learning how to tie your shoes, ride a bike, or swim, or something more abstract like completing a geometry proof, balancing a chemical equation, or using a computer program.)

2. What happened? What kinds of instructional scaffolding did the learner receive?
3. Do you feel there was enough support for the learner to acquire the new skill? Why or why not?
4. What was the outcome? Do you feel the learning was successful? Why or why not?

One of our co-authors, Mary, recalls a time in middle school when her brother Shawn tried to teach her how to do motorcycle jumps off a dirt berm. After Shawn demonstrated a few jumps, his instructional scaffolding was "just pull up when you hit the jump." Mary took off, around and through the dirt and grass track, hit the berm, and immediately crashed. Luckily, there were no injuries because she did not have enough speed to do anything other than drop, lose her balance, and career off the track. While we could debate whether teaching a sibling to do motorcycle tricks is a wise instructional move, the point here is that Mary needed a lot more information than "just pull up when you hit the jump." Speed, balance, body position, risk tolerance, and confidence are also among some of the essential aspects of completing a motorcycle jump successfully. Likewise, when reflecting through video, preservice and inservice teachers need to be told more than "reflect on your teaching" because the act of viewing video alone will not necessarily result in learning (Brophy, 2004). When preservice and inservice teachers are left to reflect on their own without support, it is a bit like saying, "just pull up when you hit the jump." What is needed is a set of scaffolded interactions with a teleological vision: What are the end goals? What support is needed for learners from a more knowledgeable other in the moment? What can learners be expected to do on their own? What is the ultimate independent action(s) that learners should be able to carry out?

Clearly, learning in an informal setting (e.g., motorcycle jumping) and in a formal setting (e.g., a preservice teacher education or professional development program) are not the same thing. But, if supports are not introduced, learners are left with trial and error. Trial and error can result in positive outcomes. But trial and error also requires a great deal of time, and in high-stakes situations trial and error can lead to negative outcomes. The practice of reflecting in and through video for many teachers is often tied to a high-stakes outcome such as teacher certification or a positive evaluation on an annual performance review. While no model ensures success, we believe that a particular model, that of the GRR (Pearson, 2013; Pearson & Gallagher, 1983), can help preservice and inservice teachers and teacher educators conceptualize the process of incremental learning over time while moving toward a future goal with the support of more knowledgeable others. This is the case in the example below where Dr. Grace Walker has introduced the GRR and a reflection framework from Jay and Johnson (2002) (also see Chapter 3) in a literacy practicum course leading to Literacy Specialist certification.

Across the semester, Professor Grace Walker (all names are pseudonyms) has been working with the Literacy Specialist students enrolled in a master's literacy program to help them apply the GRR to reflect on their own teaching within a clinical practicum. Students are familiar with the GRR Model, having been introduced to it early in their program and having encountered it in much of their coursework. On the first night of video viewing Grace introduces a video of a previous student, Rosalie, who had already completed the practicum course and master's program. In the video Rosalie worked with a child, Jeter, on a lesson that focused on modeling and breaking multisyllabic words. Prior to introducing the video, Grace has had a discussion with the students about a reflective framework from Jay and Johnson. On this night, she also provides them with a template for reflection (see Appendix 2.1) and asks them to view the video while taking notes.

After viewing the video Grace opens the floor for discussion, and because this is the first night that students are using video as a means to reflect, the students need a lot of scaffolding from Grace. Grace re-voices student responses, asks questions to prompt further reflection, and redirects students as needed throughout the conversation, helping them move from superficial comments toward more detailed explorations. For the most part, the comments are positive as students note how prepared the teacher is, how she interacts with the child, or how materials are laid out. No doubt students recognize that as current tutors in the literacy center who will be using video recording of their own teaching, they will soon be in the same position as Rosalie.

Grace leads the students through the reflective framework and encourages students to take up the critical dimension of the Jay and Johnson framework. Faith observes that maybe the steps modeled by the teacher could have been more concrete, and she explains what Rosalie could have done to accomplish this: First, tap out the syllables of the word, then draw on the "syllabication kits" that Rosalie had provided for reference; third, "look at the word" and "break it up," and then "say what set of rules applies to this word." Yet even as the students become more comfortable engaging in all aspects of the reflective typology—including a very respectful, appropriate, and constructive critique—Bailey becomes uncomfortable and interjects, "I do feel bad judging her [Rosalie] though." Grace gently reminds the class that the purpose of the exercise is to engage in constructive criticism. Turning to Bailey, she asks: "Why do you think I want you to do this?" Bailey replies, "To be able to reflect on our own video." Grace responds with enthusiasm: "Bingo! To be able to reflect on your own video. That's exactly right and at these different dimensions [using the descriptive, comparative, and critical from Jay and Johnson]."

Despite Grace's assurance to Bailey that the focus is not meant to be wholly on negative critique, this first night Bailey is skeptical, sharing her feeling that "I just felt, I don't know. I felt like we were ripping her [the teacher] apart." Another student, Brooke, is also wary, voicing concerns about being critical of others' teaching. But as an experienced educator, Grace quickly reframes the critical review of videos away from the idea of "ripping the teacher apart" and toward constructive reflection, modeling, and demonstration in addition to constructive criticism. In the following weeks Grace continues to model that critical, but constructive reflection and feedback is essential for teacher growth. In the role of a more knowledgeable other, Grace artfully supports and prompts the students to help them do with support what they are not yet able to do alone: reflect on a video of teaching through description, comparison, and criticism. Working alone on the first evening, the students struggle to find their footing with regard to *what* to talk about, but also *how* to talk about it. On this night, Grace provides extensive support as the students respond to the video because some students are clearly tentative about the use of video as a learning tool.

Over the next five weeks Grace continues to work closely with her students. In pairs, the students co-plan lessons and complete two tutoring sessions per week with their children. The teaching pairs watch and reflect on their videos together and occasionally with Grace viewing as well. As a whole group, the class also watches and reflects upon more videos of teaching, scaffolded by Grace's expertise. On a night roughly halfway into their teaching practicum, students regroup after their tutoring sessions for an open discussion time where they bring their own celebrations, frustrations, conundrums, noticings, concerns, or questionings to share with their peers in this whole-group setting. As students gather, there is enthusiasm and energy in the room and a lot of humorous banter—quite a different feel from the tentative engagement related to the first time Grace introduced the video viewing exercise. On this night, another significant difference is that Grace's role is less direct. On the first night, Grace directly and explicitly redirected talk to keep the conversation moving toward reflection, but on this night Grace, as a more knowledgeable other, is able to step back and provide less support.

One of the most compelling events of the night is the final activity. Brooke, one of the students who voiced concerns about using video for constructive criticism the first night, offers to critique her own teaching. She describes how watching video had helped her think about and change the types of feedback she provided for the child she was tutoring.

> I realized in my first [tutoring session] I can't even tell you how many times all of my responses were like 'Okay.' And then I said something like 'perfect' every time. It [the feedback] wasn't specific at all. So now I've tried to get better like "Oh I like that you made that connection. I like that you used your schema." Because literally every feedback I gave was 'perfect' and 'Oh, OK.' And then I [would] just move on.

From this and other interactions, it is clear that Grace has successfully created a Community of Practice: a space where students feel safe critiquing their own teaching and sharing with others. Not only does she encourage students to look

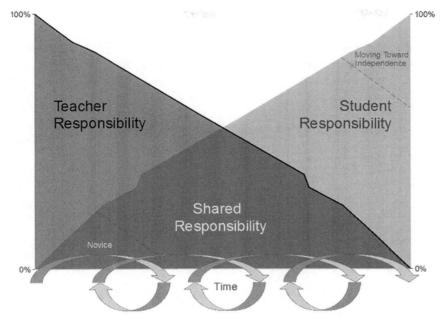

FIGURE 2.6 Teacher and student responsibility in the gradual release of responsibility over time.

at the children whom they are tutoring through the GRR, Grace models the use of the GRR as she works with her adult students; she does not merely say to them "just reflect." She has gradually stepped back as the sole leader for the group as they reflect on practice, while at the same time scaffolding her students to take on more and more of the work of reflecting using the Jay and Johnson framework as a guide. Teacher and students share responsibility for growth over time (Figure 2.6).

We recognize that both teaching and motorcycle jumping are embodied processes. While it is helpful, for example, to provide instructional scaffolds along the way, enacted practice is essential because it enables a person to physically and dynamically interact with a full range of senses in a particular environment. Such embodied action is also crucial to learning particular actions (see Johnson, 2007; McVee & Boyd, 2016 [Chapter 4]; Noë, 2009). In Grace's class, the use of video helped students re-embody and re-live their teaching and allowed Grace to simultaneously provide supportive scaffolding to help her students gain comfort with the process of reflection on practice. We explore other teaching actions more fully in later chapters.

This brings us to a third principle about teaching and learning that frames this book:

Principle #3

The GRR and video reflection help teachers explore teaching and learning as dynamic complex processes that require scaffolding.

Conclusion

In this chapter, you have been introduced to three core principles:

- **Principle #1**: Teaching and reflecting are complex endeavors.
- **Principle #2**: Learning *to teach* and learning *to reflect* are scaffolded processes. Teachers consider what learners need to learn and do in the present while looking ahead and considering what learners need to learn and do in the future (*prolepsis* and *teleology*).
- **Principle #3**: The GRR Model and video reflection help teachers explore teaching and learning as dynamic complex processes that require scaffolding.

Throughout the book, we will explore how the GRR Model is used as a mediational tool to assist in reflection across a diverse set of contexts and participants. While the ultimate goal of introducing and operationalizing the GRR is to establish independent reflection on teaching (see Chapter 6), most often, the GRR is first established within a Community of Practice (Chapter 3) or with a teacher educator, consultant, or coach (Chapter 5 and Chapter 7). In Chapter 3 we provide guidelines for establishing a Community of Practice to support and guide a pedagogy of video reflection. In Chapter 4 we explore more fully the history of reflection and the nuanced meanings of reflection and reflective inquiry. In Chapters 5–7 we provide additional examples of preservice and inservice teachers using video to reflect on teaching and learning and applications of the GRR framework as they work toward developing adaptive expertise. Chapter 8 introduces critical elements of video reflection in more detail, and provides guidance in careful examination of the intersectionalities of race, dialect, language, socioeconomic status, and other sociocultural markers that may influence teachers' analysis of video. Chapter 9 revisits the GRR Model, pedagogy of video reflection, adaptive expertise and essential elements of the text.

References

Brophy, J. (Ed.). (2004). *Using video in teacher education*. Bingley, UK: Emerald Group Publishing.

Cazden, C. B. (1983). Adult assistance to language development: Scaffolds, models, and direct instruction. In R. P. Parker & F. A Davis (Eds.), *Developing literacy:*

Young children's use of language (pp. 3–17). Newark, DE: International Reading Association.

Cole, M. (1996). *Cultural psychology.* New York, NY: Belknap Press.

Hayden, H. E., & Chiu, M. M. (2015). Reflective teaching via a problem exploration—teaching adaptations—resolution cycle: A mixed methods study of preservice teachers' reflective notes. *Journal of Mixed Methods Research, 9*(2), 133–153.

Hayden, H. E., Moore-Russo, D., & Marino, M. R. (2013). One teacher's reflective journey and the evolution of a lesson: Systematic reflection as a catalyst for adaptive expertise. *Reflective Practice: International and Multidisciplinary Perspectives, 14*(1), 144–156.

Jay, J. K., & Johnson, K. L. (2002). Capturing complexity: A typology of reflective practice for teacher education. *Teaching and Teacher Education, 18,* 73–85.

Johnson, M. (2007). *The meaning of the body: Aesthetics of human understanding.* Chicago, IL: University of Chicago Press.

McVee, M. B., & Boyd, F. B. (2016). *Exploring diversity through multimodality, narrative, and dialogue: A framework for teacher reflection.* New York, NY: Routledge.

McVee, M. B., Shanahan, L. E., Pearson, P. D., & Rinker, T. W. (2015). Using the gradual release of responsibility model to support video reflection with preservice and inservice teachers. In E. Ortlieb, M. B. McVee, & L. E. Shanahan (Eds.), *Video reflection in literacy teacher education and development* (Vol. 5, pp. 151–171). Literacy Research, Practice and Evaluation. Bingley, UK: Emerald Group Publishing Limited.

Moll, L. C. (Ed.). (1990). *Vygotsky and education.* New York, NY: Cambridge University Press.

Noë, A. (2009). *Out of our heads: Why you are not your brain and other lessons from the biology of consciousness.* New York, NY: Hill and Wang.

Pearson, P. D. (2013). *Ideas with traction: The gradual release of responsibility.* Paper presented at the annual conference of the National Council of Teachers of English, Boston, MA.

Pearson, P. D., & Gallagher, M. (1983). The instruction of reading comprehension. *Contemporary Educational Psychology, 8,* 317–344.

Rogoff, B., & Wertsch, J. V. (Eds.). (1984). *Children's learning in the zone of proximal development.* San Francisco, CA: Jossey-Bass.

Shanahan, L. E., McVee, M. B., Schiller, J. A., Tynan, E. A., D'Abate, R. L., Flury-Kashmanian, C. M., … Hayden, H. E. (2013). Supporting struggling readers and literacy clinicians through reflective video pedagogy. In E. T. Ortlieb & E. H. Cheek (Eds.), *Advanced literacy practices: From the clinic to the classroom literacy* (Vol. 2, pp. 303–323). Bingley, UK: Emerald Group Publishing.

Shanahan, L. E., & Roof, L. M. (2013). Developing strategic readers: A multimodal analysis of a primary school teacher's use of speech, gesture, and artefacts. *Literacy, 47*(3), 157–164. doi:10.1111/lit.12002.

Shanahan, L. E., & Tochelli, A. L. (2014). Examining the use of video study groups for developing literacy pedagogical content knowledge for critical elements of strategy instruction with elementary teachers. *Literacy Research and Instruction, 53*(1), 1–24.

Stone, C. A. (1993). What is missing in the metaphor of scaffolding? In E. A. Forman, N. Minick, & C. A. Stone (Eds.), *Contexts for learning: Sociocultural dynamics in children's development* (pp. 169–183). New York, NY: Oxford University Press.

Van Fleet, M. (1995). *Fuzzy yellow ducklings: Fold-out fun with textures, colors, shapes, animals*. New York, NY: Dial Books for Young Readers.

Vygotsky, L. S. (1987). Thinking and speech. In L. S. Vygotsky, Collected works (Vol. 1, pp. 39–285) (R. Rieber, & A. Carton, Eds., N. Minick, Trans.). New York, NY: Plenum. Original works in 1934, 1960).

Wood, D., Bruner, J., & Ross, G. (1978). The role of tutoring in problem solving. *Journal of Child Psychology and Psychiatry, 17*, 89–100.

APPENDIX 2.1

Topic: Modeling – Breaking multisyllable words

Clinician ID#: 12 .558S13

Before viewing the video look through the plan to familiarize yourself with the focus of the lesson.

After viewing the video clip complete the following. Below are possible areas to consider but you are not limited to these:

1. Amount of teacher talk. A LOT! Barely heard the student!
2. Types of prompts/question (open vs. closed). Are they effective?
3. Amount of wait time given to student after asking questions. Good.
4. Skills/strategies taught in isolation brought to context? Not yet, hopefully in later lesson.
5. Explicit instruction - are enough details given to the student in easy to understand language? No!
6. Other areas?

Descriptive Dimension
What positive feedback can you offer? (Be sure to include "the what & why")

Teacher	Student
• "I'll help you" • Good rapport	• Attentive, responsive, engaged
• Tying to prior Knowledge	• Asks question about "carefully" when he doesn't understand
• Modeling with "patio"	• Question about suffix
• Shows interest in student	
• Pointing to word	
• Words prepared ahead of time	

What constructive criticism can you offer? (Be sure to include "the what & the why")

Teacher	Student
• Like, um, uh	• Football story: off topic, possibly to avoid working
• Directions weren't super clear	
• Short "a" sound is pronounced weird: "eh" • More eye contact!	• Takes a bit to focus and become engaged
• Pa-ti-o, not pat-i-o?	
• Gets sidetracked w/ football	• Biting nails: distracted
• Too many rules for 1 lesson	

Comparative Dimension What the experts have to say
What connection(s) can you make to past readings from the literature? E.g. This reminds me of what Walker said about ....; this makes me think of Kibby's model...; what I saw in this lesson connects with an article we read in (course) about _____.

Kibby model: important to model for student, gradual release

556: syllabication rules

Engaging the student in instruction

Topic: Modeling – breaking multisyllable words

Critical Dimension
Where should this teacher go from here? (The action plan). If you were to teach this lesson what would you keep the same? What would you do differently?

- Steps for words would be helpful
  - Tap out syllables
  - Break up word according to syllabication rules

- I would move on to allowing the student to break up words on his own on the board, then having him read a text and breaking up words in that text. (Context)

- White board w/ magnetic letters is a great idea because student can manipulate the letters and it's fun!

- I would make my directions more explicit.

- I like that the syllabication rules are listed for easy access.

- Maybe review syllabication rules first w/o jumping right in.

- I would check for understanding more frequently

- Get the student involved more: hands-on! Be more enthusiastic.

* This clinician was a good example for reflection *

3

"I NEVER KNEW I DID THAT UNTIL I WATCHED THIS VIDEO!"

Establishing a Community of Practice to Support Collective Reflection, Risk-Taking, and Trust

Throughout Chapters 1 and 2 we shared an overview of the Gradual Release of Responsibility (GRR) showing how teachers must be supported in their initial video reflections, and we also introduced a video pedagogy of reflection. Both of these constructs are central to establishing a Community of Practice for video reflection. In Chapter 3, we consider several fundamental elements of proficient video reflection communities for you to reflect upon as you develop or participate in your own Community of Practice.

Community of Practice:
A group of people who share a concern, a set of problems, or passion about a topic, and who deepen their knowledge and expertise in this area by interacting on an ongoing basis.

(Wenger, McDermott, & Snyder, 2002, p. 4)

 Stop and Think

1. Think of an area where you consider yourself to be an expert or highly skilled. These might be hobbies or recreational activities that require specific skills. Perhaps you are an avid photographer, musician, horse trainer, knitter, runner, banjo player, book club member, traveler, hunter, sports enthusiast, video game player, or _____.
2. With regard to your area of expertise, what are some of the specialized skills you have acquired over the years?
3. What Communities of Practice helped you develop or acquire these skills?
4. What roles have you played within these Communities of Practice?

FIGURE 3.1 Collaborative video reflection.

Experts develop their expertise by gaining knowledge through an accumulation of experiences over time with others. Or, as Wenger, McDermott, and Snyder (2002) put it, experts gain knowledge through the *"residue of their actions, thinking and conversations—that remains a dynamic part of their ongoing experiences"* (p. 8). From this view, knowledge is dynamic and continuously developing instead of being a static body of information to be memorized. If we apply this dynamic view of knowledge and expertise development to a collaborative video reflection Community of Practice, we come to understand that through our conversations and actions within the video reflection community members grow by confirming, questioning, and probing one another's ideas. Importantly, having some dissonance that includes varied points of view and some disequilibrium among perspectives is a vital ingredient for the community to thrive so that expertise advances to higher levels. Members within a community must be willing to challenge one another's assumptions, perceptions, and interpretations in a dialogic manner in ways that lead to productive reflection.

The success of the video study group community does not solely rest in the use of video or gathering teachers in groups to talk about video. In order to harness the powerful reflective affordances that video offers, and the affordances of what other learners have to offer, a true Community of Practice must be formed where people in the community share a common concern or passion for what they are learning (Lave & Wenger, 1991). Learners must also develop shared understandings of reflection. In this chapter, we articulate fundamental elements of Communities of Practice related to video reflection contexts.

Shifting the Context: Moving from Individual Reflection to Reflection through Communities of Practice

Consider for a moment the contexts in which teachers are typically asked to reflect. In education courses and professional development settings, it is common to ask preservice and inservice teachers to reflect individually. For example, in teacher preparation programs, instructors often assign an article to read and ask students to respond through writing in reflective journals about such things as (a) major points in the article, (b) information that was confusing, or (c) information that changed their thinking. In a field placement or in a professional development setting, teachers might also be asked to reflect by recording their thoughts in a reflective notebook on the effectiveness of an intervention implemented (e.g., working with several students who were struggling readers). Typically, when preservice or inservice teachers are asked to reflect, usually in writing (Roskos, Vukelick, & Risko, 2001), on what they are learning or have learned, they are most commonly asked to do so individually.

There are also times in courses or professional development sessions when teachers are asked to reflect by quietly thinking, maybe doing a quick write, and then sharing their reflections with a partner in a brief activity like a Think Pair Share. The use of a Think Pair Share activity affords time for an individual reflection first that is then shared or made public. It does not afford time for dynamic conversations where teachers reflect deeply on their ideas and explore multiple perspectives. Because teachers learn through reflecting on experiences, it is critical to not only *have* experiences, but also to provide opportunities to *reflect* on those experiences in different ways. Both written and verbal reflections with others are essential because both forms potentially lead teachers to question and view their teaching from different perspectives (Woodcock, Lassonde, & Rutten, 2004). Furthermore, recent attention to teacher learning and reflection reveals that it is important for teachers to be able to construct meaning with and through multiple modes (e.g., visual, audio, gestural, linguistic, etc.) (McVee & Boyd, 2016; Miller & McVee, 2012). In this chapter, we shift the focus away from the common emphasis on individual reflections toward video reflections that occur in safe and trusting communities comprised of other learners and a more knowledgeable other who acts as an instructor. In a Community of Practice, the more knowledgeable other could be an instructor, facilitator, consultant, or another teacher in the Community of Practice who has more knowledge than other teachers in the group.

Communities of Practice can be composed of different types of members in different contexts. For instance, all of the following can be considered examples of a Community of Practice:

- an Instructional Coach and inservice teachers who meet in a school setting,
- a teacher educator and preservice teachers who meet in a college reading clinic,
- a university researcher and preservice and inservice teachers who meet at a university and in school settings.

While in educational settings such groups typically have a designated expert or more knowledgeable other, it is also possible for Communities of Practice to have distributed expertise and leadership roles. For example, a group of preservice teachers could decide to form their own video study group to help themselves prepare for the edTPA or Praxis Performance Assessment for Teachers related to teacher certification. Or a group of veteran teachers could form a study group to study their own teaching and investigate culturally relevant pedagogies in response to a student body that is increasingly linguistically diverse. While it is possible to have a video study group that does not have a designated guide or more knowledgeable other, the examples in this book are drawn mostly from Communities of Practice which begin at the instigation of a guide, expert, or more knowledgeable other (e.g., an instructor, facilitator, coach, or professional development coordinator).

FIGURE 3.2 Collaborative video reflection with a more knowledgeable other.

Communities of Practice in Context

 Stop and Think

Look back at the photographs in Figures 3.1 and 3.2.

- What do you notice about these photographs?
- What observations and inferences can you make about the people in the photographs?
- What do you notice about the grouping, body language, posture, gaze, gestures, or other modalities used for communication?
- What do you notice about the setting and where do you think the groups are meeting?

In Figure 3.1 notice the teachers' body language as three clearly have their gaze fixed on the laptop screen to view the video of a lesson with the fourth teacher is taking notes. The male teacher with the hat is gesturing as he is making a point about an event in the video. One female teacher lightly grasps the laptop to control the group viewing of her lesson. As they are watching, their body language, posture, gaze, and gestures show a high level of engagement in the community. Notice, in Figure 3.2, the teachers are sitting as a group and watching a video with a facilitator or a more knowledgeable other who leans in to scaffold their reflection on the video. Just as in Figure 3.1, the teachers have a fixed gaze on the screen. Their gaze and positive facial expressions signify high levels of participation.

Participating in Communities of Practice where video analysis is used as a tool to develop teachers' understanding has been shown to promote reflection and dialogue about teaching practices with both preservice and inservice teachers (Harford, MacRuairc, & McCartan, 2010) and can serve as a knowledge building activity (Pea & Lindgren, 2008) for teachers to understand various concepts, like a new teaching strategy. Video reflection has also been shown to develop pedagogical content knowledge (Shanahan & Tochelli, 2014). In a reflective video study group, the participants can work together as an inquiry community, collaborating to generate new knowledge about an aspect of teaching and learning that is of interest. They might explore their implementation of a new teaching technique, such as explicit strategy instruction, or examine students' understandings of a concept being taught in mathematics. Participating in this collaborative space is essential to teachers' development and ultimately student learning, because "teachers are more likely to change a behavior when they believe in and understand the change and can modify the ideas to work in their classrooms" (Tatum, 2005, p. 136).

Collegial Relationships: Social Cultural Nature of Collective Reflection

Teachers who participate in a video study group as a community are learners who contribute to and influence the reflective discussions as they learn to be a member of that community (Rogoff, 1995). Within the community, the teachers are considered to be in an apprenticeship where they are guided in their participation during interpersonal interactions with other teachers and a facilitator, consultant, or more knowledgeable other. For the remainder of this chapter we refer to the more knowledgeable other as the instructor. The teachers actively engage in these multidirectional interactions to develop a clearer understanding of the topic under study.

The instructor plays a critical role in the Community of Practice as he or she orchestrates the supports that the community of learners need in order to scaffold their knowledge construction. Support in this case can mean to challenge ideas currently held within a group or agree with the ideas put forward. Supportive scaffolds can come from other people in the community through conversation or dialogue with one another and a more knowledgeable other, and can also come from the video, reflective frameworks, and video analysis task themselves. As discussed in Chapter 1, gradually releasing the amount of scaffolding support provided from the instructor for dialogue and for the video analysis task will increase or decrease the amount of cognitive responsibility needed to learn.

 Stop and Think

- Why would collaboratively reflecting in a learning community with a group of teachers who have similar learning interests be beneficial for a teacher's learning? What is it about people's participation in a learning community that can advance their understanding?

Constructing Knowledge through Dialogue

The social interactions in a Community of Practice can promote reflection and the sharing of ideas with colleagues (Glazer, Abbott, Harris, 2004; Greene, Kim, & Marioni, 2007; Tigelaar, Dolmans, Meijer, De Grave, & Van Der Vleuten, 2006). Collaborative conversations allow participants to reflect on themes and topics of interest to them (van Manen, 1991) and can provide the opportunity to understand situations being reflected upon from new perspectives (Kahne & Westheimer, 2000; Keys & Golley, 1996; Yoon & Kim, 2010), potentially resulting in stretching and influencing others' thinking (Castle, Drake, & Boak, 1995). Willingness to reflect in a group provides opportunities for teaching and learning situations to be viewed from multiple perspectives (Greene et al., 2007) where interactions within the community guide or direct one another toward particular solutions and proposed alternatives. Stephanie shared the following about being a member of a two-year Community of Practice focused on teaching students to be strategic readers:

> But you just learn so much from talking to your peers. You do, I mean it just opens your eyes to other ways of thinking about it. It's just an opportunity to hear things from a different perspective in a way that you might not have thought of. And I loved watching other people's lessons. I think that was probably the biggest learning experience. It was like walking into someone else's classroom and seeing a different way to do it. And a way to do it at different grade levels. A different style of getting it across. I thought it was wonderful.

In order for teachers to develop new understandings, or change previously held ideas, frequent dialogic conversations with peers and mentors are necessary (Van Gyn, 1996). Taking the time to talk in a community fosters the creation of ideas that may lead to in-depth knowledge building, pedagogical changes, and/or metacognitive understandings. Participation in discussions with others has the potential to transform thinking (Allard et al., 2007). As a group reflects together, the actual reflection that is developed becomes a collective reflection and no longer resides only within the individual.

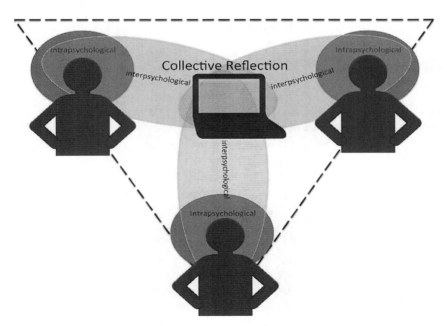

FIGURE 3.3 Depiction of the relationship between the social dimension where learning is constructed and considers individual knowledge construction during a collective reflection.

According to Vygotsky (1997), higher-level learning occurs first through interactions between people, where learning development originates in social space. In Figure 3.3 the dotted triangle signifies the social dimension or space where learning construction is happening. Vygotsky points to the importance of the relationship between the social (video study group) and individual (a teacher in the video study group) as critical to the construction and internalization of knowledge (McVee, Dunsmore, & Gavelek, 2005). Using a video study group as a social space to publicly talk provides the context to acquire and construct new knowledge for oneself. Through the process of engaging in public interaction in a video study group, teachers have an opportunity to develop their own knowledge over time as they bring ideas to the conversation (Wertsch & Stone, 1985).

 Stop and Think

1. Think of a time you have engaged in a small group discussion with colleagues or peers in a work or classroom setting.
2. How beneficial was it to work within the group or was it beneficial?
3. What social dynamics made you guarded, cautious, or vulnerable when sharing experiences or ideas? What social dynamics made you feel comfortable or more open to sharing?
4. How did the social dynamics limit or facilitate the benefits you gained, or failed to gain, from the group?

When community members take up a question or idea during discussion, this individual idea is transformed into a collective reflection. In the example that follows, the video study group community was implementing an explicit strategy instruction model called *Critical Elements of Strategy Instruction* (Almasi & Fullerton, 2012, p. 36) for teaching elementary students to be strategic readers. In the Critical Elements of Strategy Instruction model, the students learn *what* a reading strategy is, *how* to use the reading strategy, and *when* and *why* the reading strategy should be used. For instance, Liz, a third-grade teacher, was teaching her students that good readers use a reading strategy called "visualizing" and that good readers use what they know about a topic and the descriptive words from the author to create an image or movie in their minds about what is happening in the story. Her goal was for her third graders to know when the strategy of visualizing does and does not work. She explained that visualizing does not work if the reader does not have a lot of prior knowledge about what is happening in the story or if the author does not provide very many descriptive words. As Liz taught these concepts across several lessons she was supposed to leave time in the lesson for the students to verbalize (turn and talk) to one another about (a) what strategy they are working on (visualizing),

(b) how readers visualize (using prior knowledge and the author's descriptive words), (c) when readers visualize (when the author provides descriptive words and the reader has a depth of prior knowledge), and (d) why readers use the strategy (to understand the story).

During their video study community gathering, while Donna, Liz, and Nancy were in the process of learning the Critical Elements of Strategy Instruction model, they analyzed their videos and decided that they all needed to work on getting their students to verbalize their use and understanding of the reading strategies. In the example below, Donna, who teaches special education children, asked her colleagues for clarification related to two areas. First, she wondered how she could help her students verbalize a newly learned strategy, and what explicit strategy instruction might look like for students with a high need for additional scaffolding and support. As you read the example below, notice that the session becomes a joint problem-solving session with collective reflection.

LIZ: I think it's funny because all three of us were good at explaining what the reading strategy was and how to use it. We all did the reading strategy during the read aloud.

DONNA: Ok, so if verbalization of the strategy is what we all really want to focus on, how can I make verbalizing their understandings a concrete idea for my students?

NANCY: I guess first it would have to connect to your modeling.

DONNA: Right, yeah.

NANCY: Because I think we all did a really good job of modeling, and we need to gradually release it so that the students are doing more talking. We need to incorporate a turn to your partner [so students can share ideas with each other].

LIZ: And ask students to talk about what they just saw in the modeling: What did I just do? Why did I do that?

DONNA: But now how do you think I would do that type of gradual release for my students who have high needs?

NANCY: I think you do just what you were doing in the video. I saw how you would have students turn and talk to one another. And then you would get students to clarify and explore more.

LIZ: If it was my group, I would tell them: When we read, we need to be thinking about what strategies we are using and why. I hope you can share with a partner your thoughts or ideas and strategies you use after we read a section. So we want students to say: I'm asking questions now because I am confused.

This type of joint learning requires active participation and engagement (Van Gyn, 1996) by community members, such as Liz and Nancy in the example above. It also requires productive dialogue such as when Donna affirms Liz's reflection and Liz's description of how she would introduce verbalization of strategy use to her students. This example from a teacher video study group demonstrates how teachers can work together to jointly co-construct reflective knowledge that develops their expertise. Donna, Liz, and Nancy's interactions reflect a good rapport as they actively offer supportive remarks and suggestions to each other.

But how is a productive Community of Practice created? What factors should be considered in creating safe and trusting spaces where teachers can learn together as they reflect on their own instruction?

Creating Safe and Trusting Communities of Practice for Learners to Engage in Critical Reflection

To create active spaces where learners feel safe and trust one another, the following issues must be considered: (a) positioning of power and authority, (b) cultivating professional relationships, (c) using video as a mediational tool to scaffold teacher reflection, (d) apprenticing with a more knowledgeable other, and (e) avoiding risk and vulnerability when using video.

Considering Power and Authority

It's the equality of—You've got ideas, and I've got ideas, and we can find something together that works.

(Caroline, grade 1–2 multiage classroom teacher)

Collaborative reflective video study groups are more successful when the learners are positioned as authorities of their own development and feel as though they are actively collaborating with colleagues. Critical and collaborative inquiry can only occur when teachers are empowered to participate in such an environment (Greene et al., 2007). As Caroline points out in the comment above, there is equality of power and authority in effective video study groups. Everyone's ideas are valued and participants work together in a reciprocal back and forth relationship that leads problem-solving and insights into teaching.

When having the authority over their own learning, teachers value the time to learn from one another. The joint action between a teacher and other knowledgeable teachers can create a context where the learner, in this case the teacher, feels comfortable exposing his or her areas of development or ideas that are not fully developed. In the learning community, the more knowledgeable other and the teachers' roles may vary in the amount of control they have over their group processing.

For instance, when a Community of Practice has little knowledge related to teaching students to develop as strategic readers, the instructor might start out showing video clips where the lessons represent exemplary teaching and the instructor might think aloud the identification of the critical lesson aspects. Over time, the instructor will gradually release the identification and discussion of the pedagogy so that the teachers are viewing the video and making their own determinations. Eventually, once a teaching concept, (e.g., Critical Elements of Strategy Instruction, as depicted above) is built within the community, the teachers will begin to collaboratively plan their own lessons, implement them, and capture video of their own teaching to analyze and reflect on (see Chapter 6 for a more detailed account of gradually releasing teachers through video reflection).

In Figure 3.4, there are several different levels of support from the instructor related to the amount of cognitive responsibility that is shared across community contexts. Think of the settings (e.g., Instructor/Whole Group, Instructor/Small Group) like a sliding scale where the amount of understanding and cognitive responsibility from the teachers varies based on the amount of support from the instructor and other teachers in each context (McVee, Shanahan, Pearson, & Rinker, 2015). This figure can be used to think about how you want to introduce teachers to video reflection around a concept that they are interested in learning about. As you look at each setting, think about the distribution of the cognitive responsibility between the instructor and preservice/inservice teachers. A detailed description of the levels of support with an explanation of each is provided in Table 3.1.

Prior to working with your own video study group, you should consider the knowledge the teachers have as they enter into the community, as their previous knowledge will influence the amount of support the instructor provides. Recursively monitoring the teachers' knowledge and the knowledge they need to reflect upon the video will afford the instructor the opportunity

FIGURE 3.4 Amount of responsibility shared across social contexts.

TABLE 3.1 Dialogue Provides Social Support from Others

Social Support from Others	Explanation of Support	Instructor Level of Support/Community Member's Level of Thinking
Instructor/ whole group Think aloud modeling	Instructor leads whole group video analysis discussion by providing explicit detailed explanations, think aloud or modeling	Instructor provides the learners with the highest level of support and carries the higher cognitive load, whereas the learner has less of a cognitive load
Instructor/small group Think aloud/ modeling	Instructor's level of support can be high by providing explicit explanations, think alouds or modeling, but the benefit of the smaller group is the potential for more interaction with the preservice and inservice teachers. In the smaller group setting the instructor invites the teachers into the conversation	Instructor's responsibility is still higher and the teachers' cognitive responsibility is just above a mid-range so this setting still provides high levels of support for the preservice or inservice teachers
Instructor/small group	The level of support can be lower if the instructor opens up space for learners to take more responsibility by setting up the task framework and opening up the space for learners to support one another. Here the instructor orchestrates the context by taking a step back and only entering in when necessary	Increased preservice and inservice teachers' cognitive responsibility and reduced instructor responsibility as the teachers grapple with their own understandings
Trios/pairs	Preservice and inservice learners provide support to one another. Instructor's support is dramatically reduced	Increased amount of social support by other learners in the absence of the instructor. Here the instructor moves from group to group and group members distribute the overall cognitive responsibility
Individual	Individual video analysis places the responsibility of the analysis on individuals	Individuals maintain the cognitive responsibility. There is no shared or distributed responsibility, unless requested by the teachers

to strategically adjust the amount of scaffolding that is provided and needed for optimal learning to occur (McVee et al., 2015).

 Stop and Think

- Within the varied group settings, how do community members cultivate professional relationships with one another?

Cultivating Professional Relationships

> Communities of Practice accumulate knowledge and become informally bound by the value that they find in learning together.
> *(Wenger, McDermott, & Snyder, 2002)*

When teachers are cultivating relationships within the Community of Practice they tend to do so in three specific ways (Shanahan & Tochelli, 2012). Teachers who are developing relationships within a community exchange information with one another about the context of the lesson, more specifically the lesson focus, classroom, and students. They ask questions about the number of students in the class, students' familiarity with a particular graphic organizer used in a lesson/ concept taught, or the abilities of the students. Interestingly, when teachers were less familiar with one another (for example, they might teach in the same district, but in two different schools), they spent more of the reflective video study group time and conversations focused on familiarizing and contextualizing one another with the teaching and learning context with the goal of building trusting relationships.

Knowing that this exchange of information assists in cultivating professional relationships, we encourage instructors to begin each video study group by having the teachers introduce the context of their lesson with information such as, grade level, number of students, concept being taught, and where the lesson fell on the continuum from introductory to independent practice (see Chapter 6 for more information regarding the contextualizing of video). In the example described above, when teachers exchanged videos we included a space for this information on the top of the video-analysis recording sheet (e.g., name, grade level, number of students, inclusion classroom, second language learners, lesson objective, identify lesson the GRR). If instructors incorporate the contextualizing of video with preservice teachers it will scaffold their preparation for the first part of edTPA that requires preservice teachers to contextualize their video.

Teachers who taught in closer physical proximity with one another had already developed an understanding of one another and one another's teaching contexts so conversations that occurred within these groups focused on teaching right from the start, not on information related to the teaching context.

This shows the important historical nature of previous relationships between community members and how these histories shape the focus of the conversations within Communities of Practice.

> *While in a Community of Practice not only do teachers develop a body of common knowledge and common practices, they also develop personal relationships, and establish ways to interact and develop an identity.*

When our teachers came together they utilized feedback as a way to develop relationships with one another and develop knowledge. They shared compliments about specific teaching practices they observed in the video. For example, Robin, an inservice teacher, shared the following with Stephanie about her video, "Your language was so specific when you said, good readers use information from the book and from their head to draw an inference." Community members also shared approval of one another's lessons: "I was super impressed with both of your lessons" or "Wow, that was a clever way to do it!"

Another way that they began to build a feeling of togetherness and safety was that they used the collective "we" pronoun when giving a community member a recommendation. Nancy said, "*We all modeled, we read aloud, and maybe getting students to verbalize their strategy use throughout the lesson is something that we need to continue to work on.*" Note that the area of development, getting students to verbalize, was couched in a collective "we" and prefaced with positive feedback.

Once the communities developed a stronger relationship, they began to forge into the space of being more critical. Nancy asked her group: "*Do you want me to be a critical friend or do you want me to be nice and just share compliments?*" Focusing the critical friend comment on the practice they were learning was important so that the feedback did not feel personal. The most effective communities include strong personalities and welcome disagreements and debates. As Lave and Wenger (1991) share, to have an effective and productive community there must be controversy, debate and multiple perspectives.

Apprenticing with More Knowledgeable Others

What made our experience with learning the strategy instruction model unique is that the video analysis allowed us to continue to collaboratively discuss and self-reflect during the practice stage of our learning. This gave us maximum support during the "guided practice" phase of our new learning rather than only during the "modeling" phase. Not only did we have video and peer support, but we also had an "expert model" (the instructor) who was there to continue learning and support over a fairly intense and extended period of time.

(Stephanie, Reading Specialist grades 2–5)

Stephanie is referring to the instructor being there to scaffold learning during the GRR when the inservice teachers were taking on more responsibility (see Figure 3.4 and Table 3.1) for their learning in trios. Notice that although the instructor's guidance or scaffolding was less, it was still perceived as essential to the inservice teachers' continued learning as they apprenticed in learning of Critical Elements of Strategy Instruction.

As they apprenticed, teachers indicated that seeing other colleagues' lessons was helpful. Dan, a fifth-grade teacher, shared that watching the video and talking with peers:

> made me so much more aware and allowed me to see other ways of approaching the lesson I taught. However, it was also necessary to have direct feedback from someone who knew more than us.

Initially, to extend the inservice teachers' learning the instructor had to be a "critical friend" and introduce a different perspective or point of debate. The goal of educating the Community of Practice on the value of controversy was to develop the teachers' understanding of multiple perspectives and model debates that were a healthy part of the conversations and knowledge building. At times, it was necessary for the instructor to create some disequilibrium to deepen their knowledge.

 Stop and Think

- If it takes a group sustained time together to form relationships, how teachers are grouped together and the amount of reoccurring contact they have with one another becomes important. What can instructors do to add varied perspectives to debate as the communities are cultivating professional relationships?

Although the inservice teachers spent two years in their community they confirmed that directly pointing out an area of development for a peer was difficult. They knew the value of being honest, but were concerned about offending a community member's feelings. Liz, a third-grade classroom teacher, used the following analogy:

> Teachers initially used praise, praise, praise and I was looking for something to work on. This experience was like American Idol with the praise, praise, praise being Paula Abdul with her positive attitude and I wanted Simon Cowell who would tell it like it was.

One way that Liz shared how she approached adding critique into the discussion was by using a "nice sandwich," which was a genuine compliment, area of development, and another genuine compliment. The longer the community stayed together the more they were able to be critical friends.

As communities are developing, a strong instructor needs to provide varied perspectives to debate, while always being cognizant of group dynamics so that learning can occur. It is important that teachers don't turn a blind eye to other perspectives or create cliques that impede learning.

 Stop and Think

- How does an instructor assist teachers in focusing their reflections when teachers are bombarded with a considerable amount of sensory information?

Guiding Teachers through Video Reflection

> At first I didn't realize how much I would come to appreciate the guided video analysis framework. I liked time stamping points in the video when I recognized myself and my colleagues implementing parts of the strategy instruction model. It helped us to see our accomplishments and areas that needed more work. It also guided our discussions.
>
> *(Liz, grade 3 classroom teacher)*

The use of video as a mediational tool to develop teacher learning is not new. With the development of portable video equipment, teacher educators began using video in the 1960s. Recently, there is a renewed interest in video due to technological advances making video even more accessible, and in some states new teacher certification requirements expect that teachers reflect on video recorded of their teaching. Educators have learned a great deal about some of the benefits of using video to develop stronger teaching practices.

When guided through the process of watching digital video of their student teaching, preservice teachers became more reflective about their pedagogy (e.g., Harford, MacRuairc, & McCartan, 2010). However, Gelfuso and Dennis (2014) found there were significant challenges to supporting preservice teachers in the reflective process when using video from field experiences. They found that setting a purpose when viewing video was critical to teacher development. Through video reflection, inservice teachers also demonstrated improvement in their teaching skills (e.g., Rosaen, Degnan, VanStratt, & Zietlow, 2004; Zhang, Lundeberg, & Eberhardt, 2010) and shifted their focus to student learning (Sherin & van Es, 2009). In our work, we found that teachers had more comfort watching and analyzing teachers who they did not have a relationship with when they were learning something new—becoming more comfortable with video recording themselves and sharing as their understanding developed over time.

As shared in Chapter 2, a strong pedagogy of video reflection includes reflections that are self-directed. It is also important that learners have a voice in determining the purpose of their reflection. Viewing with a purpose is essential (Miller & Zhou, 2007) because when teachers watch video without a purpose for viewing, they typically attend to the teacher's personality or are overwhelmed with the amount of information available through video (Newell & Walter, 1981). Yet, we discovered that just having a purpose for video reflection did not result in teachers developing higher-level reflections. In order to move teachers' reflections beyond a descriptive level we needed to include a video reflective framework or model to guide the reflective process (Tochon, 1999).

In the reading center described in Chapter 2, literacy specialists used a reflective analysis framework aligned with Jay and Johnson's (2002) typology of reflection. Literacy specialist candidates begin video analysis reflecting on example lessons where they do not know the teacher or student and then progress to analyzing video of themselves. To prepare for the whole class reflective discussion, literacy specialists fill out the task analysis sheet (see Appendix 3.1). Here, they identify the pedagogical focus of their reflection and then draw upon Jay and Johnson's typology to move through reflective levels. For the *descriptive dimension* (lower level of thinking) they briefly describe the part of their lesson associated with their reflective goal. At the second level, the *comparative dimension* (higher level of thinking), teachers pose alternative views or perspectives drawing upon past course reading and previous experiences. Then at the third level, the *critical dimension* (higher level of thinking), the teachers create a plan of action for their next teaching.

Later in the semester, Kelsey, a literacy specialist candidate, self-selected the purpose for her reflection and then moved through Jay and Johnson's typology when reflecting with the class:

> I am focusing my reflection on wait time, and when I was viewing my first few lessons, I would ask, and I didn't even realize I was doing it at first, but I would ask maybe three questions right off the bat. And the poor kid didn't even have time to think about the first one when I've already slammed him with two more and gave him maybe a second to answer before I'm like, "it's right here," trying to help him. So now I'm paying more attention... I try to ask one question, and then wait and I'm counting in my head to three or five. Then depending on how he is reacting, I give him more time or I start to help him. I never realized I did this until I looked at the video critically. I was like holy cow I really need to work on this, but it's good. I'm getting there.

Jay and Johnson's typology is not the only reflective framework to draw upon when guiding teachers' video reflections. In Chapters 4 and 7 we present Rodgers' (2002) reflective inquiry model as another framework used to scaffold video reflections. We encourage you to ask yourself what reflective models or frameworks you might draw upon in your Community of Practice.

As one more example of video analysis frameworks, we share the Critical Elements of Strategy Instruction video analysis chart that teachers use when learning a new teaching strategy (see Figure 3.5). This analysis framework was established for use in groups of three. Each group of three is asked to view the video of their own teaching and the teaching of the two other colleagues in their trio. In this example, the teachers video recorded themselves as they implemented a new teaching strategy, Critical Elements of Strategy Instruction, and then timestamped when they saw evidence of the components of the teaching model in the lessons viewed.

Similar to Deeney and Dozier (2015), we recommend that video viewing always have a guiding question or an analysis framework to assist in setting the purpose for viewing. Additional decisions instructors need to make revolve around specifics of video use. How much video should be watched: a clip or the whole lesson? Should the teachers watch themselves, people they don't know, or their peers? Such different structures can be used when teachers view videos. For example, in some studies teachers have analyzed videos of their own practice in isolation (e.g., Rich & Hannafin, 2008, 2009) while in other studies teachers discussed the

Video Analysis Framework
Critical Elements of Strategy Instruction

Name:
Grade Level:
Strategy:
Circle where is this lesson in the gradual release of responsibility?
Modeling   Shared   Guided Trios/Partners   Independence

Timestamp the following Critical Elements of Strategy components.

CESI Component	Time	Statement
	Put the time that you observe the particular strategy component	Write the beginning of the sentence the teacher says.
What is the strategy?		
How does a reader _____ (strategy)? (e.g., Teacher describes how a good reader makes an inference?)		
Why would a reader use this strategy?		
When would be a good time to use this strategy? When wouldn't be a good time to use this strategy?		
Verbalizing Time is purposely included for student to discuss the strategy use and their understanding of the text.		
Reduce Processing Demands How was the abstract strategy made concrete?		

FIGURE 3.5 Video analysis framework for Critical Elements of Strategy Instruction.

lesson with a mentor or researcher (e.g., Powell, 2005; Rosaen et al., 2004, 2010). Another common format is where teachers selected a clip from a videotaped lesson to share with their peers (e.g., Christ, Arya, & Chiu, 2012; Zhang, Lundeberg, Koehler, & Eberhardt, 2011). All of these structures provide affordances and limitations to consider that impact teachers' comfort levels and opportunities to learn.

 Stop and Think

1. What are the advantages and disadvantages of having an instructor determine the task versus a teacher determining the task?
2. What are the advantages and disadvantages of viewing by yourself first and then bringing it to the group or analyzing the video as a group the first time you see the video?

Video analysis sessions "have the potential to help viewers be reflective and purposeful about their use of the materials and expand their personal experiences" (Rosaen et al., 2004, p. 193). In addition, using video in professional development can promote deeper discussions of teaching practices beyond what individual recollections can bring to teaching conversations (Grant & Kline, 2010) and video facilitates teachers' reflective practice. When using video, we suggest that careful decisions are made about the: purpose of viewing the video, reflective video analysis framework, amount of video viewed and whom the video is viewed with in the community.

 Stop and Think

- Now think of a time you shared when using video. What might make you feel more or less vulnerable when using video as a learning tool?

Considering Risk and Vulnerability Using Video

I think that all of us were sensitive to the fact that the video made us feel vulnerable—in the beginning we were all a little more careful about our comments and looked for positives. I think this (video study group) became a lot more natural and honest as we built trust with each other. Ultimately, I think the video really helped us to deepen our collaborative relationships because we were inviting each other into our lessons and began to rely on each other to nurture our growth. It was exciting to see our colleagues teach and experiment as well as it challenged us to push ourselves.

(Stephanie, Reading Specialist)

Although video can increase preservice and inservice teacher learning, it is critical to consider effective ways of using the video. Using video can present different degrees of vulnerability. Reflect for a minute: How do your feelings of vulnerability change when the teacher in the video is someone you don't know; someone you know but does not work in your school; someone who is a colleague in your school; or that someone is you in the video?

When using one's own video as a learning tool, its presence does influence the interactions and relationships among teachers (Shanahan & Tochelli, 2012). Educators who are considered effective by their peers and administrators revealed that initially they felt vulnerable when their colleagues viewed their video and began to reflect. Once the trust was built, teachers reflected more honestly about the teaching and learning episodes that were the focus of the reflection. As Dan, a fifth-grade teacher, shared, *"watching someone else is —dare I say it—intimate."*

Within a Community of Practice, where teachers are apprenticing together there may also be unintended power differentials between the teachers in the community. It is impossible to not have teachers' past experiences interacting with the present. Sharing one's own video may also cause discomfort resulting in a teacher feeling vulnerable due to past interactions. In the example below, the group dynamics were influenced by previous interactions with other group members.

> When we first started, Dan was the person who trained me in the essential elements when I was new to the district. So you can imagine how intimidated I was to be sharing my video with him. Then I also viewed his and was asked to provide feedback about his strategy instruction. Not to mention that Nancy was also one of my new teacher orientation trainers too.
>
> *(Robin, grades 3–4 multiage classroom teacher)*

Even though Robin was in the district for six years, those previous interactions, although not intended by Dan and Nancy, were initially present. As the instructor, Lynn (our co-author) did give some choice regarding who would collaborate in the smaller video study groups. To reduce the feelings of vulnerability, the following strategies provide important steps to developing trust.

• *Norms:* The video study group developed norms or agreed upon behaviors when analyzing one another's videos. Just like the slogan: "What happens in Vegas stays in Vegas," we decided "What happens in video study group stays in video study group." Teachers decided they would protect one another by agreeing to not share any aspects of the feedback or lesson video provided to one another with anyone else outside the study group.

- *Grouping*: When grouping the teachers, Lynn knew there would be varied levels of comfort due to their past histories so, she asked teachers for their top three people in the group who they were most comfortable sharing their teaching with, and three people who they were least comfortable sharing with. Groups were formed with their rankings in mind.
- *Purpose for viewing*: Each teacher used the video reflection guide to facilitate the focus of the reflection to meet the community's goal. The use of the video reflection guide kept reflections focused on the pedagogy. Analysis and reflection with a clear purpose is necessary for teachers to construct meaning (see Appendix 3.3). Teachers had opportunities to determine the purpose for viewing by identifying the problem space. Choice in determining the focus of the video study group discussion is important for reflection (see Chapters 4 and 6).
- *Time to reflect*: Teachers prepared for their reflective video study group community session by reflecting on the video individually prior to participating in the reflective discussion. The inservice teachers felt that individual reflection prior to group discussion was critical so that they could maintain a healthy community by thoughtfully developing their ideas, comments and questions.
- *Control*: If teachers were not pleased with how their lesson went on the video recording day, they could opt to schedule for another day. So, they ultimately had the choice to use or not use their video.

Conclusion

In this chapter, we have discussed video reflection in Communities of Practice. We provided examples from a specific Community of Practice learning a new instructional strategy in order to illustrate specific features of effective communities. In order for a community to be a productive space, members must have ownership over what they are learning and feel passionate about the learning focus of the community. If they don't feel ownership of the learning focus within a Community of Practice, they may lose interest. In situations where external assessments are in place (e.g., grades for a university teacher preparation course or evaluations from school leadership teams), participants may find themselves going through the motions rather than engaged in authentic learning. This is a time to incorporate choice and voice for the members. They can determine the focus of the video reflection by identifying the problem space.

In addition, if members fail to develop trust with other community members and consequently, fail to share ideas and learn from one another, participants may share superficial comments that do not foster engaged reflection. Relationships and collegial support within learning communities are extremely important because they are often the main determinants of change, retention, increased professionalism, and engagement levels for teachers (Daly, 2010). These strong mutually professional relationships provide critical support for an inquiry space where complex knowledge is developed through joint problem-solving. Furthermore, any learning community can also be problematic (Fernandez, Cannon, & Chokski, 2003), if teachers engage in *contrived collegiality*, a type of collaboration that maintains the status quo, instead of the construction of new knowledge (Hargreaves, 1994). In the community, the teachers themselves must take on an active role in the inquiry space, where they are creating and working toward using what is being learned with varied, approximations of proficiency.

Knowing the potential of reflecting on video as a Community of Practice, we ask that you take a moment to consider what it will take to make the reflective video study group community a safe place to develop your own knowledge and skills. We also leave you with two checklists to gain information about your participants in your community (Appendix 3.1) and a checklist to assist in your consideration of the fundamental elements of strong Communities of Practice (Appendix 3.2). In Chapter 6 we explain in detail the reflective process outlined in this chapter. In Chapter 4, we explore the nuances of reflection and reflective inquiry.

References

Allard, C. C., Goldblatt, P. F., Kemball, J. I., Kendrick, S. A., Millen, K. J., & Smith, D. M. (2007). Becoming a reflective community of practice. *Reflective Practice: International and Multidisciplinary Perspectives, 8*(3), 299–314.

Almasi, J., & Fullerton, S. K. (2012). *Teaching strategic processes in reading* (2nd ed.). New York, NY: Guilford Press.

Castle, J. B., Drake, S. M., & Boak, T. (1995). Collaborative reflection as professional development. *The Review of Higher Education, 18*(3), 243–263.

Christ, T., Arya, P., & Chiu, M. (2012). Collaborative peer video analysis: Insights about literacy assessment and instruction. *Journal of Literacy Research, 44*(2), 171–199.

Daly, A. J. (2010). Mapping the terrain: Social network theory and educational change. In A. J. Daly (Ed.), *Social network theory and educational change* (pp. 1–16). Cambridge, MA: Harvard Education Press.

Deeney, T., & Dozier, C. (2015). Constructing successful video reflection experiences in practicum settings. In E. Ortlieb, M. B. McVee, & L. E. Shanahan (Eds.), *Video reflection in literacy teacher education and development* (Vol. 5, pp. 41–57). Literacy Research, Practice and Evaluation. Bingley, UK: Emerald Group Publishing Limited.

Fernandez, C., Cannon, J., & Chokski, S. (2003). A US-Japan lesson study collaboration reveals critical lenses for examining practice. *Teaching and Teacher Education, 19*, 171–185.

Gelfuso, A., & Dennis, D. (2014). Getting reflection off the page: The challenges of developing support structures for pre-service teacher reflection. *Teaching and Teacher Education, 38*, 1–11.

Glazer, C., Abbott, L., & Harris, J. (2004). A teacher-developed process for collaborative professional reflection. *Reflective Practice: International and Multidisciplinary Perspectives, 5*(1), 33–46.

Grant, T. J., & Kline, K. (2010). The impact of video-based lesson analysis on teachers' thinking and practice. *Teacher Development*, *14*(1), 69–83.

Greene, W. L., Kim, Y. M., & Marioni, J. L. (2007). The reflective trio: A model for collaborative self-study in teacher education. *KEDI Journal of Educational Policy*, *4*(1), 41–58.

Harford, J., MacRuairc, G., & McCartan, D. (2010). 'Lights, camera, reflection': Using peer video to promote reflective dialogue among student teachers. *Teacher Development*, *14*(1), 57–68.

Hargreaves, A. (1994). *Changing teachers changing times: Teachers' work and culture in the postmodern age*. New York, NY: Teachers College Press.

Jay, J. K., & Johnson, K. L. (2002). Capturing complexity: A typology of reflective practice for teacher education. *Teaching and Teacher Education*, *18*, 73–85.

Kahne, J., & Westheimer, J. (2000). A pedagogy of collective action and reflection: Preparing teachers for collective school leadership. *Journal of Teacher Education*, *51*, 372–383.

Keys, C. W., & Golley, P. S. (1996). The power of a partner: Using collaborative reflection to support constructivist practice in middle grade science and mathematics. *Journal of Science Teacher Education*, *7*(4), 229–246.

Lave, J., & Wenger, E. (1991). *Situated Learning: Legitimate Peripheral Participation*. Cambridge, UK: Cambridge University Press.

McVee, M. B., & Boyd, R. (2016). *Exploring diversity through multimodality, narrative, and dialogue: A framework for teacher reflection*. New York, NY: Routledge.

McVee, M. B., Dunsmore, K., & Gavelek, J. R. (2005). Schema theory revisited. *Review of Educational Research*, *75*(4), 531–566.

McVee, M. B., Shanahan, L. E., Pearson, P. D., & Rinker, T. W. (2015). Using the gradual release of responsibility model to support video reflection with preservice and inservice teachers. In E. Ortlieb, M. B. McVee, & L. E. Shanahan (Eds.), *Video reflection in literacy teacher education and development* (Vol. 5, pp. 151–171). Literacy Research, Practice and Evaluation. Bingley, UK: Emerald Group Publishing.

Miller, S. M., & McVee, M. B. (Eds.) (2012). *Multimodal composing in classrooms*. New York, NY: Routledge.

Miller, K., & Zhou, X. (2007). Learning from classroom video: What makes it compelling and what makes it hard. In R. Goldmann, R. Pea, B. Barron, & S. J. Derry (Eds.), *Video research in the learning sciences* (pp. 321–334). Mahwah, NJ: Lawrence Erlbaum.

Newell, K. M., & Walter, C. A. (1981). Kinematic and kinetic parameters in information feedback in motor skill acquisition. *Journal of Human Movement Studies*, *7*, 235–254.

Pea, R., & Lindgren, R. (2008). Video collaboratories for research and education: An analysis of collaboration design patterns. *IEEE Transaction on Learning Technologies*, *1*, 235–247.

Powell, E. (2005). Conceptualizing and facilitating active learning: Teachers' video-stimulated reflective dialogues. *Reflective Practice*, *6*(3), 407–418.

Rich, P. J., & Hannafin, M. J. (2008). Decisions and reasons: Examining preservice teacher decision-making through video self-analysis. *Journal of Computing in Higher Education*, *20*(1), 62–94.

Rich, P. J., & Hannafin, M. J. (2009). Scaffolded video self-analysis: Discrepancies between preservice teachers' perceived and actual instructional decisions. *Journal of Computing in Higher Education*, *21*, 128–145.

Rodgers, C. L. (2002). Seeing student learning: Teacher change and the role of reflection. *Harvard Educational Review, 72*(2), 230–253.

Rogoff, B. (1995). *Apprenticeship in thinking: Cognitive development in social context.* New York, NY: Oxford University Press.

Rosaen, C. L., Degnan, C., VanStratt, T., & Zietlow, K. (2004). Designing a virtual K-2 classroom literacy tour: Learning together as teachers explore "best practice". In J. Brophy (Ed.), *Using video in teacher education* (Vol. 10, pp. 169–199). Amsterdam: Elsevier Ltd.

Rosaen, C. L., Lundeberg, M., Terpstra, M., Cooper, M., Fu, J., & Niu, R. (2010). Seeing through a different lens. What do interns learn when they make video cases of their own teaching? *The Teacher Educator, 45,* 1–22.

Roskos, K., Vukelick, C., & Risko, V. J. (2001). Reflection and learning to teach reading: A critical review of literacy and general teacher education studies. *Journal of Literacy Research, 33*(4), 595–635.

Shanahan, L. E., & Tochelli, A. L. (2012). Video study group a context to cultivate professional relationships. In P. J. Dunston, S. K. Fullerton, C. C. Bates, K. Headley, & P. M. Stecker (Eds.), *61st literacy research association conference yearbook* (pp. 196–211). Oak Creek, WI: Literacy Research Association.

Shanahan, L. E., & Tochelli, A. L. (2014). Examining the use of video study groups for developing literacy pedagogical content knowledge for Critical Elements of Strategy Instruction with elementary teachers. *Literacy Research and Instruction, 53*(1), 1–24.

Sherin, M. G., & van Es, E. A. (2009). Effects of video club participation on teachers' professional vision. *Journal of Teacher Education, 60*(1), 20–37.

Tatum, A. W. (2005). *Teaching reading to Black adolescent males: Closing the achievement gap.* Portland, ME: Stenhouse Publishers.

Tigelaar, D. E. H., Dolmans, D. H. J. M., Meijer, P. C., De Grave, W. S., & Van Der Vleuten, C. (2006). Teachers' interactions and their collaborative reflection processes during peer meetings. *Advances in Health Sciences Education, 13,* 289–308.

Tochon, F. V. (1999). *Video study groups for education, professional development, and change.* Madison, WI: Atwood Publishing.

Van Gyn, G. H. (1996). Reflective practice: The needs of professions and the promise of cooperative education. *Journal of Cooperative Education, 31*(2), 103–131.

van Manen, M. (1991). *The tact of teaching: The meaning of pedagogical thoughtfulness.* Albany, NY: State University of New York Press.

Vygotsky, L. S. (1997). *The collected works of L.S. Vygotsky. Vol. 4. The history of the development of higher mental functions* (M. J. Hall, Trans; R. W. Reiber, Ed.). New York, NY: Plenum.

Wenger, E., McDermott, R., & Snyder, W. M. (2002). *A guide to managing knowledge: Cultivating communities of practice.* Boston, MA: Harvard Business Press.

Wertsch, J. V., & Stone, C. A. (1985). The concept of internalization in Vygotsky's account of the genesis of higher mental functions. In J. V. Wertsch (Ed.), *Culture, communication, and cognition: Vygotskian perspectives* (pp. 162–182). Cambridge, UK: Cambridge University Press.

Woodcock, C. A., Lassonde, C. A., & Rutten, I. R. (2004). How does collaborative reflection play a role in a teacher researcher's beliefs about herself and her teaching? Discovering the power of relationships. *Teaching & Learning, 18*(2), 57–75.

Yoon, H., & Kim, M. (2010). Collaborative reflection through dilemma cases of science practical work during practicum. *International Journal of Science Education, 32*(3), 283–301.

Zhang, M., Lundeberg, M., & Eberhardt, J. (2010). Seeing what you normally don't see. *Phi Delta Kappan, 91*(6), 60–65.

Zhang, M., Lundeberg, M., Koehler, M. K., & Eberhardt, J. (2011). Understanding affordances and challenges of three types of video for teacher professional development. *Teaching and Teacher Education, 27*, 454–462.

APPENDIX 3.1

VIDEO VIEWING GUIDE EXAMPLE USING JAY AND JOHNSON'S TYPOLOGY

LAI 558: Video Viewing Guide

Name:
Lesson Topic: Writing Pass the Pen   **Date:** 3/21/17

Using Jay and Johnson's Typology, reflect upon the example lesson across all three dimensions.

Descriptive Dimension
What positive feedback can you offer?

Teacher	Student
• Reviewed with the student before they began	• Involved with teacher questions/prompts before lesson began
• Prepared with topic in case student got stuck	• Seems excited about the Pass the Pen
• Provided student with choice	• Referenced charts on the board

What constructive criticism can you offer?

Teacher	Student
• Let student get too far off topic for too long	• Shared a long story about hurting his shoulder that did not relate to his story.
• Should redirect focus on student while he writes instead of doing other things	

Comparative Dimension
What connection(s) can you make to past readings from literature? For example, this reminds me of what Walker said about…; This makes me think of Kibby's Model….;"what I saw in this lesson connecs with an article we read in (course) about…

Critical Dimension
Where should the teacher go from here? (The action plan). If you were to teach this lesson again what would you keep the same? What would you do differently?

Suggest that they complete to the story or move to a new topic.

Teacher	Student
• Reread the story each time a part is added for cohesion	• The game was engaging for the student.
• Because the student was focused on subjects and verbs, discuss subjects and verbs in each sentence and have him point them out.	• Still let him choose the topic
	• Give the student personal space/time to think while writing.

APPENDIX 3.2

INFORMATION SHEET FOR PARTICIPANTS FOR PLANNING REFLECTIVE VIDEO STUDY GROUPS

1. Have you ever recorded your own teaching? (This could be using any device from a large-style video camera, camera phone, tablet, etc.)

   a. Yes
   b. No

2. Was recording of your own teaching required (e.g., for certifications, professional development credit, practicums, class project) or was it voluntary?

   a. NA – I have not recorded my teaching on video.
   b. Required
   c. Voluntary

3. After video recording your teaching, how did you reflect on your teaching (if at all)? (Choose all that apply.)

   a. NA – I have not recorded my teaching on video.
   b. I video recorded my teaching but did not formally reflect on it.
   c. Writing (journal, reflection, description, etc.)
   d. Talking (group or paired discussion with peers; discussion with a more knowledgeable mentor, coach, instructor)
   e. Video analysis using annotation tools (marking or labelling video, commenting using video annotation tools)
   f. Other

4. If you had previous opportunities to video record your teaching, please briefly describe any benefits or positive learning experiences or outcomes.

5. If you had previous opportunities to video record your teaching, please briefly describe any negative learning experiences or outcomes.

6. (For all participants, regardless of whether you have had experience with video recording your teaching.) List 3–5 words or phrases that describe how you feel about the opportunity to video record and reflect on your teaching with your peers or colleagues at this time.
7. What do you hope to gain from the opportunity to video record your teaching and reflect on it with others?
8. List the names of several colleagues/classmates you would prefer to have in your video reflection study group.
9. List the names of any colleagues/classmates you would prefer *not* to have in your video reflection group.

APPENDIX 3.3

Questions for teacher-leaders, professional development coordinators, or teachers to consider when planning for or forming video reflection study groups.

- Have the learning community members selected their own learning topic?
- Are community members willing to be "critical friends?"
- How will you gradually release the Community of Practice so that they develop a relationship with one another and are comfortable using video as a reflective tool?
  - Consider amount of more knowledgeable other support.
  - Consider gradual release of dialogue scaffolds.
  - Consider length of video.
  - Consider who is the focus of the video.
  - Consider the video analysis task.

4

WHAT DOES IT MEAN TO REFLECT ON THE PRACTICE OF TEACHING?

Chapter 3 introduced the idea of Communities of Practice (Lave & Wenger, 1991) and the premise that in order for deep reflection to occur, a safe and trusting environment must be created for learners. This type of community is essential for learners, whether novice or veteran teachers, to step out of their comfort zones and engage in honest, and sometimes uncomfortable, examination of their own teaching practices. As described in Chapter 3, this community also requires a guide, a more knowledgeable other, who can help teachers and teacher candidates engage in video reflection through the Gradual Release of Responsibility (GRR) Model and who can scaffold reflective teacher learning across time. While we defined reflection in earlier chapters, in this chapter we explore the nuances of reflection and reflective inquiry.

Understanding Reflection in Teacher Education

FIGURE 4.1 Reflection.

re•flec•tion /ri'flekSHən
the throwing back by a body or surface of light, heat, or sound without absorbing it *'the reflection of light'* serious thought or consideration *'he doesn't get much time for reflection'*

Oxford Dictionary (2014)
www.oxforddictionaries.com/us/definition/american_english/reflection

Can any student teacher complete teacher preparation coursework without encountering the idea of reflection or writing at least one reflective response? Or more than likely, multiple reflective responses? Regardless of how many written reflections learners may compose, how does reflection help prepare teachers for the practice of teaching? How important is reflection to teaching? And what exactly are teachers being asked to do when they are asked to reflect? These are some of the questions we will consider in this chapter.

More than 100 years ago educational philosopher and psychologist John Dewey (1938/1963) argued that reflection was an essential element of the teaching process. Since that time, the construct of reflective practice, and conversations about reflective practice and the work of Dewey, have been the foundation for many teacher preparation programs and classes. Reflection is viewed as essential for strong teaching practice, in part, because effective teachers do give serious thought to their own teaching and to their students' learning—even if teachers are not always writing formal written reflections on their teaching. In Dewey's words, understanding the purpose of any experience is a "complex intellectual operation" (pp. 68–69). To say that teaching is a complex intellectual operation is an apt description, and if you recall the cartoon from Chapter 1, even more complex than banjo playing.

Dewey (1910/1933) also urged his readers to think about the "teachers who left a permanent intellectual impress" (p. 54) on them as learners. This brings to mind the question: Who are the teachers you most remember? Which teachers made the greatest impression on you and your learning? In particular, which teachers most profoundly influenced the development of your intellectual knowledge?

 Stop and Think

- Take a few minutes to recall a teacher who had a positive impact on your academic or intellectual journey. This teacher could be someone you encountered in a formal school setting (e.g., an elementary teacher or college instructor) or a teacher from an informal setting (e.g., a rabbi, Girl Scout leader, pastor, or coach).

- What actions did the teacher take that influenced your academic or intellectual growth? How did this teacher create curiosity or maintain interest? What intellectual skills, strategies, or content did you learn from this teacher?
- What types of reflection do you think this teacher might have engaged in to help reach students or learners like you?

Dewey describes reflective teachers as those who "maintain continuity of thought" while acknowledging that teaching includes sidebars and diversions that introduce "novelty and variety" (1910/1933, p. 54) in order to keep student interest. Effective and reflective practitioners keep the main learning objective or instructional goal in mind, artfully weaving in the sidebars and related topics that crop up during classroom discourse, using the unpredictable events or insights from discussion to enable teachable moments. Teachers who reflect on their practice can harness the unexpected diversions and related content ideas more fully than teachers who may not be skilled in reflection. They ultimately use such occurrences to enrich the construction of their topic. This is the outcome Dewey desired—enacting reflective thought in teaching. When enacted, such reflection represents the ability to take an idea, an interesting classroom event, or a puzzling, perplexing phenomenon and turn it over and over, examining it from all sides until coming to the point where a hypothesis can be formed and tested. From Dewey's perspective, reflective thought comes full circle when teachers form a hypothesis and take action to test it out.

The Importance of Reflection *and* Action

We do not learn from experience....
we learn from reflecting on experience

~John Dewey

Look back at the image at the beginning of this chapter. This image of the flower reminds us that reflection is not an exact representation of the real world (the flower, the pond). A reflection can be fuzzy or unclear; a reflection can distort even as it represents reality. Is the flower at the beginning of the chapter a lily or a lotus? Is the flower pink or white? Is the water flowing, or is there just a ripple in the pond? This image also shows a rather stereotypical notion of reflection as a serene, calm, and peaceful activity. While reflection can be meditative, anyone who has reflected back on a particularly challenging day can attest to the fact that reflection is sometimes stormy, anxiety provoking, and all-consuming, even when it leads to greater insights. Reflection is always created by action. Even the serene image of a flower floating on water is created by action—the action of light rebounding off the surface of the water. Typically, we do not think about the action of light reflecting when we view an image. Instead we think about the content of what we see—in this case the shape and composition of the photo representing the flower and water. In similar ways, reflection on teaching can be somewhat unclear or opaque.

Even when reflective thoughts are shared externally in writing or through discussion, such explorations are limited without connection to teaching practice. Effective teachers are those who reflect on their actions and also act to connect this reflection to instructional practices. Such ruminations include both ***reflection-on-action***, reflection after the teaching experience and also ***reflection-in-action***, reflection during the teaching experience (Schön, 1983). Interestingly, video recordings position teachers in a unique space. Through a visual and audio record of the teacher's pedagogy and students' responses, video can evoke the in-the-moment actions and feelings that a teacher may have experienced while teaching. As such, teachers can use video to reflect *in* action while they re-live or re-experience the teaching action. At the same time, teachers can pause and reflect *on* action since they can pause or interrupt teaching actions on video to discuss or debrief with peers or to reflect on their own. In this situation, video mediates or acts as a go-between, conduit, or vehicle to carry out and facilitate reflective inquiry. This is why readers of this text will occasionally notice that we describe video as a **mediational tool** that assists teachers in the reflective process.

 Stop and Think

- What comes to mind when you consider the word "reflect"?
- What types of reflection have you engaged in as part of your teaching or teacher preparation? How successful do you feel those experiences were or how successful were you at engaging in the reflective process? Are there experiences, ideas, or techniques that would have helped you to better engage in reflection?
- Find or create a still image, animation, or other representation that you feel shows what reflection about teaching should be or that represents your reflective process. Explain your representation of reflection to a friend or peer in person or through social media. What response did you get?

Look at the two definitions of reflection that open this chapter. In coursework and professional development, teachers are most likely to encounter the second definition: "giving serious thought or consideration" to their teaching, curriculum, management, learners, and so on. The first definition, "the throwing back by a body or surface of light, heat, or sound without absorbing it," is a definition that readers may recall from their study of science. Note here the emphasis on the action "throwing back." A critical hallmark of reflection is that it is an active process and a particular type of action. For this reason, the mere admonishment for teachers to reflect is not enough. For example, Russell (2013) proposed that emphasis on reflective practice in teacher education requires teacher educators to provide "extensive support that includes modeling and explicit links to teacher candidates' practicum experiences" (p. 83). So too, Shanahan and Tochelli (2014) found that even experienced teachers need support and time to express and reflect upon what is often tacit in their understandings and evaluations of classroom literacy experiences.

Clearly, the best-case scenario is to have an expert and more knowledgeable other observing or even working alongside teachers when they are still learning to teach or when they are engaged in professional development. Unfortunately, for many beginning and veteran teachers, this is not possible. Often, due to limited budgets and resources, teacher candidates are sent out into schools with little support from teacher education faculty. In some cases, even during longer student teaching or practicum experiences novice teachers may receive little support. Additionally, experienced teachers are likely familiar with the stand-and-deliver approach where an expert comes into a school or district for professional development. Often, the presenter delivers an overview of a new curriculum concept or approach to teaching, sometimes to dozens or hundreds of teachers at the same time, and teachers are then left to implement this on their own. What is often missing for both preservice and inservice teachers is the opportunity to make explicit, external links between reflection *and* the action of teaching.

Video is one tool that can be used to help teachers bridge action *and* reflection. While video reflection is never meant to be a replacement for a more knowledgeable other, we are fully aware that teachers are increasingly being asked to reflect on their teaching without support. For example, some state certification agencies now require teachers to provide videos along with reflection. In some cases, structures are in place to provide a knowledgeable coach or guide, but in many cases, the preservice or inservice teacher completes reflections independently. This assumes that all teachers know how to reflect on their own practice, as captured on video, and that expressing once-tacit evaluations of one's own teaching is relatively straightforward. In contrast, numerous practitioners and researchers have found that teacher video is a tool with particular affordances and constraints and that not all teachers know intuitively how to critique their own teaching in meaningful ways (Dozier, Johnston, & Rogers, 2006; Shanahan & Tochelli, 2014). While videos are records that can capture and represent particular teaching actions, the value of video lies neither in the embodied rendering of a teacher and classroom nor the documents produced for reflection. Instead, the value exists in the way that video and teacher reflection can be used to articulate, analyze, and interpret the action and consequences of teaching in particular ways. Added value will also be found by engaging in self-reflection through dialogue with other professionals in a Community of Practice. In sum, all teachers need to be introduced to a pedagogy of video reflection that will articulate methods of engaging in video reflection and assist teachers in employing video as a tool to aid in reflection.

The Importance of Reflective Inquiry

...reflection on a past event expands the present moment, embroidering
it with what matters most
~ *Karen Hankins in Teaching through the Storm (2003, p. 17)*

Dewey (1910/1933) defined reflective thought as "turning a subject over in
the mind and giving it serious and consecutive consideration" (p. 3). Such
rumination is a better way of thinking, from Dewey's perspective, than the
kind of disorganized stream of conscious thought in which our minds are usually engaged. Reflective inquiry involves looking back with interest and engagement, with a goal of understanding to inform future action and practice.
Dewey said reflective thought is "active, persistent, and careful consideration
of any belief or form of knowledge" (p. 9). Active consideration of knowledge
includes considering evidence that supports a particular conclusion as well as
additional or alternative conclusions. The goal is to arrive at beliefs, conclusions, and insights established on a firm basis of evidence and rational thinking.
This analysis is actually good practice for the current data-driven educational
settings in many schools.

Russell (2013) proposed that reflective practice requires teacher educators
to provide extensive support by modeling and explicitly linking reflection to
practical teaching experiences. This is where the GRR (Pearson & Gallagher,
1983) comes in. Recall from Chapter 1 that the GRR provides a staircase or
scaffold for development, with a desired outcome of full independence and
GRR for learning and doing tasks. To utilize the GRR as a framework for
developing reflection, teacher educators and professional developers first provide very specific, sometimes even directive frameworks for reflecting. Then,
teacher educators gradually remove these frameworks as learners internalize
reflective ways of thinking about their teaching practice and develop inquiry
habits of mind. Over time, teachers work toward developing expertise in the
many domains of classroom instruction such as pedagogical techniques, classroom management, and disciplinary knowledge.

Reflective inquiry is an essential component of effective teaching practice
and ***adaptive expertise***. Adaptive expertise is the ability that effective teachers
have developed to "identify instructional roadblocks, then generate and enact
successful responses" while smoothly managing the classroom and their students (Hayden, Rundell, & Smyntek-Gworek, 2013, p. 395). Teachers who
become adaptive experts are able to respond to classroom events in ways that
usually work (Hayden & Chiu, 2013), drawing on their experiences as well as
on their reflective inquiry about their experiences in order to craft effective
responses. Adaptive expertise can take many years to develop, but even the
most novice teacher can begin today to take steps toward developing adaptive
expertise.

Dewey believed that reflective thought is initiated with a moment of wondering: something that makes us pause in our busy pace and think. This pause is often initiated by an event that causes a "state of doubt, hesitation, perplexity, mental difficulty" (Dewey, 1910/1933, p. 12). But we would add that the moment of wondering can also be initiated by something that sparks our interest for other reasons than doubt: perhaps a lesson or teaching activity that went particularly well or that caused us to notice something new. The moment of wondering leads to "an act of searching, hunting, inquiring" (Dewey, 1910/1933, p. 12) to find some connection that answers the interest, resolves the doubt, disposes of the perplexity.

 Stop and Think

- Think of something that has recently caused you to pause and wonder—perhaps something one of your students said, or one of your own children. What was it that made you wonder? How did you resolve your wondering?
- Who, if anyone, experienced this event with you? Who did you share your wondering with?

Rodgers (2002a) calls such careful, purposeful, focused, goal-directed thought *reflective inquiry*. Reflective inquiry is a "complex, rigorous, intellectual, and emotional enterprise that takes time to do well" (p. 844). Rodgers' take on Dewey is useful for teachers because she puts Dewey into modern terms while emphasizing the deep understanding and length of time it takes to really connect reflective thought to teaching practice as inquiry. She emphasizes four elements from Dewey. Reflection:

1. Is a meaning making process that moves a learner from one experience to the next with deeper understanding of the relationships and connections to other experiences and ideas
2. Is a systematic, disciplined, rigorous way of thinking with its roots in scientific inquiry
3. Needs to happen in community, in interaction with others
4. Requires attitudes that value personal and intellectual growth for self and others (p. 845)

This means that the written reflection that many teachers experience during teacher preparation, which typically occurs after student teaching and consists of a review of events with very little analysis, probably doesn't even scratch the surface of true reflective inquiry.

Rodgers' (2002b) practice-oriented interpretation of Dewey's writings on reflective inquiry focused on four parts: **Presence, Description, Analysis**, and

Experimentation. These are explained in depth in the next section, but in general, the aim of Presence and of Description is to slow down the space between thinking and action so that "rich and complex" details are revealed, "paving the way for a considered response" (Rodgers, 2002b, p. 232). This is when we learn from experience, applying what we already know to what we have just experienced, turning it over and over to make sense of it and develop a reasonable response.

Presence

Beginning to drive is somewhat like beginning to teach. People who have driven a long time make it look easy, effortlessly and automatically managing actions such as checking back and side mirrors, spatially understanding where their own vehicle is in relation to other vehicles, judging speed and distance while turning onto busy roads, using signals, smoothly changing lanes, making use of the courtesy wave at a four-way stop, and so on. Novice drivers have difficulty managing all of these skills at once. Novices may remember to signal a left turn but can easily misjudge the speed of oncoming traffic, or when focusing on a smooth lane change, may forget to check if the lane is already occupied by another car. Novice drivers struggle with being present in the moment but also managing to assess multiple actions at the same time to make a judgment. Presence, whether in teaching or driving, is quite simply, learning to see in the moment, learning to perceive more in order to make an informed judgment. Presence is awareness, and it registers complexity. Rodgers (2002b) says, "A classic example … is a teacher's ability to attend to a single learner while simultaneously casting her attention, like a net, over the entire group" (p. 235).

 Stop and Think

Ms. Wang is a novice teacher. Read this description of a classroom event with her student, Jimmy.

> Jimmy seemed to take a lot of time getting out his pencil and notebook during writer's workshop. During one of my lessons, as I was excusing the students back to their seats, I asked for him to go first. I thought that maybe if he was the first one to his seat he would have all of his stuff ready by the time the rest of the students were seated and would have more time to write. This seemed to work the first day I tried it, but another day it didn't. As I was teaching on another day I thought that maybe if I were to stay closer to his area during independent writing time he would stay more on task. This seemed to work, but my

consistent checking on him and his work pulled me away from getting around to the other students. These are a couple of ideas that I tried.

Reflect: Why is there no ready-made solution to this problem? What might you advise Jimmy's teacher to try next?

We might say that in the previous vignette, Ms. Wang is learning to see or perceive more in order to make the best judgments she can about how to improve the learning in her classroom for all of her students. In her reflection, she notes that being *present* to the entire class is no easy task. Returning to our analogy of driving a car, providing guidance to 25 learners in a classroom is comparable to having to steer 25 cars at once. A teacher who can be Present in this type of moment gathers much information, and then looks for possible patterns and ways to make meaning (McCrary, 2000) in order to manage this very complex task.

Dewey (1910/1933) argues that Presence is necessary because it enables teachers to readily observe the "mental responses and movement of students" (p. 275). He notes that the challenge for students is the subject matter or content, but for teachers the challenge is that they must consider *"what the minds of pupils are doing with the subject matter"* (p. 275, italics original).

In sum, Presence requires that the teacher is "free to give time and attention to observation and interpretation of the pupils' intellectual reactions" (Dewey, 1910/1933, p. 275). The task of the teacher is to observe and be present to the experience of the students in order to determine the students' responses to the subject matter that is being taught.

Description and Analysis

Description comes from Presence: it is telling the story of an experience, without interpretation. It is objective. It attempts to get at the essence of an experience in order to name the "diverse and complex elements so that [the experience] can be looked at, seen, and told from as many different perspectives as possible (Rodgers, 2002b, p. 237). Jimmy's teacher provides an example of this objective description by listing responses she has tried and the results she has observed. Rodgers encourages teachers to engage in Description and withhold interpretation for as long as possible, so that all the details of an experience can be examined and explored. By doing this, more of the nuances and complexities of classroom experiences can be appreciated, and responses can be more carefully developed. This is also similar to the stance that ethnographers take when they are doing fieldwork. Ethnographers examine complex culturally situated interactions and attempt to describe in detail what they see and hear while also separating out questions and interpretations. Ethnographers monitor their biases in ways that help them avoid jumping to conclusions. (For an example of an observation exercise for preservice teachers using an ethnographic approach to field notes, see Florio-Ruane (1999). For a more immersive ethnographic approach, see Frank, 1999.)

 Stop and Think

View one of the movies or television shows below, and note the places where a main character slows down his/her thinking in order to become aware of the nuances and complexities in order to develop more effective responses. What types of reflective processes does the character engage in? What other individuals, if any, are part of this reflective process? How are the representations of a character's thought processes on film similar to and different from what teachers might go through when they reflect using video?

- *Premium Rush (2012)*: Staying safe as a bicycle messenger on the busy streets of Manhattan requires considerable attention to detail in traffic and in life, plus consideration of all the angles.
- *Temple Grandin (2010)*: Born in 1947 and diagnosed with autism, Grandin's ability to see in pictures is demonstrated as she visualizes solutions such as how to build better systems for handling cattle. Grandin later became a professor of animal science at Colorado State University.
- *Sherlock*: The modern British Broadcasting Corporation (BBC) television series features segments demonstrating Mr. Holmes' unique attention to detail, which allows him to select the most important bits of information before forming a judgment. Several Holmes movies (e.g., *Mr. Holmes*, 2015) also use this technique.
- Choose a movie or other digital video that you know of that uses this technique where the creators show a character's thought process.

Schön's (1983) notion of **reflection–on–action** also recommends slowing down of response and examination of a moment of pause in great detail. And while reflection-on-action is a retrospective review, looking back on an event, it is good practice for reflection-in-action: the in-the-moment noticing, responding, and thinking on one's feet that becomes the foundational work of adaptive expertise (Hammerness et al., 2005). How can teachers learn to observe, much like Sherlock Holmes, the big and small details that can provide critical information about teaching and learning?

Attempts to standardize problems, or to predict and develop fixed responses to problems did not meet with Schön's approval. Schön acknowledged the inquiry that must be present in strong teaching. His concepts of reflection-on-action and reflection-in-action take into account artistry, craft knowledge, and the complexity and decision options that are present in real world and real teaching events. Challenging

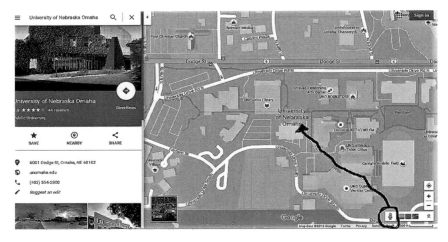

FIGURE 4.2   Google map, map view.

events in teaching do not come with solid parameters, and they don't come with ready-made solutions. Like the mysteries faced by Sherlock, there are turns and twists; unpredictability abounds. Try as we might to create procedures and recipes for teaching, there will still be events that defy one-size solutions and even categorization. These events can be complex. And complexity requires inquiry.

In real-world practice, problems don't present themselves with readily available solutions. Solutions must be constructed from the materials of situations that are "puzzling, troubling, and uncertain" (Schön, 1983, p. 40). Such construction requires extended time and focus, and the Description stage cannot be rushed by alighting on the first solution that presents itself. We use these descriptive elements to make decisions in many areas of our lives beyond teaching as well, and an illustration may be helpful here. This example shows how Description and Analysis overlap and interweave, and why cycles of description and analysis are important.

Emily, one of our co-authors, described how she often uses map-generating applications for turn-by-turn driving directions to a destination (Figure 4.2).

Because she finds the many distractions of city driving anxiety-provoking, she also uses the street view function of map applications to get a look at her destination before she starts off driving, so she will know it when she sees it. This adds another component of descriptive information. Emily has also found that simply using the street view operation by dragging and dropping the little figure to a point on the map does not give her what she needs to navigate confidently. Figure 4.3 shows the result that is gained by dragging and dropping the street view figure to the spot on the map labeled University of Nebraska Omaha. As she looks at the map, Emily asks herself:

What are the names of those particular buildings? Where is the entrance to the parking lot? And more importantly, what street will she need to take in order to gain access to the parking lot that is in the picture? Usually Emily has

FIGURE 4.3 Google map, street view.

to go through numerous descriptive steps. She uses the program arrows to turn the orientation of the street view picture and then zooms in on building address numbers before she finds the view that will help her navigate to the right spot once she gets behind the wheel of her car.

Finding the right response in teaching, as with finding the most helpful map view of a location, can take time. The first map or street view is often not adequate to solve Emily's problem of finding her way around while driving in unfamiliar areas. As she drives, she may encounter other obstacles such as detours or rush-hour traffic. Over time, and through experience, Emily has learned alternative paths to reach her destination if unexpected events occur. Stories of drivers who have followed their GPS to the top of mountain cliffs or directly into the ocean also hold an analogy for teachers: even when there is a map or guide, the description is necessary but not sufficient on its own. Drivers, like teachers, must engage in analysis to get to their destination. Analysis is an essential aspect of reflective inquiry.

Dewey (1916/1944) called this stage the "reorganization and reconstruction of experience" (p. 76) and Rodgers (2002b) believes analysis is "where meaning-making happens" (p. 244). Here, Presence (noticing) and Description (in detail) come together to generate possible actions. We reflect back on a teaching action in order to become more aware of its essence, and then create alternative actions and choose one to try (Korthagen & Kessels, 1999). According to Dewey, it is this action-plus-reflection cycle that leads us to knowledge.

Analysis encourages teachers to look through different lenses, or from different perspectives, at what was noticed in Description. If teachers have taken time with Description, resisting the urge to jump in and fix things immediately, they should have a lot to bring to this stage. Dewey said reflection needs to happen in community and with much interaction, gathering many different viewpoints for consideration. Rodgers (2002b) advocates getting and giving feedback throughout the Description process in order to provide a broad view and many alternatives for responding. Through Analysis, teachers can review many options and select one to enact. Dewey refers to this as Experimentation.

 Stop and Think

Read Ms. Wang's description of Jimmy's behavior again (below). As you read:

- Think about the events from Jimmy's viewpoint. How might Jimmy describe his avoidance behaviors?
- Think about the events from the perspectives of the other students in the class. How might they describe and interpret the situation?
- Finally, after this analysis from multiple viewpoints, what other options for responding to Jimmy could you think of? What else could Ms. Wang try?

Jimmy seemed to take a lot of time getting out his pencil and notebook during writer's workshop. During one of my lessons, as I was excusing the students back to their seats, I asked for him to go first. I thought that maybe if he was the first one to his seat he would have all of his stuff ready by the time the rest of the students were seated and would have more time to write. This seemed to work the first day I tried it, but another day it didn't. As I was teaching on another day I thought that maybe if I were to stay closer to his area during independent writing time he would stay more on task. This seemed to work, but my consistent checking on him and his work pulled me away from getting around to the other students. These are a couple of ideas that I tried.

Analysis asks us to consider all the information we have collected thus far about an event, and make some meaning out of it. Once we have clarified what we know in this way we can be ready to try out different responses and evaluate their effects. This happens during Experimentation.

Experimentation

Learning to take intelligent action and then review the outcomes of that action form the fourth part of reflective inquiry. We resist using the terms final or last, because when thinking about adaptive expertise in teaching, this process of reflective inquiry loops back on itself, so that Experimentation usually leads us directly into another round of noticing, describing, analyzing, and experimenting with a response. In the example from Ms. Wang's classroom, she described how Jimmy's behaviors were getting in the way of his learning. Her initial description noted a

FIGURE 4.4   Recognizing students' areas of interest, and experimenting with instructional approaches.

few things she had tried to change his behavior. Over time, Ms. Wang had many opportunities to talk with other novice teachers and experienced teachers and seek their advice. She wrote about the experience and talked to her instructors at the university about Jimmy. She experimented with different techniques and actions, and she engaged more with Jimmy to find out about his interests. Over a period of weeks and experimentation, she finally hit upon a successful formula for Jimmy. This involved recognizing his areas of interest (e.g., he would gladly write about penguins but resisted writing about other topics) and then using Jimmy's interests in order to build a bridge to other writing topics and areas for literacy development. Ms. Wang's approach also included more attention to writing at home for fun—a quick phone conversation with Jimmy's mom led to a plan for writing at home. And, a conversation with the occupational therapist led to trial of a pencil grip to help Jimmy hold his pencil in a position that made it easier for him to write. While this experimentation took time and effort on Ms. Wang's part, through the process of shared reflection and problem-solving, she gained specific techniques and knowledge that will be of use to her in multiple contexts. Throughout this process Ms. Wang engaged in Presence, Description, Analysis, and Experimentation and worked toward building her adaptive expertise.

Summing Up...

In this chapter, we have discussed in more detail what reflection and reflective inquiry entail. We have provided examples of Presence, Description, Analysis, and Experimentation. To illustrate these, we have used some familiar everyday examples (e.g., driving a car, navigating using a GPS) and examples related to educational settings (e.g., Ms. Wang's observation about Jimmy). In the next chapter, we continue to build on these ideas by providing examples of reflective work where teachers continue to engage in reflective inquiry as they move toward adaptive expertise. We then return to specific analysis of a video case in the context of a Community of Practice and the GRR.

Before we move on though, we want to illustrate a construct that underlies and supports everything else we have discussed and will discuss in this book, and that is the construct of scaffolding. Scaffolding is crucial to the GRR, and crucial to the instructional process. Developing Presence provides a canvas for noticing (and for learning), and this noticing and subsequent reflection can lead to Analysis and Experimentation with instructional actions that create a loop between teacher actions—student responses—teacher reflection—and renewed teacher actions (Figure 4.4). The Analysis that happens during reflection-in-practice and on-practice can lead to Experimentation with adaptations to instruction, both in the moment and when planning for future instruction, that provide the necessary support, or scaffolding, for learning to occur (Figure 4.5).

Thus, all the elements of the reflective process that we have described in this chapter are anchored in the idea of scaffolding instruction by noticing and responding to students' learning needs. Recognizing when to provide more scaffolding support, and when students can work on their own, requires close observation, utilizing Presence, Description, and Analysis in order to develop a response when needed. In the case of teaching, that response will often be Experimentation with different methods of instruction. These adaptations, formulated either in the moment of instruction in response to a puzzling or troubling

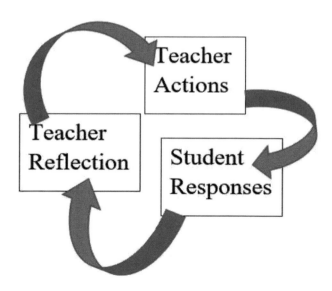

FIGURE 4.5 The feedback loop.

phenomenon; or after the moment of instruction while preparing for the next lesson, can lead to dramatically improved learning outcomes for students.

Like all human interactions, teacher-student interactions are dynamic, and knowledge is also dynamic. One day, a group of students may seem to have mastered a learning task, and the next day they may be unable to apply that learning in a new setting. Transfer doesn't always happen smoothly, and sometimes learning breaks down. Even in the moment of teaching, scaffolding can be added or adjusted.

As a teacher educator, Emily was reminded of this recently in her own practice. Her goal in a recent class was to provide preservice teachers with writing strategies that they might use to help their students understand story problems in math. In order to practice a strategy called Word Problem Roulette (Haltiwanger & Simpson, 2013) she asked preservice teachers to work in pairs to describe in writing how they could use the Pythagorean Theorem to find the length of the slanted side of a right triangle (see Figure 4.6). All of the preservice teachers had learned the Pythagorean Theorem in middle school $(a^2 + b^2 = c^2)$, which says that you can multiply the length of each straight side of the triangle by itself and then add those two sums together to get the squared length of the slanted side of the triangle (called the hypotenuse). Then, by finding the square root of that third side, you find the length of that side.

Emily's students were all comfortable with the math, and they understood the mathematical process of this task. But because Emily was asking them to use that math in a different way—to use writing to explain the process of solving the equation—some of her students became confused. It wasn't the mathematics involved that tripped these students up. Rather it was Emily's asking her students to

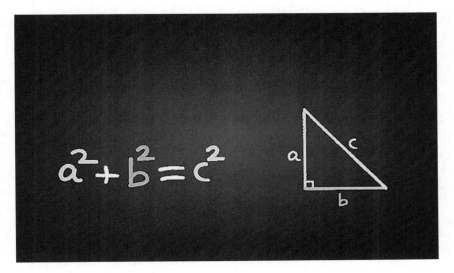

FIGURE 4.6   The Pythagorean Theorem.

combine a language focus with the mathematics that seemed to cause a learning breakdown. One pair of students became quite distressed, to the point of interspersing curse words into speech ("I'm so damn confused!") and talking about the distress in embodied terms ("My head hurts" and later "My whole body hurts".).

Clearly, Emily had misjudged the amount of scaffolding required for this activity. She had thought that she was providing enough scaffolding by using a familiar math concept with a familiar mathematical solution, and that by providing this scaffold her students could then focus on the writing strategy without becoming bogged down in the mathematical problem-solving. But for a subset of her class, this assumption was wrong.

Emily tried to adapt in the moment by adding words to the mathematical word problem in order to clarify. While this did help, it was too little too late for two of her students. They had become so anxious that they were not able to focus on the learning task. Emily had lost them. So, for the next day, Emily reflected and re-grouped. She provided more support for her students by using a less complex math problem: determining perimeter (side + side + side + side) and area (length × width) of two-dimensional shapes. By reducing the academic demands of the math task her students could focus more of their energies on the writing task. Emily also built in additional guided steps to the task, leading up to the culminating activity, which asked students to use written language to define the formulas for perimeter and area, and then describe connections between perimeter and area of two-dimensional figures using a triangular organization tool, another strategy from Haltiwanger and Simpson (2013). Emily's overarching goal was to provide her preservice teachers with practice in using writing to demonstrate knowledge of mathematical properties, and with strategies that they could use later with their own adolescent students. On this second day of instruction, Emily was closer to meeting this goal.

This vignette demonstrates the importance of scaffolding, reflecting, and adapting learning tasks. While the second day of instruction was more successful for Emily's class, the students who had struggled on the first day were less engaged on the second day. Their lack of success on the first day had diminished their energy for tackling math and writing about math on the second day. Although they completed the writing task, their hearts were not in it. If Emily had provided more support on the first day, by choosing perimeter and area instead of the Pythagorean Theorem, the outcome for her students might have been different.

In sum, providing the right type of scaffolding, and the right amount of support, is key to learning success. Sliding up and down the GRR by adapting instructional tasks and the amount of support given to find these correct amounts is what makes the GRR dynamic and responsive to the needs of students. In the next chapter, we will apply the notions of scaffolding and reflection to our discussion of the GRR, and demonstrate how thinking about the GRR Model can help teachers scaffold and adapt instruction to provide the right amount of support for learning to occur.

References

Dewey, J. (1910/1933). *How we think*. Boston, MA: D. C. Heath and Company.

Dewey, J. (1916/1944). *Democracy and education*. New York, NY: Free Press (Original work published 1916).

Dewey, J. (1938/1963). *Experience and education*. New York, NY: Collier Macmillan Publishing.

Dozier, C., Johnston, P., & Rogers, R. (2006). *Critical literacy critical teaching*. New York, NY: Teachers College Press.

Florio-Ruane, S. (1999). Revisiting fieldwork in preservice teachers' learning: Creating your own case studies. In M. A. Lundeberg, B. B. Levin, & H. L. Harrington (Eds.), *Who learns what from cases and how?: The research base for teaching and learning with cases* (pp. 201–224). Mahwah, NJ: Lawrence Erlbaum Associates Incorporated.

Frank, C. (1999). *Ethnographic eyes: A teacher's guide to classroom observation*. Portsmouth, NH: Heinemann.

Haltiwanger, L., & Simpson, A. M. (2013). Beyond the write answer: Mathematical connections. *Mathematics Teaching in the Middle School, 18*(8), 492–498.

Hammerness, K., Darling-Hammond, L., Bransford, J., Berliner, D., Cochran-Smith, M., McDonald, M., & Zeichner, K. (2005). How teachers learn and develop. In L. Darling, Hammond, & J. Bransford (Eds.), *Preparing teachers for a changing world: What teachers should learn and be able to do* (pp. 358–389). San Francisco, CA: Jossey-Bass.

Hankins, K. H. (2003). *Teaching through the storm*. New York, NY: Teachers College Press.

Hayden, H. E. & Chiu, M. M. (2013). Lessons learned: Supporting the development of reflective practice and adaptive expertise. In P. J. Dunston, S. K. Fullerton, C. C. Bates, P. M. Stecker, M. W. Cole, A. H. Hall, D. Herro, & K. Headley, (Eds.), *62nd Literacy Research Association Yearbook*, (pp. 279–296). Oak Creek, WI: Literacy Research Association, Incorporated.

Hayden, H. E., Rundell, T. D., & Smyntek-Gworek, S. (2013). Adaptive expertise: A view from the top, and the ascent. *Teaching Education, 24*(4), 395–414. doi:10.1080/10476210.2012.724054.

Korthagen, F. A. J., & Kessels, J. P. A. M. (1999). Linking theory and practice: Changing the pedagogy of teacher education. *Educational Researcher, 28*(4), 4–17.

Lave, J., & Wenger, E. (1991). *Situated learning: Legitimate peripheral participation*. New York, NY: Cambridge University Press.

McCrary, A. S. (2000). Notes from a marine biologist's daughter: On the art and science of attention. *Harvard Educational Review, 70*, 211–227.

Oxford Living Dictionaries. (2014). www.oxforddictionaries.com/us/definition/american_english/reflection.

Pearson, P. D., & Gallagher, M. (1983). *The instruction of reading comprehension* (Technical Report No. 297). Urbana-Champaign: University of Illinois Center for the Study of Reading. Retrieved from ERIC database (ED236565).

Rodgers, C. (2002a). Defining reflection: Another look at John Dewey and reflective thinking. *Teachers College Record, 104*(4), 842–866.

Rodgers, C. (2002b). Seeing student learning: Teacher change and the role of reflection. *Harvard Educational Review, 72*(2), 230–253.

Russell, T. (2013). Has reflective practice done more harm than good in teacher education? *Phronesis, 2*(1), 80–88.

Schön, D. A. (1983). *The reflective practitioner: How professionals think in action.* New York, NY: Basic Books.

Shanahan, L. E., & Tochelli, A. L. (2014). Examining the use of video study groups for developing literacy pedagogical content knowledge of critical elements of strategy instruction with elementary teachers. *Literacy Research and Instruction, 53*(1), 1–24. doi:10.1080/19388071.2013.827764.

5

TAKING THE LONG VIEW BY FOCUSING ON DESCRIPTION

Examining Agency, Bias, and the Messy Parts of Teaching

FIGURE 5.1 Full featured double rainbow in Wrangell–St. Elias National Park, Alaska.

It is hard to imagine that once a teacher has seen the stunning array of colors present in students' learning he or she would turn back to the monochromatic world of teaching as the delivery of a product. Teachers involved in … reflective development discover that life in the classroom cannot be scripted. It is therefore harder, but … full of passion and breathtaking color.
(Rodgers, 2002, p. 251)

 Stop and Think

1. Look at Figures 5.2 and 5.3. How comfortable are you reading these images? What influenced your level of comfort with reading these images?

2. Have you ever taken something complex apart and tried to understand it? How successful were you in understanding the individual parts of the item and how they worked? What helped or hindered your ability to understand?

The drawings presented in Figures 5.2 and 5.3 are often referred to as "exploded view drawings" and these are often used in technical or parts manuals. Many people are familiar with these types of 3D drawings because they often accompany items that people purchase and put together at home such as a desk, breakfast stool, computer stand, or BBQ grill. Complex depictions of such diagrams are used in a variety of fields such as engineering or auto mechanics. Engineers even have a term for taking a completed product apart to understand how it works; they refer to this as "product archaeology." This is an interesting idea because archaeology is usually associated with ancient civilizations and dusty historical sites, but in product archaeology, engineers or students learning

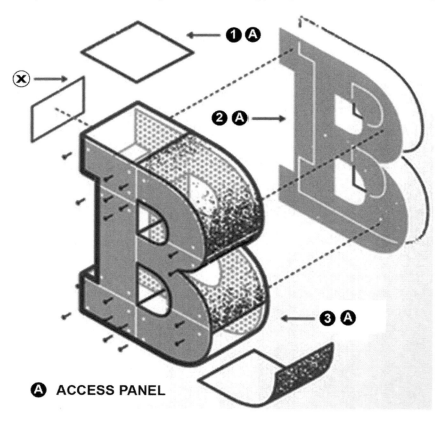

FIGURE 5.2 Matt Stevens "The Exploded Alphabet Letter B."

to be engineers disassemble a product to figure out what its component parts are and what makes it work. Drawing or understanding an exploded diagram helps to identify the component parts and understand how they fit together. As you read the various chapters of this book, part of what we want you to think about is how the varied and complex pieces of teaching fit together to form a cohesive whole.

FIGURE 5.3 Exploded view of classic cheeseburger.

Many times, teaching is viewed only in terms of the end product: what a lesson produces in terms of student learning. This all-or-nothing view ignores the many complicated components of teaching. Consider how this idea of teaching as a singular product is communicated. Some common sayings about teachers are, "Teachers are born, not made" or "Those who can, do. Those who can't, teach." These sayings and the ideologies behind them suggest that good teaching is an inborn trait or singular action: you've either got it or you don't. But what if teaching were viewed as a layered process like archaeology or an exploded diagram? Such perspectives would no doubt help learners recognize that teaching is a complex, nuanced process that is situated within our own lived histories and embodied experiences.

Video and other means of reflection can help capture the complexities in teaching. Video viewing or analysis does not merely record the process of teaching; it records the embodied, historical, socio-emotional aspects of a teacher's self. More specifically, a visual record can evoke the in-the-moment actions and feelings a teacher may have experienced during teaching. Consider the following story of a Reading Recovery lesson from Emily, one of the co-authors of this book. Reading Recovery (Clay, 1985) is a one-to-one intervention program for first-grade students. Ongoing teacher training is required, and this includes teaching "behind the glass"—that is, teaching in front of a two-way mirror while being observed and critiqued by certified teacher trainers and peer teachers. These teaching sessions are typically video-recorded for further analysis.

> Recently I uncovered a video of myself from more than 10 years ago teaching a Reading Recovery lesson 'behind the glass'. Even though it had been recorded more than a decade earlier, memories of that day came flooding back. It was a particularly busy semester, and I was serving as an administrator for my elementary school as well as teaching Reading Recovery lessons. Life was hectic! On the spring day that recording was made I was actually very sick, but knew that I could not miss my 'behind the glass' session: my teacher trainer was a stickler for attendance. I vividly remember being very hoarse, having very little voice. And I worried about trying not to breathe too much on my student or anyone else because I didn't want to make them sick. Seeing the video even brought back seemingly insignificant memories like recalling why I wore those khaki slacks that were too big and did not fit well. I chose them specifically that day because they were lined with flannel and very comforting. As I re-viewed the video it was not only my teaching interactions during the literacy lesson that were captured, it was the emotional and affective components of that lesson, that day, and the broader context. When I read about exploded drawings, I saw an immediate connection to how video allows us to pull out all aspects of an interaction whether it was helping my student to hear and record all the sounds in a word by saying it very slowly while my student wrote the letters, or the emotions and memories of that day.

Emily's story shows us that video can be a powerful memory device but also a powerful record where experiences are framed and recorded so we can pull out and examine various elements of literacy interactions.

The principles outlined in Chapter 2 reminded us that (1) teaching and reflecting are complex endeavors; (2) learning to teach and learning to reflect are scaffolded processes, and these two processes help teachers consider what learners need to do in the present and future; and (3) educators can use a Gradual Release of Responsibility (GRR) Model to scaffold learning in and through video reflection. In the same way that watching video brought back emotions and physical memories connected to the experience for Emily, teachers can review teaching actions and decisions by viewing video of their lessons as a scaffold for developing reflective inquiry and teaching expertise. We revisit each of these principles in this chapter, while considering examples of novice and experienced teachers using video viewing to position themselves to reflect *in* action while they re-experience the action of teaching and reflect *on* action. We discuss the value of spending extra time describing a teaching interaction because it helps us notice nuanced details, uncover bias, and, in the process, develop agency. In other words, we discover ways to respond to the messy parts of teaching. Finally, we introduce the use of critical incidents as a way to deepen reflection and build a bridge to the action of teaching.

Chapter 3 established the need for structure for reflection on video-recorded teaching and described the benefits of Communities of Practice to provide support in this type of analysis. While video can mediate or act as a go-between or a vehicle to carry out and facilitate reflective inquiry, structure is needed in order to focus effectively on the teaching action and results rather than the surface elements noticeable in video, like personality or behavior habits. Once the elements of the reflective cycle (***Presence, Description, Analysis, Experimentation***) are developed teachers can apply these elements to break apart and examine critical teaching interactions, emerging with new understandings that help them build more responsive teaching actions. In much the same way that design specialists use exploded drawings like those in Figure 5.2 to view parts of an item and how they go together, critical incident analysis can add depth of understanding and connect reflective inquiry to problem solving and action.

Adaptive Expertise

Principle #1

Teaching and Reflecting Are Complex Endeavors

In Chapter 4, we introduced adaptive expertise as the ability to "combine thought and analysis with action in practice" (Hayden, Rundell, & Smyntek-Gworek,

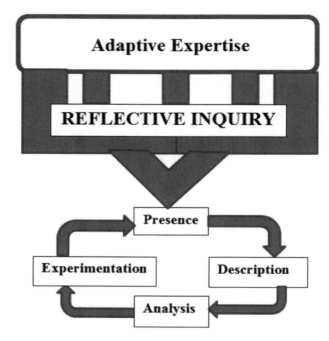

FIGURE 5.4 Elements of reflective inquiry, and how it supports adaptive expertise.

2013, p. 395), and we proposed reflective inquiry as the required foundation for adaptive expertise in teaching (Figure 5.4). In this chapter, we provide more examples of teachers using the four parts of reflective inquiry, *Presence, Description, Analysis,* and *Experimentation* (Dewey, 1910/1933; Rodgers, 2002), in order to develop teaching actions.

Early Teaching Practice: Skimming the Surface

Research on teacher development typically identifies varying levels of expertise. Early career teachers are highly focused on their own performance: Did I plan a lesson with all the elements of best practice? Did I get through all the parts of the lesson plan in the time I had? Am I doing what my administrators expect of me? Are any students misbehaving? As a result, early teachers may be less aware of their students, and they may not easily recognize when students are not engaged or when students could benefit from re-teaching. One of the first things novice teachers need to learn is to get past worrying about their own performance and focus instead on whether and how their students are learning (Hayden, Moore-Russo, & Marino, 2013). This takes time and practice, but one of the benefits of video is that it provides an opportunity for teachers to step outside of their practice and view their teaching from a more objective space. Consider Joy's vignette below. While the problems of practice she describes are very typical for a preservice teacher, or even someone in the first years of teaching practice, consider how video helps Joy get a jump on solving some of these problems of early teaching practice.

Joy

Joy, an undergraduate in her final practicum experience before student teaching, used video to record herself teaching in a kindergarten classroom on two separate occasions, once near the beginning of the three-week practicum and once near the end, for 20 minutes each time. Watching video of her practicum teaching helped Joy relive the teaching event and reflect on her actions. It provided her with an objective space where she could begin to develop **Presence**: her ability to see in the moment and perceive more so that she could make an informed judgment. Remember our discussion in Chapter 4 of Rodgers' (2002) definition: "[**Presence**] is a teacher's ability to attend to a single learner while simultaneously casting her attention, like a net, over the entire group" (p. 235).

When viewing video of her teaching, Joy first reflected on something she noticed about her teaching performance over time:

> One problem that I can identify after reviewing my videos and reflecting on my experience would be time management. I noticed that my ability to manage my time became easier once I got used to the teaching part of my lessons.

Spending time in **Description** Joy looked more closely at her time management problem, identifying contributing factors: "At first I was so worried about running into my classroom teacher's time."

Time management is a very typical problem of practice that novice teachers encounter (Hayden & Chiu, 2013), but Joy experienced it in a different way than practicing teachers do. As a practicum student, she not only felt pressure to finish the lesson, but also to do so in a time frame that did not interfere with her mentor teacher's schedule. This is an important consideration, because the mentor teacher was Joy's evaluator as well as her guide. A practicum student or student teacher must manage these additional pressures while also working to master lesson delivery, classroom management, assessment of learner needs, and so on.

After describing the problem, Joy went on to **Analysis**. This is where her reflection shows the power of spending time, because Joy noticed the impact her teaching was having on her students. She began to recognize that rushing through lessons inhibited her students' learning.

> [When I] read stories to get through them, [it] made my students have to rush their work at the end of the lesson because I couldn't balance everything out as well at first. As time went on, I was able to better judge the length of my story and the length of my student work so that they were able to complete and share their work. This was great because then I was able to see their learning through their sharing.

Video helped Joy build a bridge from reflection to action because she then used *Experimentation* to create a solution to try in her future teaching.

> A routine that I would develop for myself to avoid this problem would be to read through the story a few times first. Then, I would put my questions that I want to ask my students in the book so that I don't have to try and remember them. Next, I would allow a 5-minute brain break to partner share in my lesson. Finally, I could fill in the whole worksheet to see how long it takes me to complete [to get a ballpark estimate]. If at this point there is extra time, I could include a share portion at the end or a whole group activity throughout the lesson. This could help me better regulate my time.

Spending time developing *Presence*, using *Description*, and trying out *Analysis* and *Experimentation* is powerful for a preservice/novice teacher, and it helped Joy notice how her teaching actions impacted her students' learning. While these types of insights may be typical of someone who is just learning to teach, using video as a mediator for such reflection jump-starts the process. It takes time and practice in teaching to move beyond concern about one's own performance and toward noticing and responding to students' responses (Hayden et al., 2013). Using this structured reflection process with video helped Joy notice and name some of the problems of early teaching practice, and helped her begin this shift from self to students before moving into student teaching.

Reflecting "After the Moment" as Practice for "In the Moment" Principle #2

Learning to Teach and Learning to Reflect Are Scaffolded Processes Where Teachers Consider What Learners Need to Learn and Do in the Present and in the Future

By looking at teaching interactions and specific challenges over extended periods of time, teachers at all experience levels can generate more instructional choices. This is empowering and develops a sense of agency as well as an awareness of one's impact. Video plus time in *Description* gives teachers a "space" to view and think critically about the challenges and complexities in a teaching interaction. In Konnor's reflection below, both video and Rodgers' reflective framework or cycle scaffold his reflective process.

Konnor

Konnor, a certified teacher working toward a literacy specialist endorsement, used video-supported reflection for a more extended period of time than Joy. Over eight weeks of teaching in a reading center, Konnor critiqued his development of *Presence* and expanded his use of *Description*. He set two goals for his teaching practice during these eight weeks: first, improving his ability to take anecdotal notes on his student's reactions during lessons, and later, to improve his questioning techniques. By spending time in *Description* throughout the term while using video and a structured reflection format, Konnor developed adaptive responses and began to see opportunities to apply the GRR and turn over more of the learning tasks to his student, Jerry.

Rodgers (2006) called *Description* "the most challenging aspect of reflection for teachers" and notes that description "*after the moment,*" as in video viewing, can be practice for seeing "*in the moment*" (p. 216, italics added) in later teaching interactions. In week one of the eight-week tutoring term Konnor first focused on developing procedures for capturing anecdotal observations of his student's actions and confusions, and then on using these observations to plan teaching responses. He viewed video of his teaching to describe, *after the moment,* what he saw.

> At no point during the lesson did I observe myself taking notes … However, there were multiple instances where I should have been. The first was at 6:27 PM when I had Jerry sort words with affixes into columns for prefixes or suffixes. While I watched and provided feedback, I should have noted whether he was able to place each word in the correct column or not—especially because he placed the last word in the wrong column but self-corrected a few seconds later.

Video enhances the amount of information teachers can collect and reflect on by supplementing anecdotal notes and filling in the gaps that remain even after careful observation and *Presence* during instruction. With video as a material scaffold, Konnor was able to see important aspects of his student's learning that he did not capture on his anecdotal notes. While describing his notetaking on student responses, he also described his questioning techniques, noting missed opportunities for effective questions.

> While some of it [questioning] is planned and other times it is sponta-
> neous, I noticed that there were multiple instances [when] I asked minor
> questions during the lesson to assess whether or not Jerry was retaining
> what I had explained or understanding the material. For example, at 6:29
> PM I asked whether suffixes are added to the beginning or end of the
> word, after I had explained it a few minutes earlier. Jerry hesitated, but
> again I failed to note this.

As Konnor continued to work on anecdotal notetaking in week two, engaging in video viewing while also spending time in **Description** revealed some
roadblocks.

> As I watched … I recalled what I was thinking at the time. I remember
> feeling as though Jerry might become self-conscious of me taking notes.
> I also felt that stopping the lesson to jot down notes might have wasted
> time, which was precious that night …and I thought it might interrupt
> the flow of the instruction. Therefore, while I did have the observation
> sheet in front of me and went to take notes, I [did not] write everything
> I needed.

Using video of his teaching helped Konnor recall the emotions and thoughts
of the teaching interaction, and describing these helped inform his **Analysis**.
Konnor decided to develop his own kind of shorthand, with abbreviations
for common words to use on the anecdotal note sheet. After reaching this
solution, he moved to focusing on his questioning techniques. In week four,
he described how he could refine his questions to better assess his student's
learning:

> After this week's Wednesday discussion as a group [with my peers and
> course instructor], I left wondering what my abilities were with ques-
> tioning the student. While I was still very much focused on the anecdotal
> notes, I did pick up a few interesting observations from my questioning
> Jerry. At 6:08 PM during the Monday session I noticed that at the begin-
> ning of the lesson I was asking quite a few recall questions. This is some-
> thing that needs to be done because he needs to improve on his ability to
> recall information, but it should not be the only focus. I also need him
> to understand why it is important to understand the material and strat-
> egies we are teaching him. In addition to having Jerry recall what was
> previously taught I may want to begin asking more inference questions.
> At 6:03 PM during Wednesday's session I asked Jerry, "Do you remember
> what we covered last time?" A better way to frame this question would
> have been to ask "What two characteristics of fluency have you been
> practicing?" I need to name the strategies more often.

Here, Konnor reflected on the support of the Community of Practice formed by the other teachers working in the reading center and the center supervisor. The Wednesday discussion group with these teachers, held after tutoring, provided fuel for his exploration of questioning techniques. He also noted the value of anecdotal notes for reflection *after the moment* and for planning with his teaching partner. These teaching conversations, supplemented by notes and video, lead to thoughtful teaching adaptations for future lessons. What is important to note is that the conversations with others along with the notes and video all served as scaffolds when Konnor engaged in the reflective process.

> As I improve in my recording anecdotal [notes], I have seen the improvement in the conversations I have with my clinical partner after each session. We both reference our notes and recall specific examples that enable us to make informed decisions about where the instruction should head in the future. For example, the other day I recorded notes on significant miscues that [Jerry] was making during a read aloud. I noted that he was breaking multisyllabic words into chunks but failing to blend those chunks together into the full word. I [wrote] specific examples that I used to explain my thoughts, [and] I can use these words when teaching Jerry to blend syllables into words because I know that he has struggled with these words.

By week six, Konnor's time in **Description** and reflection *after the moment* was helping him develop adaptations for better use of questioning with his student as well as helping him understand why these techniques were important.

> Before starting the new book at 4:37 PM I asked Jerry if he remembered reading a chapter out of the book when we completed the diagnostic assessment [at the beginning of the tutoring term]. He did not remember and what I should have done is asked him to make predictions. Especially because we have read from the Magic Tree House series and he has an understanding of their format. When we have asked him to make predictions ... he often repeats the title as his prediction, but occasionally when given enough time to respond, he comes up with a very strong and creative prediction. Not only would it be highly beneficial to provide him with practice in predictions but it would require him to use higher order thinking. Another example of a missed opportunity was when I asked, "how do you feel about the strategy, does it help you?" Instead I could have asked, "how might this strategy help you comprehend the text better?" [This] would have given me much more information on his understanding of the [strategy].

Konnor described the value of giving his student wait time and of asking questions that require more than a yes or no answer. Using video to scaffold his understanding, he was able to see that sometimes, "when given enough time," Jerry would come up with a stronger, more creative prediction than just repeating the title. Konnor also was able to see that asking Jerry to think metacognitively about where and when he could use a particular strategy (e.g., "How might this strategy help you comprehend the text better?") is more beneficial than just labeling a strategy as helpful or not helpful.

Clearly, Konnor is a strong teacher. None of the teaching actions he described were inadequate or unhelpful. However, by spending extended time in *Description* with the mediation of video, he was able to see ways to improve and refine his teaching, thus improving and refining his student's learning. In our work with teachers at all levels of experience, we have emphasized this cycle of reflection as a way to manage the complexity of daily practice and develop agency. Teachers can transform the "raw data" they receive from teaching—the responses of students to curriculum, content, and instruction—into mindful instruction for student learning. By the end of Konnor's eight-week tutoring term he had ideas for how to gradually release responsibility for learning to his student, Jerry.

> At 6:33 PM Jerry made a text to text connection. He asked if Blackbeard had been discussed in the book because he saw a [TV] show on sunken treasure, and they were trying to find Blackbeard's treasure. While I allowed him to talk about this, there were so many opportunities that I could have taken advantage of to get him to use higher order thinking. For example, I could have asked how the topic of the show relates to the book we were reading. It would have been the perfect opportunity to compare and contrast what was taking place in both stories. At 6:45 PM there was [another] opportunity: Jerry asked a question about the shipping records, and I immediately explained their purpose in discovering the treasure. I could have used prompts to have him logically determine why the shipping records were important to the explorers. This would have been much more valuable than just telling him.

Principle #3

Educators Can Use a Gradual Release of Responsibility Model to Scaffold Learning in and through Video Reflection

Coming in the final week of Konnor's tutoring experience, this reflection provided just a glimpse of *Principle 3*. When thinking about using video within the GRR Model, setting up the reflective process so that preservice or inservice teachers have multiple forms of scaffolding is important. Space to engage in conversation with others and the use of reflective frameworks when reflecting on video both have the potential to scaffold the reflective process.

We'll return to this principle later in the chapter, but it is important to note that Konnor came to this realization after several weeks of reflecting on his teaching, using video, conversation with a teaching partner, and time in *Description*. He then began to use *Analysis* to explore how and why he might apply the GRR.

> Sometimes I feel that I might hold back from asking Jerry higher order questions because I am not sure if he is capable of comprehending at that level. Not only is this not fair to the student but they will not improve if I do not allow them attempts at answering these types of questions. In the case of the shipping records I explained their significance without allowing Jerry the opportunity to figure it out for himself. Peterson and Taylor (2012) suggest that, "The teacher could then respond by modeling how to give a higher order response" (p. 297). Therefore, what I should have done is asked Jerry higher order questions to see if he could figure out the significance of the shipping records. If he was unable to, then I could have modeled how to answer the question. From there we could have read on, and I could possibly have found another topic in which I could ask a similar question. This way he has an opportunity at answering a higher order question immediately after I modeled how to answer one.

Take some time to begin working with elements of reflective inquiry as discussed and demonstrated in this chapter and in Figure 5.4. You will find guiding questions and suggestions in **Appendix 5.1**, which lists activities to begin working with video and reflective inquiry.

Messing with the Details, and Messy Problems

One reason Rodgers (2002) called the *Description* phase of reflection "perhaps the most difficult" is "because it asks [teachers] to withhold interpretation of events and postpone their urge to fix the embedded problems until they can 'mess about' with the details of their stories" (p. 238). Joy spent very little time describing her problem of time management, just skimming the surface, but this was enough to help her notice that her students' learning was affected when she rushed through her lesson. Konnor spent eight weeks in *Description* mediated by video, and at the end of that time he could begin to plan ways to release responsibility for learning to his student, reflecting Principle 1 (teaching and reflecting are complex endeavors) and Principle 2 (these are scaffolded processes). They take time, space, and support. In this case, the support or scaffolding was Rodgers' reflective framework, conversations with another teacher, and the material scaffold of the video.

With more complex challenges, or the messy parts of teaching, spending more time on **Description** becomes even more important. By asking teachers to pay attention to **Description** we ask them to look at all the diverse and complex elements at play. By doing this, they develop **Presence**, noticing their subject matter, their teaching actions, and their students' responses; all within the larger teaching context which includes elements of bias, assumptions, conflict, and resolution. Noticing and describing all these elements of a teaching interaction increases a teacher's ability to support instructional choices, meaning that teachers will be better able to provide reasoned responses to questions from administrators, parents, and outside stakeholders. This can go a long way toward increasing feelings of confidence or efficacy—feelings which are quite frequently under attack within school and from outside of school these days. Spending more time in **Description** can help us notice and respond to the biases we all bring to teaching.

Using Critical Incidents to "Explode" Description

We all bring our own experiences and perspectives to our interactions with others. We all bring biases. Using critical incidents as a reflective framework in teaching can help us think about how those biases might shade our decision making. Critical incidents are significant vivid events that are remembered and that have impact (Brookfield, 2012; Tripp, 1993). They don't necessarily have to involve classroom instruction. For example, Chad shared this story about his time working for an in-school tutoring program in a high poverty, high needs urban school where most of the students were African-American. Not only is Chad a White male, his last name is also "White." As a certified Social Studies teacher, Chad had a passion for history and was committed to principles of social justice, but at the time he had had few opportunities to work with African-American students. On one of Chad's first days in the school, a group of boys teased him about his name, saying things such as, "He's White, and his name's White, so he's **Mr. White**."

Chad later reflected on this story and his response to his Black students' overtly drawing attention to his white skin color—something that Chad was unused to. Despite the focus on race and skin color—two topics often considered taboo in White, middle class culture—Chad responded back that yes, he was "**really**" Mr. White, a play on both his name and his skin color. This led to laughter from the boys and continual ribbing across the following weeks related to more word play from students on the words "white" and Mr. "White." Chad related how this one small moment came into focus for him in retrospect, as he thought about a University class he had completed that had focused on language, literacy, and culture. In this class concepts such as race, whiteness, literacy, and teaching had been discussed. Race was "put on the table" rather than "swept under the carpet." Chad observed that many White teachers have not been given that opportunity to deeply and reflexively explore the intersectionalities of race, class, and beliefs about teaching. Without such an opportunity to explore his own racialized positions, Chad pondered, would he have been as likely to respond to humor with humor? Or, he wondered, would he have misread humor as disrespect or even a threat from young Black men toward a new teacher? Having been part of a Community of Practice where participants considered their own racialized positions, Chad had become aware of his own position as a teacher who was White and male. As described above, this was a critical incident: a significant, vivid set of events that were remembered and had impact.

Using a critical incident approach to consider teaching interactions encourages learners to stay in *Description* longer, and the longer learners stay in *Description* the more that can potentially be noticed (Dozier, 2008; Dozier & Rutten, 2005). Describing a critical incident is akin to making a detailed illustration of a teaching event, something similar to exploded view drawings such as those provided in Figure 5.2 at the beginning of this chapter. When learners use the critical incident steps to stay in *Description* longer, they can provide a highly detailed view of a teaching interaction (Figure 5.5). The process looks like this:

Observation and description of a teaching incident is followed by creating an explanation that includes naming assumptions and biases as well as identifying other ways to view the incident. After this examination, teachers take a position and develop a responsive teaching action based on their "exploded" view of

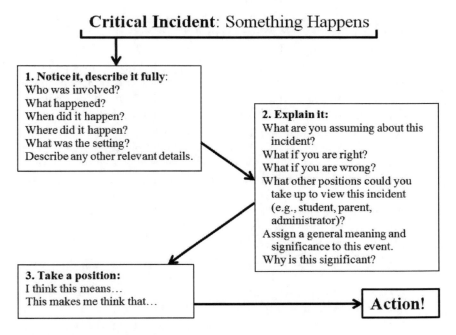

FIGURE 5.5 The critical incident framework.

the critical incident. Appendix 5.2 provides the Critical Incident Guide that you can use to begin examining a critical incident you have experienced. Here is a critical incident written by Karen, a White high school English teacher.

Karen's Critical Incident

Notice it, describe it

One of my students, Josh, is African-American. Josh's mom works at a bank, and his older brother was arrested this past summer and is currently in jail. Josh's standardized testing placed him at the 3rd grade reading level, and he has multiple accommodations to help him be successful in the classroom. He also has a detailed behavior plan as he struggles with dishonesty, rude and disrespectful speech towards adults, and "shutting down" as a coping mechanism.

Early in the year we were working on writing paragraphs using the stoplight paragraph structure: topic sentence (green: GO!), key idea (yellow: Slow down!), and supporting detail (red: Stop!). We use this language all year, really focusing on it in the co-taught classes since many students have disorganized writing or don't use any supporting details. Using a graphic organizer and color-coding his sentences, Josh turned in a paragraph that was similar to: "My summer was fun. I went swimming. It was fun. I ate food. It was fun. See, my summer was fun." Josh was on the right track, and had technically followed the paragraph format, but my next goal for Josh and all my students was to expand on details in their writing. I asked all students to revise their first drafts.

When I sat down with Josh to explain that I wanted him to work on adding and expanding his supporting details in his revision, he immediately shut down and said, "I did what you said. I'm not doing it again." Even after he would listen to what I was asking him to do ("Can you be more specific about swimming? Why was it fun?" Etc.), he would just look at me, shrug, and say, "I don't know. I can't do this."

Explain it: Examination of assumptions, biases, and other lenses

In these power struggle moments, I'm never fully sure what to do. Argue? Demand it happens? Send the student to the Dean for not following directions? Give him a pass and let him just sit there? I will admit I've done all of the above to varying degrees of success depending on the situation, but with Josh, I wonder if my assumptions of him, his home life, his capabilities, etc. affect how I treat him.

Josh's abilities are low, he doesn't have a father in his life, his older brother is in jail, he has a negative response towards adults, and he doesn't hang out with the "best crowd." I assumed many things about Josh based on these bits of information. I assume he doesn't get much educational support at home, that he doesn't have many positive role models in his life, that he may be "acting out" to impress others, that he may have been exposed to a multitude of criminal behaviors due to his brother, etc. Are any of those true? I don't actually know. Lisa Delpit, in "Lessons from Teachers" (2006), warned of the dangers of "being nice". When I just let Josh sit in class and not do what I was asking of him, was I giving up on him and "being nice"? Was I afraid of his eight-page-long behavior plan and what further disciplinary action may result in? Was I more "afraid" of looking like a racist if I sent him to the Dean?

What was Josh assuming about me by choosing to behave so defiantly? Did he assume I wouldn't "get it"? Was he just afraid of looking stupid in front of his peers and needing my help? Did he think I was judging him or treating him differently because I'm a White female and he's a Black male?

I also wonder if part of Josh's low ability stems from a lack of experiences in his life to build schema, but then again, this is an assumption I'm making based on what I know about his home life and minimal comments he's made in class. Often Josh struggles with adding relevant details to his writing, perhaps because he doesn't have much schema to help him put language to his experiences. Josh also has trouble comprehending texts.

I don't have access to Josh's individual testing results, but I have noticed that he has trouble "hearing" if grammar is incorrect. Often students can hear mistakes if I read their writing out loud, but Josh can't tell why "They box last night" is wrong, in formal grammar assignments, even if I lead him by prompting him to think about a certain word. Maybe Josh has phonemic difficulties and this weakness has "fanned out" to affect all other aspects of reading as well? Maybe he has to spend so much time decoding that comprehension is short-changed? I keep switching between reading and writing because they're so related. Rarely have I had a student with a great discrepancy between their reading and writing skills.

Take a position, and develop a plan of action

Thinking about how I interact with Josh is significant because there are so many students like him in my classroom. Students that are different than I am, and students that struggle. Since these students whose reading and writing skills are far below grade level will not be leaving my classroom, it is up to me to figure out how to meet them where they are and go from there.

First of all, I need to continue to take the time to assess my biases, my actions, and my words in order to critically evaluate how I'm treating my students. Instead of fearing "the other," I need to work to embrace the cultural (and all other types) of diversity within my classroom while still holding the same expectations for all students. This reflection and self-evaluation takes humility, honesty, and processing time, and would be beneficial to discuss with my co-teacher too.

In order to actively help Josh and other students like him, my co-teacher and I must work more effectively together. Ultimately, these students who are reading at 2nd and 3rd grade levels need access to texts that they can navigate on their own at least weekly, if not every day. My co-teacher and I also need to become better at breaking the kids into groups to do more individualized instruction to help students improve their weaknesses and build upon their strengths.

Adaptive Expertise .... in Real-Life Teaching

Karen's critical examination of her interactions with Josh raises many uncomfortable questions. How do our assumptions about students impact our daily, minute-to-minute instructional decisions? Once we've uncovered some biases, as Karen does here, what should we do next?

Since both Karen and Emily (the instructor for the graduate-level class Karen was enrolled in) are White women, it is also important for them to consider Josh's position as an adolescent Black male. For example, as an English teacher, Karen may be viewing Josh's grammar usage only through the lens of the formal grammatical rules set out by the high school English curriculum, without considering aspects of African-American Vernacular English (AAVE) that Josh may be using. Adding consideration of AAVE means that Josh's grammatical usage is not a deficit, just a difference. On the other hand, Karen's desire to know more about his phonological processing and decoding skills also seems valid. Since Josh has difficulty reading and writing, knowing more about his skills in these areas could help Karen target her instruction for him.

In helping to think through reading difficulties, Tatum (2005) recommends a number of what he calls "close-ups", which include "cognitive close-ups, pedagogical close-ups, psychological close-ups, and in some cases physiological close-ups" (pp. 125–126, see also 126–128). Karen seems to be incorporating several of these close-ups: cognitive, pedagogical, and psychological. While Tatum writes specifically with Black male adolescents in mind, most of his recommendations apply to struggling readers of any ethnic or racial background and across genders. Tatum (2013) also writes about the importance of helping students hear the voices of those who have come before and find their voice among them.

 Stop and Think

1. What do you think Karen should do next? Why?
2. What would you do to reach Josh? Why?
3. How do you think Karen's process of reflection might be assisted through video reflection?

Video Connections and Extensions

Question: How could Karen's reflective process have been expanded or enhanced if she had been able to view video of her interactions with Josh? What additional affordances might video reflection offer?

Since reflection on teaching is often not visible externally or readily seen by others, video evidence can help teachers like Karen, as well as teacher educators, articulate specific practices regarding how and when teachers reflect and adapt, as well as reveal the instructional conditions that support these processes (Parsons, 2012). In Karen's case, the concreteness and objectivity of video could make viewing from different perspectives easier. After using the critical incident framework to help identify, describe, analyze, and plan an action, what if Karen could then utilize video to capture specific moments of interaction with Josh? She could use these specific video moments and the objective space they provide to deepen her analysis and critique of her teaching as well as refine her plan of action.

While this book foregrounds video recording as a means of reflecting on one's teaching, audio recording can also be helpful. Even having an audio recording of Josh might be helpful. Remember Karen's comment about Josh's grammar:

> I have noticed that he has trouble "hearing" if grammar is incorrect. Often students can hear mistakes if I read their writing out loud, but Josh can't tell why "They box last night" is wrong, even if I lead him by prompting him to think about a certain word. Maybe Josh has phonemic difficulties and this weakness has "fanned out" to affect all other aspects of reading as well? Maybe he has to spend so much time decoding that comprehension is short-changed?

As stated earlier, Karen may have failed to recognize a common grammatical rule of African-American Vernacular English (AAVE) where consonant clusters at the end of a word "boxed" (e.g., /bɔkst/) are often dropped (e.g., /bɔks/). Thus, a speaker using AAVE might say, "They box last night." If Josh is a speaker of AAVE, this could be one reason he does not recognize "They box last night" as incorrect when reading it aloud because in the rules of AAVE, it is acceptable because it is correct. If Karen were able to listen to Josh reading, she could listen and watch for these patterns and support Josh's learning through exercises in contrastive analysis (Wheeler & Swords, 2004, 2006) where students study their own language systems in comparison to formalized ways of speaking and writing English. Such analysis enables learners to view their own languages or dialects as different—not inferior or wrong—but they also provide tools for children to think about linguistic systems for formal and informal communication. As Karen rightly notes, it is not enough to be the "nice" teacher who affirms a student. Authors such as Delpit (1988) and Wheeler and

Swords (2006) acknowledge that explicit instruction and teaching is necessary to help learners think about varieties of language as well as to make implicit rules explicit.

The Gradual Release of Responsibility

One of the worst things that can happen in an incident like this is for Karen to feel like she has no response, and no agency to act in a way that will advance Josh's learning. However, an "exploded view" of the critical incident asks her to develop an action plan. Karen ends her critical incident with a plan to work with her teaching partner to group students for skill building and find more accessible texts. It's a start. Additionally, if Karen (along with her partner) continues using a reflective process of developing **Presence**, spending time in **Description**, and using **Analysis** and **Experimentation,** she will build her Adaptive Expertise over time.

Unlike Joy and Konnor, Karen wrote this reflection in the context of a graduate level literacy leadership class without a matching practicum component. In the description of Joy's teaching, the structure of Joy's teacher training program provided the fertile ground for her to practice her teaching skill. The Community of Practice and teaching partnership that Konnor experienced in the reading center provided support for examining his teaching over time. This was not the case for Karen. In Chapter 3, we mentioned the importance of choice when reflecting. Karen had the opportunity to choose this incident from her teaching practice. Some of the responsibility was thus released to her for choosing when to practice the reflective cycle as well as what to reflect on. However, the way she reflected was still structured with the critical incident format (see Appendix 5.2), and Karen was prompted to think about her biases and her assumptions as well as to ask herself, "What if I'm right in the way I am viewing this? What if I'm wrong?" This structure resulted in reflection that was more nuanced, demonstrated risk-taking, and perhaps was more honest.

Principle 3: Educators Can Use a Gradual Release of Responsibility Model to Scaffold Learning in and through Reflection

The structure of the "Explain it" section pushed Karen to begin to confront her biases by naming them and examining them. We could say that she has done a pretty good job of this. Karen admits that what she believes she knows about Josh's home life influences her view of the incident with him in addition to her view of his abilities. She admits that she has some fear about pursuing a disciplinary path with him because such action may be perceived as racist. She doesn't deny that there may be racial undertones at play in her interaction with Josh: she says it, and she thinks about it, although she stops short of directly asking the next difficult question that lurks below the surface: Is race playing a part in my decision making or my opinions of Josh? As a teacher, she considers her options for proceeding, and she develops a teaching response only after this complex analysis of the interaction.

After weighing options, including disciplinary measures, Karen develops an Action that instead focuses on developing supports for Josh and other students who need more help with skill building—adapting the instructional approach. Karen opts for what she can attempt to do as a teacher instead of punishing Josh and perhaps further cementing biases that will work against him and his success. Karen's Action comes out of the deeper understanding and critique that comes from "exploding" the *Description* part of reflection to look at all the working parts of this incident. It brings more of her expertise to her teaching of Josh.

Jump-Starting or Boosting Growth

Research on teacher development typically identifies varying levels of expertise. While novices are more focused on their own performance and less aware of the feedback from their students, adaptive experts are the opposite. Adaptive experts are more keenly aware of the effectiveness of their teaching performance, and they are able to monitor, check, innovate, and modify (McNaughton, 2011). They notice features that may escape the attention of novices (Bransford, Darling-Hammond, & LePage, 2005).

The use of video and the GRR Model can mediate this development, because teachers of all experience levels can more readily examine the effectiveness of their teaching performances as well as the responses of their students. The objective space of video scaffolds or supports teachers to examine the concrete evidence of their teaching practices as well as student responses, as Joy and Konnor demonstrated at the start of this chapter. But learning to teach and learning to reflect are complex processes that need to be scaffolded. The reflective cycle or framework of *Presence, Description, Analysis,* and *Experimentation* is a scaffold that supports the development of adaptive expertise. When the critical incident framework is practiced as a way to "explode" the *Description* process, teachers spend more time uncovering and confronting biases as they work to develop action plans, as Karen did. The "Explain It" part of the critical incident prompts teachers to name and examine their biases, pushing towards a level of awareness many of us don't take to naturally. However, this awareness is essential for teachers when working in the diverse environments of schools.

Using critical incidents is a way to spend more time in *Description.* The collegial setting of a teacher group (for Joy, Konnor, and Karen, a college class) provides support for this exploration. A group of colleagues who "live" the reality of school life establishes a base of understanding for the kinds of incidents described here.

Continued Growth

Teachers, teacher educators, and professional developers need to consider sound pedagogical knowledge at all levels of development and experience. We need to look for ways to support examination of biases and questioning of assumptions about our students as well as our teaching. Otherwise, we run the risk of having our initial teaching experiences insulate us from growth—and from our students (Henry, Bastian, & Fortner, 2011).

References

Bransford, J., Darling-Hammond, L., & LePage, P. (2005). Introduction. In L. Darling-Hammond & J. Bransford (Eds.), *Preparing teachers for a changing world: What teachers should learn and be able to do* (pp. 1–39). San Francisco, CA: Jossey-Bass.

Brookfield, S. (2012). *Teaching for critical thinking: Tools and techniques to help students question their assumptions.* San Francisco, CA: Jossey-Bass.

Clay, M. M. (1985). *The early detection of reading difficulties: A diagnostic survey with recovery procedures.* (3rd ed.). Auckland, NZ: Heinemann.

Delpit, L. (1988). The silenced dialogue: Power and pedagogy in educating other people's children. *Harvard Educational Review, 58*(3), 280–298.

Delpit, L. (2006). Lessons from teachers. *Journal of Teacher Education, 57*(3), 220–231.

Dewey, J. (1910/1933). *How we think.* Boston, MA: D. C. Heath and Company. (Original work published 1910).

Dozier, C. L. (2008). Literacy coaching: Engaging and learning with teachers. *The Language and Literacy Spectrum, 18,* 11–19.

Dozier, C. L., & Rutten, I. (2005). Responsive teaching toward responsive teachers: Mediating transfer through intentionality, enactment, and articulation. *Journal of Literacy Research, 37*(4), 459–492.

Hayden, H. E. & Chiu, M. M. (2013). Lessons learned: Supporting the development of reflective practice and adaptive expertise. In P. J. Dunston, S. K. Fullerton, C. C. Bates, P. M. Stecker, M. W. Cole, A. H. Hall, D. Herro, K. Headley (Eds.) *62nd Literacy Research Association Yearbook* (pp. 279–296). Oak Creek, WI: Literacy Research Association, Incorporated.

Hayden, H. E., Moore-Russo, D., & Marino, M. (2013). One teacher's reflective journey and the evolution of a lesson: Systematic reflection as a catalyst for adaptive expertise. *Reflective Practice: International and Multidisciplinary Perspectives, 14*(1), 144–156.

Hayden, H. E., Rundell, T. D., & Smyntek-Gworek, S. (2013). Adaptive expertise: A view from the top, and the ascent. *Teaching Education, 24*(4), 395–414, doi:10.1080/10476210.2012.724054.

Henry, G. T., Bastian, K. C., & Fortner, C. K. (2011). Stayers and leavers: Early-career teacher effectiveness and attrition. *Educational Researcher, 40,* 271–279. doi:10.3102/0013189X11419042.

McNaughton, S. (2011). *Designing better schools for culturally and linguistically diverse children: A science of performance model for research.* New York, NY: Routledge.

Parsons, S. A. (2012). Adaptive teaching in literacy instruction: Case studies of two teachers. *Journal of Literacy Research, 44*(2), 149–170.

Peterson, D. S., & Taylor, B. M. (2012). Using higher order questioning to accelerate students' growth in reading. *Reading Teacher, 65*(5), 295–304.

Rodgers, C. (2002). Seeing student learning: Teacher change and the role of reflection. *Harvard Educational Review, 72*(2), 230–253.

Rodgers, C. (2006). Attending to student voice: The impact of descriptive feedback on learning and teaching. *Curriculum Inquiry, 36*(2), 209–237.

Tatum, A. W. (2005). *Teaching reading to Black adolescent Males: Closing the achievement gap.* Portland, ME: Stenhouse Publishers.

Tatum, A. W. (2013). *Fearless voices: Engaging a new generation of African American adolescent male writers.* New York, NY: Scholastic.

Tripp, D. (1993). *Critical incidents in teaching: Developing professional judgment.* New York, NY: Routledge.

Wheeler, R. S., & Swords, R. (2004). Codeswitching: Tools of language and culture transform the dialectally diverse classroom. *Language Arts, 81*(6), 470–480.

Wheeler, R. S., & Swords, R. (2006). *Codeswitching: Teaching standard English in urban classrooms.* Urbana, IL: NCTE.

APPENDIX 5.1

ACTIVITIES TO BEGIN WORKING WITH VIDEO AND REFLECTIVE INQUIRY

1. Use websites such as Teaching Channel, TeacherTube, Edutopia, or another website that houses free video to identify a video of a literacy-related teaching event. With your peers explore the video using the ideas of *Presence, Description, Analysis,* and *Experimentation*.

   a   https://www.teachingchannel.org/
   b   http://www.teachertube.com/
   c   https://www.edutopia.org/videos

2. If you have access to a classroom, literacy center, or tutoring situation, record your own literacy teaching. Explore the ideas of *Presence, Description, Analysis,* and *Experimentation* (see Figure 5.4). Then share your video and your reflections with a peer or a group of peers.

3. From your own teaching or classroom experience, pick a critical incident. This could be something you experienced while teaching, something you observed, or something you experienced as a student. Write up this incident using the outline that Karen used:

   • Notice it, describe it.
   • Explain it: Examination of assumptions, biases, and other lenses
   • Take a position, and develop a plan of Action

Also see Appendix 5.2 on the following pages for the Critical Incident Guide.

APPENDIX 5.2

CRITICAL INCIDENT GUIDE

Critical incidents are *significant vivid events that are remembered and impact people* (Brookfield, 2012; Tripp, 1993). Examination of critical incidents can lead us to *ACTION!* because they enable us to arrive at a position.

> The vast majority of critical incidents … are not at all dramatic or obvious; they are mostly straightforward accounts **of very commonplace events** that occur in routine professional practice **which are critical** in the sense that **they are indicative of underlying trends, motives and structures.** These incidents appear to be 'typical' rather than 'critical' at first sight, but *are rendered critical through analysis.*
>
> *(Tripp, 1993, p. 24–25)*

Critical Incident: Something Happens

1. Notice it, describe it fully: *Who was involved? What happened? When did it happen? Where did it happen? What was the setting? Describe other relevant details.*

2. Explain it: *What are you assuming about this incident? What if you are right (or wrong)? What other positions could you take up to view this incident (e.g. student, parent). Assign a general meaning and significance to this event. Why is this significant?*

3. Take a position:

Action!

6

USING VIDEO FOR REFLECTION AS AN INDEPENDENT LEARNER IN A FIELD-BASED PRACTICUM

FIGURE 6.1 Reflection of the complexities of teaching and learning.

During my undergraduate studies, I kept countless journals and was asked to reflect throughout my coursework and in my sophomore and junior participation experiences I was asked to reflect daily on my lessons. Typically, I wrote down what part of the lesson was successful and what should be changed for next time. My reflections rarely dug deep into the complexities of teaching and more importantly student learning. I did not critically reflect on my own understandings;

instead I picked a teaching practice that was easy to talk about. Frankly, I was going through the motions and checking off the box on the assignment. I knew how to do school.

(Barbara, preservice teacher)

Historically, state education departments use standardized tests that are decontextualized from teaching to determine if candidates earn their teaching certification. Recently, many states have shifted away from decontextualized tests to also include performance-based assessments (e.g., edTPA, Praxis Performance Assessment for Educators) that require teacher candidates to demonstrate if they are qualified to teach in more authentic ways. One artifact that is being used to capture a teacher candidate's competency is video. Teacher candidates are being asked to capture video *learning segments* (ILA, 2010), which are three to five consecutive lesson segments, as artifacts of their teaching competence; they subsequently compose written reflections (sometimes called commentaries) that show their knowledge. Through this process, candidates need to provide documentation of what they intended to teach, artifacts (such as video) of their enactment of teaching, and finally, documentation of the impact of their teaching on student learning (Figure 6.1).

These new requirements not only impact teaching candidates, but they also depend on teacher educators' examination of how their programs prepare their preservice teachers to be reflective. In Chapter 3, we began by asking teacher educators to consider developing a cohesive and coherent path of reflection across their teacher education program that gradually releases preservice teachers through the reflection process. It is critical for teacher educators to self-examine their programs to provide insights into their effectiveness in preparing preservice teachers to reflect independently on artifacts, such as video, as part of state education certification requirements with the goal of developing highly competent teachers. Keep in mind that although we focus our conversation on video, it is only one tool teacher educators may use to develop preservice teachers' reflective practices.

In this chapter, we also ask preservice teachers to critically think about times when they were asked to reflect on their own learning and teaching. Our goal is to create a space where teacher educators and preservice teachers can collaboratively consider how the teaching of reflection as a construct is gradually released across their program. To fully prepare our next generation of teachers, teacher educators, as well as preservice and inservice teachers need to know how they are being asked to demonstrate their competence (Figure 6.2).

FIGURE 6.2   Collaborative reflection.

After considering the development of reflection in the teacher education program, through an example from Lori, one of our preservice teachers, we then follow Caitlyn, a student teacher, into her field-based practicum. Caitlyn engages in reflection using digital video along with other scaffolds to revisit her teaching practices. What is important to remember is that Caitlyn is at the end of her program, meaning she should be able to reflect more independently if her reflective practices were developed across her undergraduate program.

Our goal was to collaborate with Caitlyn to determine an alternative reflective format for the practicum. While most researchers and teacher educators argue that support should be provided in the field, this case provides evidence that critical reflective inquiry can occur even with support that is not immediate (e.g., an instructor providing feedback on teaching experiences prior to and after teaching and reflection). This is particularly important because in times of shrinking resources, ongoing supervision, and feedback for preservice teachers in the field may not be present in every preservice program. Instead, preservice teachers might only get intermittent feedback. This case study typifies many of the experiences of preservice teachers who are asked to reflect independently while in the field.

Critical Components to Consider: Developing Reflection across a Program

 Stop and Think

In this Stop and Think we ask preservice and inservice teachers questions titled "Student Reflective Questions" and teacher educators questions titled "Teacher Educator Reflective Questions." Our goal here is to create a dialogue between teacher educators and preservice and inservice teachers.

1. **Student Reflective Questions:**
   a. Think of a time you were asked to reflect on your teaching when the reflective process was meaningful and informed your practice. What made that reflective experience meaningful?
   b. Now, think of a time you were asked to reflect when the reflective process was not meaningful, and instead, you just went through the motions similar to Barbara in the opening vignette.
   What made that reflective experience less meaningful or less significant?
   c. What were you asked to do during the more meaningful reflective process that was different from what you were asked to do in the less meaningful one?

2. **Teacher Educator Reflective Question:** Think of a time when you read a student's reflection and felt that it was mostly comprised of summary, never reaching higher levels of critique (e.g., including next steps or introducing a teaching action). What strategies did you use or could you use to raise the level of reflection?

When our literacy faculty first began discussing our expectations for reflection, we realized that we all included experiences for preservice teachers that developed their reflective practices, but we did not have an intentionally designed cohesive and coherent way to develop reflective practitioners across our program. Through our self-analysis, we realized that our preservice teachers' reflections rarely included detail beyond the descriptive level. We knew they were capable of much more than this, so we reflected and asked ourselves what we were doing programmatically to develop a culture of reflection from the time preservice teachers entered the program through when they were asked to demonstrate their competencies in more complex teaching experiences. Developing a culture of reflection required faculty, who design undergraduate and graduate teacher education programs, to come together and intentionally design instruction in how to

FIGURE 6.3 Strategically planning to develop a culture of reflection.

reflect as well as how to thread such reflective instruction throughout the program in a cohesive way. We begin by highlighting some critical components suggested for teacher educators who strive to develop a culture of reflection (Figure 6.3).

Was There Cohesion and Coherence on How Preservice Teachers Were Taught to Reflect?

When reflecting on our program, we began by considering the end goals for our teaching candidates. As most would expect, we wanted our preservice teachers to:

- Understand theoretical and evidence-based foundations of reading and writing processes as well as instruction
- Use a variety of instructional approaches and materials to support student learning
- Develop knowledge about assessment and its connection to instruction
- Develop awareness and ability to teach in ways that respect and value differences in our society (e.g., racial, ethnic, gender, or socioeconomic status)
- Develop knowledge of curriculum and standards
- Create a literate environment that fosters reading and writing

These goals are commonplace in teacher preparation programs and so is developing reflective practitioners. One critical factor influencing how preservice teachers are prepared to reflect is the new set of certification requirements, which necessitates the use of video as a way to capture evidence of candidates' competency. This means that both reflecting and use of video as a mediational tool for reflection play integral roles in demonstrating one's competence and ultimately obtaining certification. One of our long-term goals in both our undergraduate and graduate teacher education programs was always to develop reflective practitioners who were prepared to make informed decisions about teaching and learning. In *Performance Practice for Educators* (2015), this type of reflection is referred to as a disposition where "The teacher takes responsibility for student learning and uses ongoing analysis and reflection to improve planning and practice" (Educational Testing Services, p. 8). Developing preservice teachers who independently reflect on video is key given the current landscape of teacher certification. With this in mind, teacher educators must consider instructional design that is teleological, meaning that the coursework is designed intentionally with specific purposes that are linked to long-term program goals. As a result, we wondered how we should teach the construct of reflection cohesively and coherently across our teacher education program, so that our preservice teachers were prepared for more complex teaching situations, like field-based practicums and student teaching. If we did not consider our own practices, the end result could be the development of teachers who were not critical thinkers and problem solvers, and who were, perhaps, less prepared for the complexities they would encounter in classroom teaching. After all, "it is imperative that teacher education programs develop creative, effective ways to prepare the teaching population to meet the needs of a diverse student population" (McMillon, 2009, p. 119).

 ## Stop and Think

- **Student Reflective Question:** When you were asked to reflect as a student, what kind of guidance or scaffolding, if any, was provided to you so that your reflection was more than description?
- **Teacher Educator Reflective Question:** When you ask preservice teachers to engage in reflection, what scaffolds do you strategically use when teaching the reflective process?

When conceptualizing the GRR Model as well as video reflection, we need to consider the different ways to support preservice teachers through the reflective process. In Chapter 2, we pointed to the following scaffolds:

- Conversations with peers,
- Conversations with more knowledgeable others,
- Use of reflective cycles and/or frameworks with guiding questions,
- Use of video analysis with specific goals.

In what follows, we briefly discuss these scaffolds with requirements of performance-based assessments that include video as an artifact, knowing that strategic scaffolding is critical to the Gradual Release of Responsibility (GRR).

Preparing to View Video: Context, Purpose, and Video Selection

Just as there can be multiple interpretations of words that are read, there can also be multiple interpretations of images that are read. Interpretations of all text types (e.g., video, print book) are influenced by context. As touched on in Chapter 3, preparing preservice teachers to view video should include providing them with relevant information about the teaching and learning context they will see in the video. The depth of discussion on context needed will vary by audience. The instructor, who is the more knowledgeable other, will need to strategically slide up or down the GRR depending on the preparation and needs of the audience viewing the video.

If the video is being shared with teachers who are familiar with the context, less information will need to be shared. However, if the viewers are not familiar with the context, it is important to share contextual information to support the interpretation. Below is a list of potential information to consider when contextualizing a video.

* Type of School
  * Elementary, middle, or high school
  * Urban, suburban, or rural
  * Charter, public, private, or magnet
* Grade Level
* Objective of lesson and discipline being taught
* Classroom Setting Examples
  * Teaching model or support: co-teaching, consultant teaching model, bilingual team teaching, or teaching assistant
  * Whole group, small group, or intervention
  * Ability grouping or tracking
  * Instructional program(s)
* Student Composite
  * Number of students in class; males versus females
  * Students with Individualized Educational Program (IEP); or a 504 plan for students with disabilities; inclusion students, second language students, specific language needs
  * Students who need more challenging work
  * Students working at, on, or above grade level
  * Racial and ethnic backgrounds
  * Socioeconomic status (e.g., percentage of free and reduced lunch students in school)

Providing information about context assists the viewer in the interpretation of the events that occur in the video.

Just as we set purposes for reading a book, the same principle holds true for viewing video. Teacher educators need to clearly identify the reason for viewing the video, which will help set the purpose for engaging in video reflection. We caution that "setting purpose" does not mean that teacher educators should control the identification of the problem space. Here is another place where the GRR can be utilized to scaffold the reflection process. For example, the teacher educator can pose a more open-ended question at the start, and gradually release the responsibility of identifying the problem space to the preservice teacher.

We suggest starting with video of others early in teacher preparation programs and gradually lead up to preservice teachers viewing video of themselves and their own teaching, because watching oneself places a preservice teacher in a vulnerable situation when they are also in the process of forming a community of learners (Shanahan & Tochelli, 2012). Research points to the fact that when preservice and inservice teachers learn to reflect on video, they initially focus on what the teacher is doing more so than on what the students are doing and learning (Sherin & van Es, 2009). Scaffolding preservice teachers early in the processes of video reflection can orient them to focusing on student learning and how the teacher's practices seen in the video are impacting that learning. Another benefit to video viewing of others early in an education program is that it increases preservice teachers' ability to connect classroom interactions viewed through video to pedagogical concepts and principles they are learning in coursework (Bausmith & Berry, 2011; Shanahan & Tochelli, 2014). Grounding pedagogical practices by viewing them in action through video assists preservice teachers in conceptualizing best practices.

Initially, the teacher educator will most likely pick the focus of video reflection in a methods course based on its objectives. However, after using video of others to teach various instructional practices as well as the reflective framework, it is essential to have preservice teachers begin to determine their own focus for reflection. Developing preservice teachers' ability to identify a central focus of video reflection is critical, because gradually releasing teachers in determining this problem space in the video gives them voice and choice in the focus of their reflection. Having voice and choice is critical for ownership and will also prepare them to write their reflective commentary for their performance-based assessment. Eventually, preservice teachers should move from reflection on the practices of others to reflecting on their own practices.

Programmatically Committing to Using a Reflective Model

So far in this book, we have shared several reflective frameworks (e.g., Rodgers' Reflective Cycle Critical Incidents; Jay and Johnson's Typology) that can be used to guide the reflective experiences both preservice and inservice teachers engage in while in their teacher education programs. We became interested in learning about multiple reflective frameworks because we recognized that it was more typical for our preservice teachers to stay at the descriptive level in their reflections. Upon this reflection, our action was to explicitly teach a reflective framework, the Jay and Johnson Typology (2002), to determine if the explicit teaching of a reflective framework would scaffold the preservice teachers' levels of reflection. Regardless of the framework used, we recommend that the reflective framework be taught early in the program when teachers are watching video of instructional practices that are not of their own teaching. Having preservice teachers analyze video of exemplary practice while using a reflective framework is a setting to begin cultivating a culture of reflection. For example, for teacher certification purposes in states using the edTPA assessment, preservice teachers will be asked to view their video to evaluate their instruction. Below are several tasks that edTPA requires of teacher candidates.

- Explain how you elicited and built on student responses to promote thinking and apply the essential literacy strategy using related skills to comprehend or compose text.
- Explain how you modeled the essential literacy strategy *and* supported students as they practiced or applied the strategy to comprehend or compose text in meaningful context.
- Explain how the teacher's instruction engaged students in developing foundational literacy practices.

Teacher educators can set purposes for viewing, like those described above, and have preservice teachers analyze the video applying Jay and Johnson's (2002) three dimensions. If preservice teachers are at the end of their program, they can determine their own problem spaces and purposes as well as apply a reflective framework or cycle (e.g., Jay and Johnson, 2002; Rodgers, 2002; Reichenberg, 2017—see Chapter 7).

What follows is an example of written reflection or commentary from Lori, a preservice teacher, analyzing her own video when she and her co-teacher were instructing Junie (student pseudonym), an eight-year-old girl in third grade at the Center for Literacy and Reading Instruction. In her written reflection, Lori selects her own problem space and uses the Jay and Johnson Typology (2002) to guide her through the reflective process. Lori's reflection shows the intersection of the Jay and Johnson framework and her own selection of the problem space. Using this reflective structure, Lori selects her own problem space: wait time.

Lori's Reflection Using Jay and Johnson's Typology

In the next section, Lori's reflection is separated into Jay and Johnson's (2002) three dimensions (descriptive, comparative, and critical) (see Appendix 2.1 for information on each of these dimensions) with the guided questions included. When you read Lori's reflection, take a moment to reflect on the guiding questions at each dimension and analyze Lori's response focused on wait time to determine how she is addressing the reflective dimensions. Keep in mind that there are multiple scaffolding threads running through and supporting this work as Lori moves through the reflective process. Some of these scaffolds are:

- Video itself as a tool for reflection
- Jay and Johnson Typology (2002) with the guiding questions
- Assigned task that includes the preservice teacher determining the central focus or problem space of the reflection
- Lori's discussions with her co-teacher

Descriptive Dimension

As a reminder, the *descriptive dimension* is meant to decide the focus of the reflection by describing what is happening and determining a problem space. Several of the guiding questions used during video reflection are:

- What is happening?
- Is this working, and for whom? Whom is it not working for? How do I know?
- How am I feeling? What am I pleased and/or concerned about?

Lori's Written Commentary for the Description Dimension

Since we used the "Mystery Bag" for the first time as an instructional tool, I surrounded the introduction with teacher talk. At points, Junie (student) interjected her own thinking. Retrospectively, I am wondering if Junie was adding in her own thinking on top of mine specifically because I had not been providing her with enough talk time while launching the lesson. One thing I noticed about my teacher practice upon playback was how frequently I rephrased questions. What struck me, too, was how quickly I chose to restate a question when little time had passed for Junie to respond. The key example that surprised me was the following. While prompting Junie to generate an item that she could compare to a stretchy rubber band, I said:

Time Stamp	Clinician Questions
6:38:<u>15</u>	"What's something that's stretchy like a rubber band that we can compare it too?"
6:38:<u>17</u>	"What's something that's stretchy?"
6:38:<u>20</u>	"Hmm. What's *really* stretchy?"
6:38:<u>24</u>	"… that you can pull or twist?"

When coding the difference in times between questions asked before rephrasing, I calculated that the average wait time that I used before rephrasing the question was 3 seconds. I also noticed that after asking the initial question, I truncated the restated one by approximately 70%, shortening the question from 14 words to 4 words. In addition, I used filler ("Hmm") as if I were thinking myself about the question's answer during the third restatement. At this time, I also added emphasis ("*really*") to convey the meaning. Again, I reduced the number of words in this restatement to three. Finally, I added in a definition to describe what the term "stretchy" meant ("… that you can pull or twist?"). Within 10 seconds, I restated the question four times. In review, I am thinking that Junie knew what the word "stretchy" meant, but merely needed think-time to thoughtfully generate an item that shared a rubber band's elasticity.

 Stop and Think

- Pause for a moment and as a group (preservice teachers and teacher educators together), discuss how Lori addressed the guiding questions in the descriptive dimension using your analysis.

  ➤ What is happening?
  ➤ Is this working, and for whom? Whom is it not working for? How do I know?
  ➤ How am I feeling? What am I pleased and/or concerned about?

Just as shown in Chapter 5, with **Description** and **Presence** in Rodgers' (2002) model as well as in Schön's (1983) work, the descriptive dimension provides a space for the preservice teacher to put parameters around a problem of practice. Here, Lori noticed and identified a problem space as her lack of wait time for the learner. Having Lori, a preservice teacher, independently identify the focus of her reflection and make the connection with how her actions influenced the student's learning was powerful, because it gave her voice and choice. In addition, her reflection was grounded in evidence from video of her teaching.

Comparative Dimension

In her written reflection, Lori then moved on to the *comparative dimension*. The goal in the comparative dimension is to reframe the problem space in light of alternative views, others' perspectives, and research. Knowing this goal, we asked our teachers to consider the following questions for the comparative dimension:

- What connections can you make to past readings from literature? (e.g., This reminds me of what [an author] said about…This makes me think of [author's name] model... What I saw in the video connected me with an article we read in [course name] about...)

Below, we share the second part of Lori's written reflection on the comparative dimension. Once again, we ask that you consider the guiding question above when reading the written reflection or commentary and determine how Lori is moving through her reflection at the comparative dimension.

Lori's Written Commentary for the Comparative Dimension

While I found my mere 3 second wait time on average to be startling, I was interested to find in research that 3 seconds is the typical amount of wait time students are allotted by teachers. According to Wasik and Iannone-Campbell (2013):

> As teachers, we tend to jump in to answer our own questions when a child does not respond immediately. Providing wait time for children to answer a question allows them to gather their ideas and then communicate them. However, because our typical wait time is usually about three seconds, teachers must understand the importance of wait time and how it can be used to support young children's thinking and learning (p. 330).

In a sense, Wasik and Iannone-Campbell's work was comforting as I learned that I was not alone in the profession with super-speed questioning; however, through their work, I have now become more cognizant of wait time when questioning. As a person, I know that I often feel uncomfortable in silence, so I wonder if I automatically perceive the wait time as time to fill with teacher talk; this may be one way to explain the amount of times I restated the question earlier. In addition, if a student does not respond right away, I may have the perception (truly a misconception) that the student needs to hear the question in a new way with different words. I am thinking that for some lessons this may be true, but in this particular one I think Junie simply needed wait time to process the question. Shortly after, she did come up with a headband and ultimately settled on a sweater as an item that could be stretchy like a rubber band.

 Stop and Think

Pause for a moment and as a group (preservice teachers and teacher educators together), discuss how Lori addressed the guiding question in the comparative dimension, using your analysis. What connections can you make to past readings from literature?

Through the comparative dimension, Lori connected a course reading explicitly to practice. The comparative dimension provides an opportunity to make research-to-practice connections. Furthermore, what is not seen here in the written reflection is that perspectives or points of view of others were brought to the table through video study group discussion. As teacher educators, we need to create spaces where connections can be made and comparative views can be applied to practice through discussion with peers. Lori co-taught Junie, so she had a peer to collaborate with throughout the process. Having others to talk with during the reflective process is generative (Shanahan & Tochelli, 2012), making reflection a self-extending system.

Critical Dimension

According to Jay and Johnson (2002), the *critical dimension* entails considering the implications of the problem under study and establishing a renewed perspective or, in this case, course of action. We asked our teachers the following questions to shift their reflection to action. After you read the next vignette, analyze Lori's reflection to see her connections to these guiding questions.

- Where should the teacher go from here? What's the action plan?
- If you were to teach this lesson what would you keep the same? What would you do differently?

Lori's Written Commentary for the Critical Dimension

Moving forward, I will be more purposeful about providing wait time for Junie to respond. One professor of mine last spring suggested one strategy to use for think time. She said after asking students a question to discreetly and slowly draw a tiny hashtag symbol on a piece of paper (#). With each line drawn, the teacher reminds her or himself to wait before calling on students to respond. I have used this strategy in the past and could use it more frequently after asking a question and before restating a question. In their research, Wasik and Iannone–Campbell (2013) found that:

> Providing a child with a 15-second wait time allows the child time to respond and also allows the teacher time to think of a scaffolding question to encourage the child's response without the silence of waiting becoming overwhelming (p. 330).

In my philosophy of education statement, I write that I value student thinking. Through this reflection, however, I noticed that I am placing student thinking on a timeline by not providing Junie with enough opportunity to think before I restate the question for her to respond. My short-term goal will be to increase my wait time after I ask a question and before restating to six seconds; this will double the amount of current wait time I provide. I will try this by discreetly drawing (#) with my finger on the table. Our mentor has noted how much Junie enjoys sharing her thinking with both Miss Flower and I on topics ranging from content to even lesson planning, so it is important for me as a teacher to provide her with opportunities to respond and provide her with access to an appropriate amount of wait time.

 Stop and Think

Pause for a moment and as a group (preservice teachers and teacher educators together), discuss how Lori addressed the guiding questions in the critical dimension, using your analysis.

- Where should the teacher go from here? What's the action plan?
- If you were to teach this lesson what would you keep the same? What would you do differently?

In the critical dimension, Lori identifies an action plan based on her observation, course reading, and advice given to her by a more knowledgeable other.

Through Lori's reflection, our goal was to illustrate how a predetermined reflective framework (in this case, Jay & Johnson, 2002) could scaffold the reflective process when the preservice teacher determines the problem space. By choosing a reflective model with guiding questions, preservice teachers understood our expectations for reflection. It also helped us, as teacher educators, programmatically define what we meant by reflection. We strategically and purposely scaffolded the reflective process through:

- Using video
- Adopting a model of reflection that included guiding questions
- Having preservice teachers work in partners
- Releasing preservice teachers to determine the central focus or problem space of their reflection.

 Stop and Think

1. **Student Reflective Questions:** Think about how you are asked to reflect on video. Visually map how video reflection was introduced and developed across your program. In this map, identify what courses

used video reflection and how you were gradually released through the process. Think about what types of scaffolds were put into place to support you as you engaged in the reflective process (e.g., guiding questions, reflective frameworks, discussion with peers).

2. **Teacher Educators Reflective Questions:** Reflect on how your current program develops a culture of reflection, specifically through video reflection. Visually map how video reflection was gradually released across your program by identifying the courses that use video reflection and the purposes of video reflection in those courses. Think about: How is the use of video introduced? Do you use a reflective framework with guiding questions? If so, how do you scaffold the preservice teachers' understanding of that model? Do you gradually release preservice teachers in the use of video as reflective tool? If so, how do you do this?

Planning for Gradually Releasing Responsibility to Preservice and Inservice Teachers through the Reflective Model

Once a reflective model is adopted, teacher educators should consider how they will gradually release preservice teachers' experiences with the reflective model so that reflection becomes a self-guided habit leading to action. Scaffolding is crucial, and is the thread that runs throughout the GRR Model. We leave teacher educators and video study leaders with the following scaffolds to consider when gradually releasing preservice teachers through the reflective process:

Step 1: Read and critique written reflections done by preservice teachers in previous semesters in order to learn to identify the components of the reflective framework.

Step 2: Score the written reflections on a rubric (Appendix 6.1). Begin by having the preservice teachers scoring the same written reflection in partners. They should provide evidence to support the score they have assigned, and then participate in a whole group discussion about the scoring.

Step 3: View someone else's teaching. Then, draft a written reflection on the video clip using the guiding questions using the reflective framework. As a class, compose one written reflection with the instructor's scaffolding to guide the process. Score the reflection on the rubric.

Step 4: Because our teachers co-teach when they tutor in an afterschool clinic, we first ask them to collaboratively reflect through each dimension and then create a common written reflection. Then, preservice teachers self-assess their reflection using the course rubric.

Step 5: Each preservice or inservice teacher reflects independently using Jay and Johnson's (2002) reflective framework, attending to the guiding questions. Once again, they should refer to the rubric as a way to self-analyze (Figure 6.4).

FIGURE 6.4 Develop a culture of reflection by leaving time in the day to collectively reflect.

Creating Reflective Spaces

Knowing that our goal was to develop a culture of reflection, we asked ourselves where, within, and across our coursework we purposely provided spaces for our teachers to engage in reflection. Individual reflection as well as conversations with others and a more knowledgeable other are critical to developing the culture of reflection (Deeney & Dozier, 2015) (see Chapter 2). Some essential points to consider:

- In the beginning of a program, the role of the teacher educator might be to model the reflective process, but the ultimate goal is to develop a reflective community where the role of the teacher educator is to facilitate. This means that the preservice teachers will have both choice and voice in selecting the problem space during the reflective process. The facilitator can assist or scaffold raising the preservice teachers' awareness as they reflect.
- When reflecting on video cases use guiding questions that (a) lead the teachers to define a problem space, (b) look at that space from multiple points of view, and (c) determine a plan of action so that there is transfer between research and practice.
- Use complex cases for preservice teachers to reflect upon.
- Leave space for collaborative discussions so that knowledge can be co-constructed by the preservice teachers.

In the second part of this chapter, we share lessons we learned when we worked with a preservice teacher named Caitlyn on re-conceptualizing the reflective assignment in the final practicum course of our literacy specialist program. Reflecting upon our preservice teachers' feedback required us to trust our own gradual release of the reflective process. If we were effective, our preservice teachers should have been able to reflect more independently and authentically.

Lessons from a Preservice Teacher: Gradually Releasing the Reflective Task

When I first began teaching the final summer literacy practicum, I interviewed preservice teachers who had previously taken the course. They shared that the written reflections took hours and that more times than not it interfered with their planning because they would run out of time. Knowing that time is a constant and they were committed preservice teachers, I myself had to take a moment to reflect on their words. Hearing their message and knowing that both the preservice teachers and I valued reflection, I collaborated with Caitlyn on modifying the reflective process in the practicum.

(Lynn Shanahan, teacher educator)

The literacy practicum is a complex learning space where preservice teachers are trying to balance more responsibilities as well as reflecting recursively over time. The preservice teachers viewed the crafting of a polished written reflection throughout the practicum as detrimental because it left them with minimal time to design upcoming lessons. Through this collaboration between Caitlyn, a preservice student and Lynn, a teacher educator, they designed another set of procedures for the reflection assignment in the practicum. We first share (a) information about Caitlyn, (b) Caitlyn's reflective procedure, and (c) Caitlyn's reflections along with what we learned about gradually releasing our preservice teachers during video reflection.

Caitlyn

I did not feel prepared to teach students how to read and write after taking only two undergraduate literacy courses.

(Caitlyn, preservice teacher)

Let us take a moment to introduce you to Caitlyn. Caitlyn had limited teaching experience when she was enrolled in the School-Based Literacy Practicum. The practicum was designed for candidates to work in no more than a 1:6 ratio with struggling readers who all qualified for Title 1 reading support. The elementary aged students who ranged in age from five to ten years old attended summer school for six weeks, Monday through Thursday from 8:00 to 11:00 am. Each grade level team of preservice teachers was assigned a supervisor who provided scaffolding to them in meeting their goals, such as: (1) working on classroom management, (2) lesson planning, (3) formative and summative assessment, and (4) establishing teacher and student goals.

The format of Caitlyn's reflection differed from previous classes in that she did not submit a written commentary or reflection like the one shared in the beginning of this chapter. Instead, she gradually released to (1) watch herself teach on video, (2) determine the problem space, (3) memo about her teaching and the students' learning, and then (4) audio record her reflection. She submitted these audio reflections to her supervisor, and it became the content of their discussions. In this scenario, the supervisor had access to her video recorded lesson and audio recorded reflection. No written artifact was submitted.

Problem Space

Caitlyn determined that the setting for her video reflection would be during guided reading (i.e., small group instructional reading at the student's reading level). She began recording her guided reading lessons and viewing them daily with the goal of identifying the problem space, which would be the focus of her reflection. The performance assessments for teacher certification focused on three to five lesson segments. Fortunately, teaching students all semester provides preservice teachers with a much broader view beyond their three to five lesson segments; they can also observe change over time—in this case, over six weeks. When reflecting over six weeks, Caitlyn's problem space changed multiple times as her teaching proficiency grew.

As teacher educators, we were curious about what would happen to Caitlyn's reflective levels if we opened up a more flexible way to reflect. What follows are transcripts from the audio recorded reflections in one problem space, classroom management, that Caitlyn selected to focus on during guided reading.

 Stop and Think

Similar to the multiple Stop and Thinks earlier in the chapter, read Caitlyn's reflection and see if you can identify where Caitlyn reflected at the descriptive, comparative, and critical dimensions.

Problem Space: Classroom Management

Many of the classroom management issues I dealt with surfaced from the students' poor self-confidence and task avoidance.

(Caitlyn's Reflection)

When Caitlyn first began exploring her classroom management she began to see student behaviors from a different perspective. She realized that student behaviors in guided reading were directly connected to their identity. Consider Caitlyn's reflection:

As I began reflecting on my guided reading group the first week, I quickly learned that I would need to be stern yet supportive in order to maintain and move the students forward in their reading abilities. I had a group of students who were talkative and energetic. However, as I listened to and intently watched my video recorded lessons at night I heard a complex story. For example, Nalah said, "I'm not a good reader. That's why I'm here." Other students jumped into the conversation and also verbalized their struggles with reading. That same week, one day Erik hid under the table and said, "Just pretend that I am not here. I don't want to guess." This task avoidance clearly showed how he did not feel he would succeed. It was at this moment that a glaring realization became apparent: reading really is a socially constructed activity. Through my coursework, I read about this and discussed identity, but had never made a real-life connection to the notion of reading being a socially constructed activity. Because many of the classroom management issues emanated from the students' poor self-confidence and task avoidance, I had to attempt to build their confidence by having them experience success in small intervals that were very close together.

 Stop and Think

Pause for a moment and as a group (preservice teachers and teacher educators together) using your analysis, discuss how Caitlyn addressed the descriptive, comparative, and critical dimension within a less structured reflection format.

What we noticed in Caitlyn's reflection was that she

- Identified the problem space and described what happened (descriptive dimension).
- Provided descriptive evidence to support what she had learned although she did not stop to cite a particular reading; compared her interpretation with previous coursework (comparative dimension).
- Critically determined a teaching action (critical dimension).

Ultimately, we wanted our preservice teachers to reflect in authentic ways, similar to how they might reflect as a practicing teacher, and this modified process seemed to support our goal.

This pattern continued over the six weeks of the practicum. During the third week, Caitlyn identified her use of passive language in directing students as a problem space that contributed to her classroom management issues. Caitlyn exclaimed that:

> I became very conscious of my passive language in the classroom. I felt that I was not being the stern, fair disciplinarian that the students needed. I am beginning to realize how much passive language I am using. I always blanket it in a question like, 'Do you think that's a good idea? Or make another choice?' It's always this passive roundabout thing. I guess I've just realized that my language is really wishy-washy in the classroom. And that I really put on this 'I want to be your friend, not your teacher' thing. And that's not what I want to put across because I want the students to behave and be focused in a way that helps every student learn. And I've realized that my language is hindering that and maybe sending mixed messages. I needed to take action and use very clear and explicit language when giving directions. I decided to write my directions out in my lesson plans until this became more natural.

Notice that in this reflection Caitlyn

- Identified the problem space and described what happened. She also shared whom this was working for and not working for, as well as how she was feeling (descriptive dimension).
- Did not include information that could be used as evidence that she thought around the problem from different perspectives (comparative dimension).
- Did determine an action or next steps. Although this is a first step, it is not enough. So this is a time when the more knowledgeable other might step in to scaffold Caitlyn in determining next steps (critical dimension).

Caitlyn expressed that the process of observing and reflecting on the video recorded lessons allowed her to listen to the language that she used in the classroom. She said,

> If not for this process, I never would have known my language was not conveying my thoughts to the students in an accurate way. After realizing this I was able to internally monitor my comments and redirections made toward the students.

Scaffolding by a More Knowledgeable Other: Shifting Reflective Focus

Knowing that Caitlyn had spent a great deal of time reflecting on classroom management, her supervisor wanted Caitlyn to shift her awareness away from classroom management at the three-week mark. Her supervisor wanted to facilitate the reflection so that Caitlyn would become metacognitive about her instructional modifications made throughout the lesson.

As discussed in Chapters 2 and 7, a more knowledgeable other can be used to push learning to a different level. At this three-week mark (halfway through the term), Caitlyn's supervisor observed that Caitlyn's pacing of her guided reading lessons was too slow. The result was that Caitlyn was not able to move through all the components of guided reading, even though her lessons extended to 45 minutes, which was well beyond the 25-minute time frame. Knowing that part of the classroom management issues Caitlyn was experiencing was tied to lesson pacing, and that Caitlyn had expressed that she "struggled to keep the students' attention and focus for the entire lesson," her supervisor decided to provide scaffolding by resetting her problem space. She added some guiding questions for Caitlyn to consider while viewing video:

- Give examples of where you specifically taught to your guided reading lesson objective. Give examples of where you were off task.
- Time stamp each component of your guided reading lesson. What was the proportion of time in each area? How do those times compare to the model? Was too much or not enough time spent in each component area?
- What were the most effective and least effect aspects of your lesson?
- What potential modifications will you make to increase instructional effectiveness?

At this point, her supervisor was playing the role of the more knowledgeable other and shifting Caitlyn's focus to an important area for her teaching development. Her supervisor strategically moved up and down the GRR (see Chapter 9) as she stepped in to scaffold Caitlyn. There are times that it is critical for the more knowledgeable other to scaffold the preservice teaching during the reflective process. Caitlyn expressed the following about the change in guiding questions.

> The new format focused my attention to whether objectives were met and what modifications were made to increase student learning. I quickly saw that my lessons were unfocused and did not meet my objectives. The least effective thing was that this lesson really didn't have any focus. Although the objective was to focus on chunking, I didn't really get to it. So in lieu of not really working on chunking too much, I think that I worked on sight words.
>
> In retrospect, I put the chunking activity at the end of the lesson, which due to my pacing I rarely got to. Therefore, I did not consistently meet my objective. The new reflective format allowed me to see that I was struggling with pacing because I was not meeting the objective or focus of my lessons.

Two weeks later Caitlyn observed the benefit of her reflections:

> During guided reading two students helped one another with the chunking of an unfamiliar word without my prompting. Nalah and Haley were partner reading and Nalah goes, 'I'm stuck. I don't know this word!'

And Haley goes, 'Try to chunk it, Nalah." so that was like an epiphany moment. Like, oh my goodness, they're actually seeing this as a strategy and that it can help them.

As Caitlyn's reflection continued, she went on to share what she had learned about pacing:

> Pacing includes more than the speed of the lesson. Good pacing occurs when the teacher has a clear structure and organization for the lesson. This helps the teacher to make the lesson flow and know when to speed up or slow down. In addition, the teacher may be more successful in reaching students if an objective is formed and met on a consistent basis. Students who are experiencing difficulties in reading and writing will have many areas of development; however, it is not feasible for the reading teacher to fix every problem at once.

Conclusion: Lessons Learned

Throughout this experience with Caitlyn, we learned that it was possible to modify written reflective commentaries when preservice teachers came to the end of their program because they had spent considerable time across their program writing them. Like Caitlyn, preservice teachers would still be able to transfer and show their reflective capabilities through different modes, like audio. After working across the course together to determine an alternate way to share reflections with supervisors, Caitlyn shared:

> I believe that the process of video-recording lessons, observing and reflecting on the lessons, provides teachers with rich student data that can be used to improve instruction. The process of observing and reflecting allows the teacher to take a second look at student actions and assess their learning.

Although the mode of reflection was audio, video reflection afforded Caitlyn an opportunity to understand herself and her students in ways that might not be possible when reflecting in action (Schön, 1983). Caitlyn used multiple modes (e.g., visual, audio, gestural, linguistic, etc.) to construct meaning reflections (McVee & Boyd, 2016; Miller & McVee, 2012).

Caitlyn also reminded us that we, as teacher educators, couldn't forget that other preservice teachers have much to offer one another in the scaffolding process. As Caitlyn so eloquently shared with us when the course was concluding:

> One of the most beneficial things I did this summer was to watch a lesson with two friends who are educators. They were able to look at a behavior problem I was having in a new way and offer alternative ways to curb the distracting behavior. The process of observing and reflecting on instruction can be a powerful catalyst for change.

Caitlyn asked us to recognize that the instructor was important, but creating spaces for other preservice teachers or peers to scaffold one another also has the potential to be generative, fostering a strong Community of Practice (see Chapter 3). This point is critical because we are currently in a time when resources are shrinking in teacher education programs. Although we cannot discount the importance of the teacher educator pushing preservice teachers when they need to see a problem through a more complex lens or alternative point of view, we must also remember that the connected experiences across the program with peers, as well as the scaffolds identified in this chapter, collectively develop the culture of reflection that we strive to establish.

References

Bausmith, J. M., & Berry, C. (2011). Revisiting professional learning communities to increase college readiness: The importance of pedagogical content knowledge. *Educational Researcher, 40*(4), 175–178.

Deeney, T., & Dozier, C. (2015). Constructing successful video reflection experiences in practicum settings. In E. Ortlieb, M. B. McVee, & L. E. Shanahan (Eds.), *Video reflection in literacy teacher education and development* (Vol. 5, pp. 41–57). Literacy Research, Practice and Evaluation. Bingley, UK: Emerald Group Publishing Limited.

Educational Testing Services (2015). *The praxis performance assessment for teachers: Reflective handbook.* Princeton, NJ: Educational Testing Service.

International Literacy Association (ILA) (2010). *Standards for reading professionals-revised 2010.* Newark, DE: International Literacy Association.

Jay, J. K., & Johnson, K. L. (2002). Capturing complexity: A typology of reflective practice for teacher education. *Teaching and Teacher Education, 18,* 73–85.

McMillon, G. M. T. (2009). Pen pals without borders: A cultural exchange of teaching and learning. *Education and Urban Society, 42*(1), 119–135.

McVee, M. B., & Boyd, R. (2016). *Exploring diversity through multimodality, narrative, and dialogue: A framework for teacher reflection.* New York, NY: Routledge.

Miller, S. M., & McVee, M. B. (Eds.) (2012). *Multimodal composing in classrooms.* New York, NY: Routledge.

Reichenberg, J. S. (2017). *A model of joint action for literacy coaching with video self-reflection* (Doctoral dissertation). Retrieved from ProQuest.

Rodgers, C. (2002). Seeing student learning: Teacher change and the role of reflection. *Harvard Educational Review, 72*(2), 230–253.

Schön, D. A. (1983). *The reflective practitioner: How professionals think in action.* New York, NY: Basic Books.

Shanahan, L. E., & Tochelli, A. L. (2012). Video study group: A context to cultivate professional relationships. In P. J. Dunston, S. K. Fullerton, C. C. Bates, K. Headley, & P. M. Stecker (Eds.). *61st Literacy Research Association Conference Yearbook* (pp. 196–211). Oak Creek, WI: Literacy Research Association.

Shanahan, L. E., & Tochelli, A. L. (2014). Examining the use of video study groups for developing literacy pedagogical content knowledge for Critical Elements of Strategy Instruction with elementary teachers. *Literacy Research and Instruction, 53*(1), 1–24.

Sherin, M. G., & van Es, E. A. (2009). Effects of video club participation on teachers' professional vision. *Journal of Teacher Education, 60*(1), 20–37.

APPENDIX 6.1

Name: _____   Date: _____

RUBRIC FOR EVALUATING PERFORMANCE: REFLECTION

Criteria for Assessment	*S*	*U*
Reflection turned in on time		
Completed coversheet is the first page of the reflection		
Reflection goal stated at the top of page		
Reflection goal is appropriate for the clinician and is an ability the clinician needs to develop		
Reflection aim stated at the top of the page		
Reflection aim is appropriate and directly relates to the reflection goal		
Reflection includes 3 dimensions: descriptive, comparative, critical		
Descriptive dimension includes background knowledge on the lesson and information related to the reflection goal		
Comparative dimension reframes the situation by including information from other perspectives and/or research		
Critical dimension includes an action plan that states what the clinician will do differently and keep the same and why		
Reflection clearly demonstrates that the clinician viewed his or her video, by including time stamps and specific information/ statements in the reflection		
Mentor feedback addressed in reflection		
Reflection is well written		
Reflection is fully de-identified		
Action plan is evident in future lessons and implemented during tutoring		

GRADING KEY:
S = signifies satisfactory (adequate) completion of criterion
U = signifies unsatisfactory completion of criterion because of partial completion or criterion is not evident

7

THE GRADUAL RELEASE OF RESPONSIBILITY FOR SELF-REFLECTION

Transitioning from a Literacy Coach to a Social Studies Teacher

With Jennifer Reichenberg

The bell rings signaling the end of third period. As Isabella's tenth-grade students pack up their belongings, they head toward the classroom door chatting with one another in Nepali, Pa'o Karen, Arabic, French, Spanish, and other languages. Isabella quickly cleans up her materials from class, grabs her bag, and walks to the school library. Today, she has a meeting with Jennifer, her literacy coach, during her planning period.

As Isabella opens the library door, she sees Jennifer (second author) sitting at their usual table with her computer open. Jennifer greets Isabella with a smile and asks, "Did you bring the popcorn?" Today, Jennifer and Isabella will look at video from a lesson Isabella taught during the previous week. Together, they will use the video to reflect on the challenges and complexity of teaching social studies to tenth-grade students from diverse ethnic, cultural, and linguistic backgrounds.

Isabella works at an urban high school in a mid-sized school district in up-state New York. Almost 70 percent of the student body speaks a first language other than English. In this school alone, over 40 different languages and language variations are spoken. Isabella's third period social studies class is comprised entirely of students classified as Students with an Interrupted Formal Education (SIFE). SIFE means that these students speak a first language at home other than English, had at least two years less schooling than their same age peers, functioned at least two years below expected grade level in reading and math, and may have been preliterate in their native language. The students' varied backgrounds enrich the culture of the school community, and Isabella enjoys the challenge of teaching her students the state social studies curriculum and helping them prepare for the state social studies exam at the end of tenth grade. These students are working to learn conversational English, in addition to academic English and secondary level content in multiple subjects. To help meet this challenge, Isabella volunteered to be part of a small cohort of teachers to participate in a three-year professional development initiative between a large research university and her public high school.

 Stop and Think

- Think of a time you had the chance to work with a coach, whether it be a coach for a sports team or the classroom (e.g., literacy coach or math coach). What did the coach do that supported your ability to successfully learn and implement a new skill?

Have you ever had someone explain to you how to do something, but you didn't really understand until you saw it in action or even tried it for yourself? Recall Mary's experience of attempting a motorcycle jump from Chapter 2. Her brother Shawn demonstrated the jump for her and even gave her advice to "pull up," but this was not enough scaffolding for Mary to complete a successful motorcycle jump. Similarly, inservice teachers are often given directives to implement instructional techniques, curriculum modifications, or other professional activities with limited scaffolding and differentiation. The lack of differentiation in scaffolding with experienced teachers is common. As one inservice teacher in Fenice's graduate course shared with her: "I wish our professional developments were of this level rather than continually repeating the same basic knowledge or only touching the surface" (email communication, 3/8/17). Oftentimes, however, teachers participate in excellent professional development workshops presented by knowledgeable and engaging speakers. Teachers witness examples of strategies, and they receive curriculum materials. But when they return to their classrooms with great enthusiasm about what they learned, on their own and isolated from the professional development facilitators, they realize that they have many unanswered questions when attempting to implement their new learning and no one to help them. Thus, the one-shot approach to professional development is generally not very effective (Yoon, Duncan, Lee, Scarloss, & Shapley, 2008).

The Gradual Release of Responsibility (GRR) Model used by a literacy coach can better prepare teachers to address this shortcoming in professional development. Applying Au and Raphael's 1998 Model (Figure 7.1) to the description of one-shot professional development above, we see that only explication and perhaps modeling have been provided through this approach. Teachers can benefit from a full application of the model, beginning with explicit instruction and moving through modeling, scaffolding, facilitation, and participation. This is true whether they are in their third year or thirtieth year of teaching.

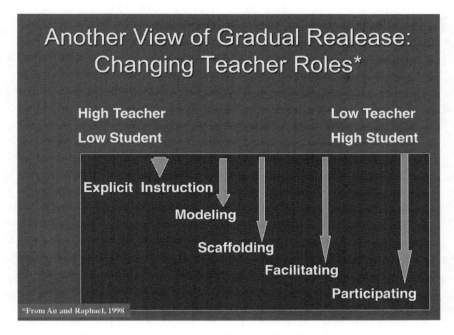

FIGURE 7.1   Gradual release of responsibility and changing teacher roles
Source: Au & Raphael, 1998.

In this chapter, we will reveal how literacy coaching with video enabled one teacher to shift her thinking about pedagogy. We will examine how the GRR can support inservice teachers' reflective growth throughout this process. In the spring of the professional development initiative described above, Jennifer designed a reflective framework (Reichenberg, 2017) (see Figure 7.2) based upon the writing of Dewey (1933) for use with video. She planned to use the framework to guide her video reflection sessions with Isabella and to use the GRR when applying the framework. Jennifer began by using one coaching session to model reflection while viewing video of a lesson she had taught in Isabella's class during one of her classroom visits. During the next coaching session, Jennifer and Isabella engaged in collaborative reflection as Jennifer released some of the responsibility to Isabella for reflecting upon her own instruction and continued to support her through dialogue. Finally, Jennifer released responsibility to Isabella to reflect upon her own teaching with video. While this brief description makes the process appear linear, in reality, the type and amount of scaffolding provided to Isabella by Jennifer varied within and between sessions depending on Isabella's instructional needs and what Isabella deemed important for her students' learning.

Principles of Productive Video Reflection: Collaboration with a Framework

Teachers benefit from having a framework to guide their reflection (Chapter 3). However, research suggests that many teachers must be coached in order to become reflective practitioners (e.g., Wallace, 1996). Deaton (2012) found that when teachers were provided with a written reflective framework and video of their own teaching, they were often unable to identify inconsistencies they exhibited between their beliefs and teaching practices. She suggests that more individualized guidance is necessary for teacher growth in reflection. Conditions necessary for reflection to be useful include scaffolding or guiding reflection, reflecting and getting a response, and creating a link between action and reflection (Reimann, 1999). Simply asking teachers to reflect upon video without these kinds of supports is not likely to be effective.

As shared in Chapters 3 and 6, teachers also benefit from collaborative support and guidance as they develop reflective practice. One way this can happen is through informal or formal Communities of Practice, such as the one described in Chapter 3. Another way is through working with a more knowledgeable other, as in the partnership described above between Isabella and Jennifer. Collaborative reflection stimulates a teacher and coach to ask thoughtful questions that can serve to scaffold new thinking patterns about teaching practices (Cheliotes & Reilly, 2010) and planning (Pylman, 2016). Rather than simply reflecting on a video without having the benefit of a response, collaborative reflection can spur dialogue and raise questions in productive ways to offer ideas for further consideration.

Knowing this information, Jennifer created a seven-step reflective framework based on Dewey's (1933) writing about the reflective process with the goal of scaffolding Isabella's reflection with video (see Reichenberg, 2017). Because the amount of information available through video can be overwhelming, Jen's reflective framework begins by focusing reflection on a specific challenge in the lesson. First, Jennifer modeled thinking through video of her own instruction for Isabella.

Reichenberg's Reflective Framework

Step 1: Identify a moment in the lesson that is intriguing or presents a challenge.
Step 2: View and describe the video clip associated with that moment while explaining your reasoning.
Step 3: Create a question to articulate the central challenge suggested by the video clip.
Step 4: Generate alternatives to deal with the challenge and explore reasoning for each.
Step 5: Choose an alternative.
Step 6: Enact.
Step 7: Evaluate.

Dewey (1933) suggested beginning the reflective process by identifying perplexity because without perplexity there is nothing upon which to reflect. He compared this perplexity to a "forked road situation" (p. 14) (Step 1). Next, he said that we should "metaphorically climb a tree" at that fork in the road to gather more information about the situation (p. 14) (Step 2). Formulating a question based upon this observation focuses and frames the reflective process (Dewey, 1933; Schön, 1983) (Step 3). Dewey also suggests we assume an attitude of open mindedness to multiple possibilities to address that question, not rushing into one before entertaining several (Step 5). Enactment brings to fruition our reflective process, providing a critical link between reflection and action (Dewey, 1933) (Step 6). Finally, we must return to the beginning of the process to reflect once again (Step 7).

 Stop and Think

1. Create a three-column chart with the following headings: Rodgers, Jay and Johnson, and Reichenberg.
2. Write down the components of each phase of the reflection models under each column being mindful of how the phases of reflection are similar and different.
3. Discuss the affordances and limitations of each one of the three reflective frameworks shared in this book. Select one framework that resonates with you and explain why.

In what follows, we show how Jennifer applied the GRR to steps two and four of Reichenberg's Reflective Framework to support Isabella as she reflected on her own teaching using video as a mediator, over an extended period of time.

Strategic Pedagogical Moves When Modeling Video Reflection

Pearson and Gallagher (1983) write that at one extreme, the more knowledgeable other (in this case Jennifer, the coach) takes most of the responsibility for a cognitive task through modeling and thinking aloud. As time goes on, more of this responsibility is shared with the student (in this case Isabella, the classroom teacher) in the form of "practicing" or "applying" that strategy. What comes between these two is the GRR from teacher to student, scaffolded by guided practice. Whether teaching students or facilitating reflective activities with veteran teachers, modeling is an important component of this process. As the coach releases responsibility to the teacher, she continues to provide support, enabling the teacher to work through new ways of thinking. As the teacher becomes more accomplished at exercising aspects of reflective inquiry, less scaffolding is needed over time to engage in reflective practice.

In the transcript that follows, you will read a conversation in a coaching session where Jennifer modeled reflection for Isabella. The video they focused on is from a lesson Jennifer taught in Isabella's class during the previous week. She was showing Isabella a way that she might help students learn to organize their writing about primary source documents in social studies using a topic sentence, support from the document, and then an explanation of that support. In her lesson, Jennifer used familiar content, the seasons of summer and winter, to first teach students the structure of the writing. Jennifer began this portion of the lesson by sharing a paragraph she wrote about the harsh winter they had all experienced together that year.

Modeling: Describing Instructional Moves. Jennifer first showed Isabella how she would describe, and not judge, what she saw in the video. Careful observation helps us to achieve a clear formulation of the nature of the situation (Dewey, 1933). In this case, Jennifer had first identified a moment she found perplexing in her instruction. She wanted to view the part in which she modeled this for the students because she felt it was not as clear as she had intended.

Notice when Jennifer pauses the video to model describing without judgment. Dewey suggests that suspending judgment is necessary to maintain open-mindedness. Obviously, teachers are not able to pause action as they teach a lesson in the same way as one might press the pause button on a digital device. The pause button on a device however, allows Jennifer and Isabella to pause the action of the lesson so that they can relive the instructional moves through the video. First, Jennifer pauses the video and thinks aloud about what she is doing. She then resumes the video, for a few seconds, and pauses it again, raises a question, and describes her actions. Listen in on what Jennifer and Isabella discuss during this first phase of the reflection:

[ISABELLA AND JENNIFER WATCH THE VIDEO OF THE LESSON TOGETHER.]

[JENNIFER'S VOICE IN THE VIDEOTAPED LESSON]: I want you to think before you write anything. What are two reasons I told you that winter has been hard? Two main reasons.

[JENNIFER PAUSES THE VIDEO]

JENNIFER (THINKING ALOUD): So, here I asked the students to identify two main reasons winter has been hard. Now I have lots of opinions in my head already... but I'm trying to withhold judgment until the end of my five-minute clip.

[JENNIFER PLAYS THE VIDEO FOR ANOTHER MOMENT AND THEN PAUSES IT AGAIN.]

JENNIFER (THINKING ALOUD): What am I doing? So, I'm walking around and checking to see if everyone has marked their papers correctly.

We offer this scenario to show that Jennifer made a judgment call about when to press the pause button. What caused Jennifer to press the button at that moment, and not the one before or the one after? It was in fact the instructional move, the question that she had asked students in the video that prompted her to pause the action. This moment is important because the instructional moves we make as teachers, such as the questions we ask and how we ask them, fundamentally impact students' learning. By pausing the video at the moment when Jennifer asked the students "What are two reasons I told you that winter has been hard? Two main reasons," she was communicating to Isabella that she needs to think about each instructional move she makes. Jennifer's ultimate goal for Isabella, of course, was to help her think about her instructional moves in moment-to-moment instruction. Pausing the video served to scaffold the development of reflection-in-action (Schön, 1983), and Jennifer modeled this process for Isabella.

After pausing the video, Jennifer engages in what Rodgers (2002) called "telling the story of the experience" (p. 237). She narrates what she had just seen: "So, here I asked the students to identify two main reasons winter has been hard." She also explicitly mentions both her instinct to pass judgment, and her decision not to: "I have lots of opinions in my head already... but I'm trying to withhold judgment until the end of my five-minute clip." It is in our nature to want to judge what we see and hear, especially while watching ourselves teach with another person sitting right next to us. Rodgers (2002), too, points out the difficulty in describing while withholding judgment, naming it as the most difficult phase in the reflective cycle; yet, she notes that the "discipline of description" is a powerful element of reflection (p. 238).

As the video continues, Jennifer continues to tell the story: "So, I'm walking around and checking to see if everyone has marked their papers correctly." Rodgers (2002) points out that the very act of telling a story is an interpretive act. Details we choose to include or exclude communicate our interpretation. In this case, Jennifer chose to mention that she was circulating to check on students' learning. The fact that she includes this detail is important. It communicates to Isabella that her movement among the students was intentional: she was gathering feedback about the students' understanding of her task directions (identify two main reasons that the winter was hard).

Gradual Release Supports Video Reflection: From Jennifer to Isabella

During video reflection, questioning teachers like Isabella about their teaching moves and providing them with the opportunity to take up and expand their reasoning, as well as clarify the context and the moves made, facilitates the GRR. Strategic questions centered on teaching moves provide a space for a teacher to develop metacognitive knowledge of instructional decisions.

During a coaching session held about one week later, Jennifer and Isabella watch the video of a lesson Isabella taught on the causes of World War II. Jennifer questions Isabella about her teaching moves. In turn, Isabella takes up and expands on her reasoning to clarify the context for the word *position*, the concept of *blame*, and the next step to help students internalize and apply the vocabulary words she discussed in the lesson. Read the transcript excerpt below to see how these elements evolved during the coaching session.

[WATCHING VIDEO]

JENNIFER: So you were reading them the question, and you got to the word *position* and stopped and – whatever it was about that word, it made you stop and feel like you needed to provide context.

ISABELLA: Yeah, because *position* … they were all thinking of it as a location, as a geography, you know France's position next to Germany. But this is talking about taking a stance on something, and I knew they had absolutely no idea what that was.

JENNIFER: So the prompt for this teaching move was the word *position*.

ISABELLA: No doubt.

As they continue reflecting through the video, Jennifer raises a second strategic question that supports Isabella to elaborate on the context of her instructional decision. In the video, Isabella is giving her students a real-world concrete example of one sibling blaming another for breaking a teacup. She uses this to scaffold her students' understanding of the word *blame* as a concept and links it to the social studies topic and content. As you read this excerpt, notice how Isabella springs into description of her instructional decision.

[VIDEO CLIP: Isabella talks about *blame*. She was blamed for [a] broken teacup by her brother as a child.]

JENNIFER: So, what were you doing with that teaching move?

ISABELLA: I'm relating it to real life.

JENNIFER: So, a real-life example.

ISABELLA: Yeah…

JENNIFER: Of a concept?

ISABELLA: Of *blame*, of guilt, of Germany getting blamed. And not only are they [Germans] going to get blamed, they are going to get punished. And this is going to lead to World War II and Hitler.

This example illustrates the role of the coach in scaffolding teachers' reflection through strategic questions. Jennifer's questions lead to Isabella's explanation of how the real-life example relates to the concept of blame leading to World War II. Pausing the video allowed Isabella to slow down the action of the lesson and notice students' understanding of the vocabulary word *blame* in context as related to Germany. Using the video as evidence, Isabella is also processing whether or not her students have a firm grasp of the vocabulary and concepts. Additionally, as Isabella narrates her lesson, she not only notes what strategies her students were using and her scaffolding (providing a real-life example and underlining text), but she gives a brief account of what led to World War II, which was connected to the word *blame* as a concept that she was teaching her students. In this way, video and Jennifer's strategic questions supported Isabella's ability to notice and to explore her thinking.

In the next excerpt Jennifer calls attention to an instructional move Isabella makes in the video. As she describes the action, Isabella joins in recounting a specific strategy (i.e., underlining) students are using, the objective behind it, and how a previous instructional move supported the students in carrying out the strategy in the video.

[WATCHING VIDEO]

JENNIFER: So that's another teaching move right there. You are writing on the text. And specifically you're having them mark.

ISABELLA: They're underlining keywords and then associating that phrase with the country of Germany, and I put a question mark next to it annotating that this maybe … isn't totally accurate.

JENNIFER: Okay so they're underlining the keyword and then they're thinking about the significance of that keyword, okay.

ISABELLA: And to whom it applies.

As you may have noticed, Jennifer's role shifts. Although she is still responsible for describing the teaching actions that Isabella is demonstrating in the video, Isabella elaborates about her moves, and specifically notes what her students were doing and why. More importantly, here we see Isabella describing why she put a question mark "next to it …" because she notices that students had not yet internalized what *blame* meant as related to Germany. This suggests that not only is Isabella paying attention to her teaching moves, she is involved in her own reflective process during the coaching session and during the act of teaching. Further, in these three video reflection transcript excerpts, we see that Isabella has taken up parts of the reflective process. She now describes on her own, providing more context and explanation of her teaching moves.

Released to Take Responsibility: From Jennifer to Isabella

In this section, we present examples of how Jennifer releases the responsibility for video reflection to Isabella by giving her space to take the lead in identifying her teaching moves. This third coaching session occurs two weeks after the example above. Previously, our examples of reflection encompassed Jennifer's purposeful strategic modeling of the use of Reichenberg's

Reflective Framework and giving Isabella opportunities to work through and process her teaching moves beside Jennifer. McVee, Shanahan, Pearson, and Rinker (2015) suggest that a well-articulated and understood purpose for reflection is necessary in order for teacher reflection to move beyond a purely descriptive level to a deeper level of critical analysis. They argue that, "In video reflection, it is essential that learners have the opportunity to work together to learn how to view and respond to video in order to interpret and learn from video text" (p. 69). In this section of our chapter, we show how Isabella takes the lead on self-reflecting while watching video of her teaching with Jennifer.

In the transcript segments that follow, notice how Isabella first describes the writing activity, which involves defining government, and then proceeds to explain *how* the definition will better support the students to distinguish between the three types of government. Isabella moves from explaining the purpose of having students write definitions (so that they understand the different types of government), to telling a story about her challenge to help students understand the concept of representative government. In this way, she begins to explore her pedagogical reasoning. As Isabella tells the story, Jennifer takes a less active role in modeling and questioning: she has gradually released responsibility for these steps to Isabella.

[WATCHING VIDEO]
ISABELLA PAUSES THE VIDEO.
ISABELLA: So we are writing the definition of government. Partly because I believe in the reading they're going to be introduced to three different types of government: absolute rulers, democracy, and a coalition. So I really wanted them to have the definition.
JENNIFER: I see. Right.
[WATCHING VIDEO]
ISABELLA PAUSES THE VIDEO.
ISABELLA: I was trying to … I knew they were going to… This [how voting plays out in a representative government] is a tough concept. We do it in Global 9 [ninth grade class], and it continues to be tough in Global 10— because we don't directly vote. For example, that's why we have the Electoral College, you know. But I wanted them to get the idea of representative government. Because that's the whole idea with "coalition" is that they're representing this whole mishmash of ideas, that doesn't succeed. A representative government is an extremely difficult concept for them. And, I'm not sure even now that they understand. But definitely, on ancient Rome they just definitely don't get the concept of a representative government. Because we are a Republic, you know, and the distinction between a democracy and a republic is very tough. So I'm trying to tease that out.
JENNIFER: Right.

[WATCHING VIDEO]

ISABELLA PAUSES THE VIDEO.

ISABELLA: I use the word characteristic. I want them to know what characterizes democracy. Because again I want them to know what characterizes a
coalition, which is the idea that lots of different interests are being represented, you can never get a majority.

As you can see, Jennifer's role is minimal as Isabella describes her teaching
moves and decisions resulting in an increase of responsibility on Isabella's part
(Collet, 2013). The reflection began with Isabella identifying a point in the
lesson and then describing that segment in detail while watching the video.
As Isabella analyzes the lesson, she raises issues that she struggled with which
related to how to better support her students' understanding of the complex
concepts of different government systems. Isabella is honest and transparent
about her challenges to convey this content for her students. Remember
that at the beginning of this chapter, we briefly described the rich cultural
and linguistic backgrounds of the students in the high school where Isabella
works, where 70 percent speak a first language other than English and over
40 languages and language variations are spoken throughout the school.
Teaching students the structures of various government systems is complicated
for native English speakers; can you imagine what it must be like for Isabella,
whose students might speak English as a second, third, or maybe even a fourth
language? Through video reflection, and with the support of a literacy coach,
Isabella was able to describe and critique the challenges she faced during her
teaching moves.

Differential Support While Generating Alternatives

Teachers may need different levels of support across the reflective process. For
example, Jennifer noticed that Isabella was strong in identifying an alternative
to deal with the central challenge she identified. However, she also noticed that
Isabella needed support to suspend final judgment of the best solution before
entertaining multiple ideas. Dewey (1933) refers to this as the willingness to
"sustain and protract that state of doubt" (p. 16).

Step 4 of Reichenberg's Reflective Framework entails generating multiple
alternatives to address the challenge identified in the lesson and exploring
pedagogical reasoning associated with each. This step supports teachers to
thoughtfully plan their next teaching moves rather than relying upon routine
(Dewey, 1933).

Here, Isabella begins to generate alternatives for the lesson Jennifer taught
(mentioned earlier) on writing with a topic sentence, supporting facts, and
details.

ISABELLA: I just had an idea. We could almost use a visual.

JENNIFER: Do you need to write on something?

ISABELLA: Yeah like if we had winter. Say winter is the lintel of the post the lintel thing, the supports would be snow and cold. And the bricks inside it...

JENNIFER: I love that.

ISABELLA: ...would be the details ... [drawing bricks]

JENNIFER: Great visual.

ISABELLA: I don't know what you think ...

JENNIFER: Yeah!

ISABELLA: And that way they know that these two supporting—almost like support members—are the concept of winter and then we use the bricks. Let's try maybe playing around with that maybe.

Isabella takes the lead with an idea that she wants to try out with her students during a coaching session. While Isabella is explaining her thoughts, Jennifer offers her something to write on, and this is when the visual that Isabella first mentioned evolves.

As the conversation continues, Jennifer models maintaining open minded-ness to multiple alternatives instead of seizing the first option Isabella suggested. Jennifer does this by thinking aloud, making her internal thought processes externally visible to Isabella. Making thought processes externally visible pro-vides a strong degree of support to Isabella, who first engages primarily through listening and then by taking up where Jennifer leaves off. Isabella then begins to discuss her pedagogical reasoning, and to make her thoughts explicit and visible in a similar way to what Jennifer had previously modeled.

JENNIFER: And now just to ... come back to this for one second, we have to generate lots of ways. So that's one of the things, like I love that idea so tying the consistent use of supports to some sort of a visual. As you were talking I was thinking sometimes when we work at the paragraph level it's too much.

ISABELLA: Oh definitely.

JENNIFER: Start with one piece of support. Without explanation and just keep it that simple.

ISABELLA: Topic sentence supporting details. I mean even some of these kids struggle [with] writing sentences.

JENNIFER: And so in that lesson, maybe I should not have had two pieces of support, but just one. Another idea I had was I meant to model that first one, and actually not get the kids involved. And I did. I ...

ISABELLA: ... didn't model it.

JENNIFER: I got them involved too soon. Now I don't know if that would be too much talking at the students, on the flipside.

ISABELLA: No, not if we kept it short and sweet enough, and I think like with the photographs yesterday. We've never done something like that, but I think that's why it was a success.

JENNIFER: Because we modeled that … so that's another option. Also I was thinking of having the kids turn and talk before marking anything down just to explain the difference between the green, the yellow, and the red in their own words. I didn't know if they had enough knowledge to do that at that point, but … it might be a nice place to insert thirty seconds of native language use. Also I thought the paragraph could've been more black and white. You know snow and cold … I thought maybe if it was like describing a person. They're funny and they're a really good cook … snow and cold are so closely related I didn't know if that was confusing for the kids. Also I didn't know if maybe I used a color-coded paragraph that was already color-coded, and showed that first rather than showing them one white paragraph. If they could see the color pattern first, it might've helped.

ISABELLA: I also saw with the yellow that they almost didn't need to underline the entire sentence. You get your topic sentence snow cold and make it a little simpler than that. And then have the details be the explanation be in red and be a complete sentence, but I didn't think you really need to do that for …

JENNIFER: In yellow …

ISABELLA: Maybe keep yellow brief

JENNIFER: So there we generated four, five, six, seven, eight different modifications from that one five-minute clip.

This example is valuable for a couple of reasons. First, we see Jennifer continuing to model her thinking about her own teaching. Issues that she raises are when there may be too much information for students learning English and getting students involved in the lesson too soon before actually modeling what she wanted them to do. Realizing that modeling also increases the amount of teacher talk, Jennifer contemplates whether or not that would be too much "talking at" students.

We also see Isabella exhibit one of her strengths as a teacher, generating an alternative to deal with the central challenge Jennifer identified in the lesson. However, Jennifer then pushes Isabella to suspend action in favor of continuing to generate ideas before deciding upon action. Jennifer puts several options out on the table for Isabella's consideration: (a) having students turn and talk in their native language for a few seconds, (b) color coding paragraphs to better support students in their writing, and (c) thinking about different ways to use descriptive language. Jennifer models, Isabella leads, and Jennifer provides support by talking through and generating alternative ways to teach Isabella's students the new idea.

Conclusion

As a whole, our examples of Jennifer coaching Isabella show the interplay between the coach's support, Reichenberg's Reflective Framework, and the GRR during video self-reflection. Taken together these also align with many of the recommended standards for coaches and literacy teachers. (You can explore connections to the standards through the activity in Appendix 7.1.)

The reflective framework provided a structure, informed by theory, to guide the coaching sessions with video. (In Chapters 3, 4, 5, and 6 various other reflective frameworks were presented, and these have been summarized in Appendix 7.2.) Jennifer employed the GRR for the framework across coaching sessions. Consequently, she used a variety of scaffolding techniques such as strategic questioning to support Isabella's participation in video reflection. We noticed that Isabella required different amounts of support in different aspects of reflection. This illustrates that the GRR Model does not proceed in a linear manner, but rather, it is recursive and responsive to the teacher's needs in a particular coaching session. We are always working to release more responsibility to the student (in this case, Isabella) but we are always prepared to slide up and down the diagonal, and to share responsibility with the student at different levels of support at any time during a teaching interaction (Figure 7.2). Scaffolding is the key, and thoughtful analysis of our actions guides every step of the way.

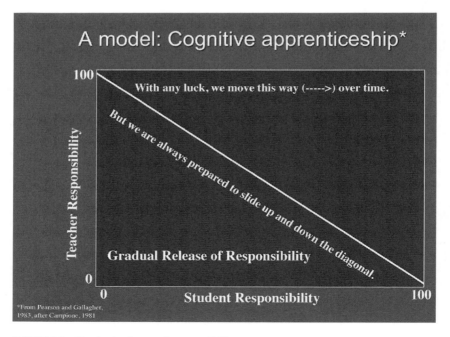

FIGURE 7.2 Gradual release of responsibility
Source: Pearson & Gallaher, 1983.

As teachers deal with the fast-paced action that occurs in their classrooms every day, it is challenging to take a step back and think deeply about teaching and learning. The application of the GRR to literacy coaching with video self-reflection has the potential to support teachers like Isabella to take time to reflect on their practice in order to better meet their students' needs. The GRR afforded Isabella new ways of thinking about her classroom practices, support in thinking through these new ideas, and space to think out ideas on her own.

References

Au, K. H., & Raphael, T. E. (1998). Curriculum and teaching in literature-based programs. In T. E. Raphael & K. H. Au (Eds.), *Literature-based instruction: Reshaping the curriculum* (pp. 123–148). Norwood, MA: Christopher-Gordon Publications.

Cheliotes, L. G., & Reilly, M. F. (2010). *Coaching conversations: Transforming your school one conversation at a time.* Thousand Oaks, CA: Corwin.

Collet, V. (2013). The gradual increase of responsibility model: mentoring for improved intervention. In E. Ortlieb & E. H. Cheek Jr. (Eds.), *Advanced literacy practices: from the clinic to the classroom* (pp. 327–351). Bingley, UK: Emerald Group Publishing.

Deaton, C. (2012). Examining the use of a reflection framework to guide teachers' video analysis of their science teaching practice. *Electronic Journal of Science Education, 16*(2), 1–22.

Dewey, J. (1933). *How we think: a restatement of the relation of reflective thinking to the educative process.* Boston, MA: D.C. Heath and Company.

Jay, J. K., & Johnson, K. L. (2002). Capturing complexity: A typology of reflective practice for teacher education. *Teaching and Teacher Education, 18*, 73–85.

McVee, M. B., Shanahan, L. E., Pearson, P. D., & Rinker, T. W. (2015). Using the gradual release of responsibility model to support video reflection with preservice and inservice teachers. In E. Ortlieb, M. B. McVee, & L. E. Shanahan (Eds.), *Video reflection in literacy teacher education and development: lessons from research and practice* (pp. 59–80). Bingley, UK: Emerald Group Publishing.

Pearson, P. D., & Gallagher, M. C. (1983). *The instruction of reading comprehension* (Report No. 297). Champaign, IL: University of Illinois at Urbana-Champaign.

Pylman, S. (2016). Reflecting on talk: a mentor teacher's gradual release in co-planning. *The New Educator, 12*(1), 48–66.

Reichenberg, J. S. (2017). *A model of joint action for literacy coaching with video self-reflection* (Doctoral dissertation). Retrieved from ProQuest.

Reimann, A. J. (1999). The evolution of the social roletaking and guided reflection framework in teacher education: recent theory and quantitative synthesis of research. *Teaching and Teacher Education, 15*, 597–612.

Rodgers, C. R. (2002). Seeing student learning: teacher change and the role of reflection. *Harvard Educational Review, 72*(2), 230–253.

Schön, D. A. (1983). *The reflective practitioner: How professionals think in action.* United States of America: Basic Books.

Wallace, M. (1996). Structured reflection: the role of the professional project in training ENL teachers. In D. Freeman & J. C. Richards (Eds.), *Teacher Learning in Language Teaching* (pp. 281–294). New York, NY: Cambridge University Press.

Yoon, K. S., Duncan, T., Lee, S. W., Scarloss, B., & Shapley, K. L. (2008). *Reviewing the evidence on how teacher professional development affects student achievement.* Washington, D.C.: Institute of Educational Sciences.

APPENDIX 7.1

BECOMING FAMILIAR WITH COACHING OR LITERACY STANDARDS RELATED TO ENGLISH LANGUAGE LEARNERS AND RACIAL, ETHNIC, AND CULTURAL DIVERSITY

Read and review standards for coaching and learning as they pertain to diversity and teaching literacy for students from diverse language, cultural, ethnic, and racial backgrounds. Schools, districts, and states often have their own standards. Many literacy organizations have published their own standards. For example:

- International Literacy Association (formerly International Reading Association) Standards for Reading Specialists/Literacy Coaches
- International Literacy Association (formerly International Reading Association) Standards for Middle and High School Literacy Coaches
- NCTE/NCATE Standards for Initial Preparation of Teachers of Secondary English Language Arts, Grades 7–12

Use the search and find function to search some of the key terms **bolded** below. As you read through standards, consider:

1. What role does **reflection** play in the standards?
2. What role does **video** play?
3. How do the standards position teachers? students?
4. How do the standards attend to the needs of diverse language learners (e.g., **English Language Learners**)?
5. How do the standards attend to **diversity** in terms of **race**, socio-economic **class**, **linguistic**, **cultural**, and **geographic** diversities?
6. What do you notice about the standards and what they include?
7. What do you notice about the standards and what they exclude?
8. Why is it important to know the standards related to literacy?
9. How could these standards be used by teachers in reflecting upon teaching?
10. How could these standards be used by coaches/teacher educators in assisting teachers with reflection?

COMMON ASPECTS OF THREE REFLECTIVE FRAMEWORKS

	Rodgers (2002)	Jay and Johnson (2002)	Reichenberg (2017)
Presence	• Learning to see • Seeing learning, differentiating its parts, giving it meaning, and responding intelligently • State of mindfulness		
Description of an Experience	• Learning to describe & differentiate • Differentiation and naming of an experience's diverse and complex elements	*Descriptive* • Describe the matter for reflection	*Steps 1–3* • Identify an intriguing or challenging moment • Describe video & explain reasoning • Create a central challenge
Analysis of an Experience	• Generating a number of different explanations for what is being observed • Look at evidence from various perspectives and question rigorously to develop explanations • Unearthing assumptions	*Comparative* • Reframe the matter for reflection in light of alternative views, others; perspectives, research, etc. • Seeking to understand others; points of view, which may not align with one's own	*Step 4* • Generate alternatives to deal with the challenge and explore reasoning for reach
Experimentation	• Use alternatives to decide on ideas for action that must be tested	*Critical* • After reflecting on alternatives establish renewed perspectives • Making a judgement and decision to act	*Steps 5, 6 & 7* • Choose an alternative • Enact • Evaluate

Common Premise Across Models: Schon (1983) & Dewey (1933)

Setting a problem space

Putting parameters around a situation

Define what is to be understood

Puzzling, troubling, interesting phenomenon, framing experiments, identifying a perplexity

Bodily expression of the mental condition

Assume an attitude of open-mindedness

Non-linear process

8

LOOKING BEYOND WHAT YOU SEE

Critical Inquiry and Video Reflection through
Positioning Analysis and Story

> Look beyond what you see.
> ~Rafiki in *The Lion King*

In the classic Disney film *The Lion King*, Rafiki is a wise old mandrill who
lives in a baobab tree. In the sequel *The Lion King 1½*, he helps the meerkat
Timon find his way, urging Timon to "Look beyond what you see." This is
good advice not only for meerkats wanting to understand their destiny, but also
good advice for teachers engaged in video reflection. In this chapter, we invite
you to "look beyond what you see" and uncover characteristics of classrooms,
learners, and teachers that can be masked or hidden in the video reflection
process. We also ask you to consider the different perspectives and positions that
may be available (or unavailable) through video recordings and representations
and how these are linked to the ways that teachers narrate events on video
(or avoid even avoid discussing particular events). You will explore positions
and perspectives through several **Stop and Think** activities, but also through
the **Ethnographic Video Viewing Activity** in the Appendix at the end of
the chapter.

Stories and Positions

> For we dream in narrative, daydream in narrative, remember, anticipate,
> hope, despair, believe, doubt, plan, revise, criticize, construct, gossip,
> learn, hate, and love by narrative. In order really to live, we make up
> stories about ourselves and others, about the personal as well as the social
> past and future.
>
> *(Hardy, 1968, p. 5)*

Throughout this book there have been many stories. In Chapter 7, the opening narrative of Isabella's classroom helped ground the interactions described between Isabella and Jennifer. Karen's critical incident in Chapter 5 was reflexive and analytic but structured predominantly as a narrative description of events with judgments, questions, inferences, and possible solutions, outcomes, and alternatives. Such narratives are more than mere stories. Psychologist Jerome Bruner (1986, 1990) argued that narratives are one way in which individuals learn and that narratives are sites for identity construction as well as representation. Even though we may describe events in a linear, sequential fashion, our narratives represent multiple positions taken up across interactive and dynamic storylines over time (Davies & Harré, 1990; McVee, Brock, & Glazier, 2011). Across these multiple storylines, we enact many different facets of ourselves, our lives, and our identities.

The challenging thing about stories is that while they can be powerful tools, they can also be limiting. Writer Chimamanda Ngozi Adichie (2009) describes the limitations and affordances of narratives in a powerful TED talk called "The Danger of the Single Story" (https://www.ted.com/talks/chimamanda_adichie_the_danger_of_a_single_story). When Adichie came to the United States from Nigeria to attend college, she found that,

> My American roommate was shocked by me. She asked where I had learned to speak English so well, and was confused when I said that Nigeria happened to have English as its official language. She asked if she could listen to what she called my 'tribal music,' and was consequently very disappointed when I produced my tape of Mariah Carey [a pop singer]. She assumed that I did not know how to use a stove.

In this case, the dominant narrative of Africa that the roommate possessed (e.g., catastrophe, poverty, tribal communities) caused her to position Adichie as someone who must be unfamiliar with modern conveniences such as a stove or contemporary music. In other words, the roommate's comments and the positions inherent in those assumptions made clear that she had constructed a deficit-oriented narrative of Nigeria and Africa, as well as of African students such as Adichie.

Adichie also points out how pervasive these types of narratives and positions are, describing how she herself was not immune to them. As her talk unfolds Adichie tells how back home in Nigeria, she had made similar assumptions about Fide (Fee-day), a boy from a nearby village who worked for her family. Adichie assumed that Fide was poor and had nothing. Rather than seeing connections to Fide and his family, Adichie's position was one of *self-opposed-to-other* (McVee, Baldassarre, & Bailey, 2004). Adichie saw her own life as dissimilar and disconnected, oppositional in terms of resources and achievements in a way that led to pity for Fide and his family rather than respect for the family's hard work and achievements. But after visiting Fide's village and home, Adichie realized that poverty, the deficit-oriented narrative and assumptions she had relied upon were not the single story of Fide and his family.

Adichie's stories and all of the stories in this book related to literacy instruction and video reflection are linked to this concept that Harré and van Langenhove (1991) call *self-other positioning.* All human communicative interactions position both the self and others. Even when people choose silence or no responsive action, they are positioning themselves and others. Within self-other positioning, many different types of positioning may occur (McVee et al., 2011). Every video of teacher–student interaction holds multiple layers of positioning, and every video tells a story. Even if we see only a small snippet of video, human fondness for stories causes us to place that story within a narrative frame, aligning it with other narratives we have seen or heard. These narrative frames are often referred to as *grand narratives* or *metanarratives* (Lyotard, 1984; McLaren, 1993). Chimamanda Ngozi Adichie's stories provide examples of metanarrative. Metanarratives are the equivalent of a single story of cultures, races, genders and so on. Metanarratives are over-arching storylines built over time through language and cultural practices that suggest that particular people or groups—the self and the other—must behave or respond in certain ways. Over a lifetime, these suggestions can become unseen and unexamined lenses that filter our beliefs about others and the decisions we make about others even before we encounter these groups or individuals. Thus, within metanarrative frameworks, individuals or groups can be subject to *pre-positioning* (Moghaddam & Harré, 2010, pp. 8–9), which "involves attribution of qualities of character, intellect, or temperament" to a particular individual or group. Pre-positions can influence or even bias our expectations about the identities and agency of particular individuals or groups.

One of the challenges of pre-positions and metanarratives is that they are typically invisible. Like the air we breathe, we seldom take notice of them, but they are ever present, helping us interpret our experiences. Metanarratives are just as prevalent in education as they are elsewhere, and they can be extremely challenging to confront. Metanarratives can cast a positive light, such as the "model-minority myth" which positions Asian youth with the expectation for high achievement and excellence in school (Lee, 2009). Metanarratives can also be negative. For example, children speaking Spanish and English are frequently positioned as if they have a cognitive deficit in reading because they speak two languages, even though bilingualism has been shown to increase metalinguistic awareness (i.e., the ability to think about one's own reading and language processes) (Harry & Klingner, 2014).

In the following sections, we share an example of how one of our co-authors, Mary, came to understand how a metanarrative or single story was framing her adult students' responses to a video. The video was used during a reflection activity that asked these students to take up a position as an ethnographic observer.

Taking an Ethnographic Stance Toward Video

Ethnographers study culture as enacted by individuals through speech, action, artifacts, and practices. Ethnographers are trained in what anthropologist Clifford Geertz (1973) called *thick description*. This is similar to the idea of description presented in Chapters 4 and 5.

Thick description is the process of carefully describing actions, behaviors, speech, and other cultural interactions as fully as possible. Just as an artist might layer on coatings of paint to create an image—think of Van Gogh's well-known *Sunflowers* or *The Starry Night*—ethnographers use thick layers of details to describe cultural behaviors. A first step in thick description is to focus on describing the actions and behaviors that are actually carried out, rather than leaping to interpretations or inferences about what such behaviors mean. Such observations and descriptions are challenging because one of the greatest skills humans possess—a skill that is learned from an early age—is the ability to recognize patterns and apply these across a variety of contexts in problem-solving. Anthropologist James Spradley (1980) writes that "People everywhere learn their culture by making inferences" (p. 10). A challenge for all humans—educators among them—is that sometimes the mind becomes so good at recognizing patterns and making inferences that people don't realize that what they perceive as factual "observations" may actually be "inferences." Remember in Chapter 5, Rodgers (2002) referred to description as one of "the most difficult" aspects of reflection because it requires teachers to "withhold interpretation of events and postpone their urge to fix the embedded problems" (p. 238).

 # Stop and Think: Guiding Questions

As you read the story below keep the following questions in mind. When done reading, revisit these questions:

1. Who are the characters in this story?
2. What positions are represented by the characters? Keep in mind that positions can be dynamic, changeable, and even contradictory.
3. As you consider characters and positions, what aspects of self-other positioning are present?
4. Which characters do you most identify with and why?
5. Over time, what metanarrative or single story becomes apparent to Mary as a teacher educator? How is time an important element of this narrative?
6. What pre-positionings did Mary feel her students brought to their video viewing?
7. How could Mary have used a Gradual Release of Responsibility to better scaffold her students' learning?

Metanarrative Frames during an Ethnographic Viewing of a Literacy Event

When I (Mary) began teaching courses in literacy methods to preservice and inservice teachers early in my career, I frequently used video clips in my classes. These activities positioned preservice and inservice teachers as ethnographers who viewed video of classrooms or teaching interactions, noting their observations and inferences throughout. As students in classes studying childhood (elementary) literacy methods, they discussed their observations and inferences, and also reflected on literacy practices.

One video showed a third-grade student Unesha discussing her writing with her teacher Nancy. Prior to discussing the video, I provided the student's grade level but no other information about the student's background or literacy skills. I wanted the viewers to rely upon what they observed and also on recent readings about literacy development, language, and teacher–student conferencing. For the activity, students were asked to divide their paper into two parts, putting their observations on one side and their inferences on the other. After viewing the video, I would ask: What did you see? What observations do you have?

The first few times I did this exercise, I expected that teachers or teacher-candidates (I had both groups in some classes) might struggle with observations versus inferences. After all, teaching is about making judgments in the moment (e.g., Schon's *reflection-in-action* in Chapter 4). In addition, I knew from using similar activities with doctoral students studying research methods that the idea of observation versus inference was deceptively simple. It sounds easy, but in reality, separating one's judgments of things seen from things felt, believed, or assumed is much harder than it appears. Frequently, when learners believe they are stating an observation about teaching reflected in a video, they are actually stating inferences or assumptions, and I found this was often the case when asking preservice and inservice teachers to comment on video.

What I noticed over a period of time in using this activity with a variety of students (preservice or inservice teachers, or in combined groups) was that responses followed a somewhat predictable pattern. Students would begin by commenting on clearly observable behavior, how the teacher or student pointed to the artifacts they were discussing, how the teacher referred specifically to the student's portfolio of writing as well as to specific writing conventions, or how the teacher and student sat in a relaxed, comfortable posture. But comments such as the following would also surface when I asked students to state their observations (again, not inferences, but what they observed):

- The student is below grade level.
- The student is not paying attention.
- The student has a learning disability.
- The student needs to be put in special education.

These comments would surface with both preservice teachers, inservice teachers, and mixed groups. After viewing the video, I would reveal more information about the student (e.g., that she was originally from Botswana, that she primarily spoke Setswana but that in her home English was also frequently spoken because it was the official language of Botswana). After providing additional information, I would ask the class to view the video and again work to separate observations from inferences and also to look at a sample of Unesha's writing.

Over time, I noticed a persistent pattern. Comments that might be considered deficits, such as those mentioned above, tended to focus on the student. Few, if any, negative or critical comments would surface regarding the teacher. Often the additional information gained through examining written artifacts or gained by learning about the context did little to persuade participants to change their original interpretations or judgments. In many instances, the most adamant interpretations were provided by teachers with the most experience. It seemed that rather than additional information providing an opportunity for teachers to revisit or rethink their original inferences, the additional information was used by some teachers in targeted ways to reaffirm their initial inferences and judgments. This happened regardless of what the video showed or how much the context differed from their original assumptions.

Not all comments were negative. Participants did make insightful comments and recommendations, and they also raised authentic and insightful questions. But what troubled me over time was the deficit-oriented positioning of the student. These responses were upsetting to me on two levels. First, for many years before becoming a university professor and teacher educator, I had been a teacher of students who were learning English as an additional language. Over the years, I had occasionally seen classroom teachers position English language learners in the same way. That is, English language learners were measured by what they could *not* do rather than what they were accomplishing in the moment. Second, as the pattern of response became clearer over time, I realized that part of the reaction from those viewing the video was based on perceptions of what teachers thought they were seeing: a Black child with an accent whose literacy ability and achievement would not be on par with other children, particularly White suburban children.

While the video of Nancy (a White teacher) and Unesha (a Black student) was not from a local school, part of what framed the context of the video was that class participants were living and working near or in a large urban area which had one of the highest poverty rates for mid-sized cities in the United States. The urban core of this city was home to a predominantly African–American population of students labeled "underachieving" and "at-risk." This context helped to form an over-arching narrative—a metanarrative—that positioned preservice and inservice teachers' interpretations of the video and what they felt they were seeing. As viewers, they were largely unaware of their subconscious positionings. For example, while all English speakers speak with an accent of some kind, the student was positioned as deficient because her accent was not "standard" or "normal." In other words, it was not the accent of mainstream middle (mostly White) America. In addition, the viewers were unaware of how their own lived histories (e.g., the towns or suburbs where many of these teachers grew up, their racial positions, their socioeconomic backgrounds, their gender, and other factors) deeply influenced their interpretation of this one interaction between a child and her teacher.

An easy response to this narrative would be to dismiss the preservice or inservice teachers who responded with deficit-oriented views of Unesha as ignorant or even racist, and to assume that those of us reading (or writing) this narrative "know better." In many instances, I knew those inservice and preservice teachers responding to the video to be thoughtful and caring individuals who set high standards for their own learning and teaching. Yet it was upsetting to see how these same teachers could conflate inferences with observations, and assumptions with evidence, in their responses to the video and in their positioning of Unesha and Nancy. In other projects, writings, and discussions, course participants had revealed themselves to be knowledgeable and curious about literacy practices and children. At the same time, I was cognizant that most of these teachers were White women, mostly in their 20s or 30s, who were most often raised in monolingual, middle- or upper-middle-class homes in suburban areas. In many ways, they were representative of teachers that many scholars have written about whose own racial, ethnic, linguistic, social, and economic upbringings pose a challenge to their vulnerability, ability, or willingness to grapple with such issues as race, class, linguistic diversity, or bias (Rogers & Mosley, 2008). The challenge also lies in another metanarrative frame that many White middleclass women are taught: don't rock the boat. Many research studies have documented that White women have learned through prior experience that in particular settings, it is best to maintain what McIntyre (1997) has labelled a "culture of niceness" (p. 40) rather than to breach protocol by openly discussing matters related to class, race, economic and social status, or even gender.

I was not only troubled by my students' responses—I was troubled by my own lack of response. While I was able to sometimes scaffold conversation and more complex explorations of the contextual factors surrounding the video, I struggled with how to raise open and honest conversation around responses as well as patterns that, over time, I came to see as based on assumptions about race and language use. I knew from prior experience and research how difficult it could be to have such conversations. Direct engagement or confrontation were typically ineffective, as both often led to silence and closing-down conversations. I had spent several years investigating how to foster such discussion, and I considered myself somewhat adept in helping deepen teachers' conversations around student diversities in response to narrative and literature. But in those first years of my work as a teacher educator in response to the video, rather than step into any "hot lava" (McVee & Boyd, 2016, p. 85), I avoided direct discussion of race, language use, and the positions that seemed to under-gird the deficit-oriented inferences in some of my students' responses to this video of Unesha and Nancy.

Over the years, as I have reflected back on this situation, I am most disappointed not in my former students, but in myself. I was the more knowledgeable other in this situation. I had read, discussed, and listened to the arguments made by many scholars on the need to have more honest discussions about race and literacy (e.g., Delpit, 1988; Ladson-Billings, 2006), and I shared many of these same readings with my preservice and inservice teachers. I understood that nothing was gained by allowing teachers to maintain a myth of colorblindness. Indeed, I considered myself to be someone who was committed to exploring hot lava and upholding conversations related to social justice and education for all students through literacy practices that challenged the status quo. In retrospect, as challenging as conversations around difference can be, it was my responsibility to scaffold the preservice and inservice teachers in my courses in this conversation. Simply put, I did not provide the scaffolding for students to engage in the conversation and examine their own positions and the ways they positioned others.

When you have finished reading, remember to revisit the Guiding Questions in Stop and Think that preceded this vignette.

Affordances and Limitations of Video

The vignette above raises a number of tensions: When observing teaching and learning, how can we avoid falling into pre-positioning of others based on our beliefs about their outward appearance as marked by language use, skin color, age, gender, or socioeconomic status?

What is the responsibility of the more knowledgeable other (i.e., a teacher educator, a professional development coordinator, a video group leader) in helping to address occurrences of pre-positioning (or what may be bias, assumption, or prejudice)? What can we do in conversations or responses to video if we feel that conversations around pre-positioning or bias are being avoided? Ultimately, we must also ask: what are the limitations of video as a tool for reflection?

The Oxford English Dictionary defines an affordance as "a characteristic of an object, especially relating to its potential utility." At the same time that tools have affordances, they also have limitations. Look back at the exploded diagram of the letter B in Chapter 5 (Figure 5.2). If you were assigned the task of putting this letter B together, you would need to know whether the screws that hold the parts together required a Phillips head, the screwdriver for cross-recess screws, or a flat-blade screwdriver. Each tool (i.e., flathead or Phillips head) has affordances, but each tool is also limited. Anyone who has tried to use a flathead screwdriver to remove a screw that requires a Phillips screwdriver has experienced what happens when a tool is inadequate. Occasionally the screw is removed, but often the incorrect tool (i.e., the flathead screwdriver) fails to accomplish the task.

Throughout previous chapters, we have highlighted the affordances of video recording as a tool that can be used in reflective teaching practice. For example, in Chapter 5 with Karen's critical incident narrative, we considered that if Karen had had access to video, it could have provided further opportunities for reflection on action as well as additional data to consider in considering her teaching and her interactions with Josh. Having video of her classroom pedagogy could have provided Karen with more opportunities to look across her teaching and would have provided more opportunities for Emily to scaffold Karen's learning by documenting Karen's teaching interactions, speech patterns, and self-other positionings of Josh. Yet, video recording does not guarantee that Karen would have captured the dilemmas she wanted to capture in her teaching. This is partially because many of these dilemmas involve attitudes, beliefs, and values as much as they involve enacted teaching practices within the classroom. In contrast, problems are more technical and more readily resolved (Cuban, 1992; Hayden & Chiu, 2013).

Problems versus Dilemmas

According to Cuban (1992) **problems** are the more routine, predictable, or structured challenges to teaching. An example might be that when a bell rings and students should settle down, they are instead still milling about, chatting with their friends, checking their digital devices, and not paying attention to the teacher. Anatoly, the novice teacher in this situation, realizes that he is spending 10 minutes of valuable instructional time getting his class settled down. While this type of behavior management is critical to resolve in classroom teaching, it is a technical problem that has a solution as well as an element of predictability. It may be a challenge for novices, but once structures are identified and set in place, solutions for more experienced teachers are typically routine and straightforward.

A comparable example in literacy instruction might be the problem of teacher wait time after asking questions. For example, in Chapter 3, Kelsey identified wait time as a problem after watching a video of herself tutoring. She noticed that instead of allowing time for the child to answer, she quickly moved to ask several questions in a row. Kelsey did not adequately scaffold the child's responses because she introduced so many questions that it was difficult for the child to answer. In her written reflections, her discussion with classmates, and her course instructor, Kelsey followed the "technical process of identifying the problem, generating feasible solutions, choosing the one that best reaches the goal (that is eliminates the problem), and putting the solution into practice" (Cuban, 1992, p. 6). Kelsey was able to monitor her future teaching; she attended to her questions and how much time she allowed for student responses by counting to herself after asking a question. She intentionally monitored and interrupted her own desire to immediately step in and ask more questions if the child did not respond immediately. In the end, Kelsey was able to address the problem she had encountered. This does not mean that the problem is resolved forever. Kelsey may find that in another context (e.g., large group instruction) she may fall back into her old habit of asking too many questions in a row. But even in a different context, she could follow a similar process to monitor her own teaching and address wait time.

Karen (Chapter 5) and Mary (this chapter) raise what Cuban would describe as *dilemmas*. These are difficulties that teachers encounter that are messy, untidy, complex, intricate, and often unpredictable. Conflict and discomfort can be a part of both problems and dilemmas, but dilemmas are "far messier, less structured, and often intractable to routine solutions" (p. 6). Dilemmas often involve moral choices which do not lead to neat solutions but to compromises that must be "good enough" often leaving behind a sense of discomfort, perplexity, or dissonance. Dilemmas "are conflict-filled situations that require choices because competing, highly prized values cannot be fully satisfied" (p. 6). For example, in the vignette earlier in this chapter, Mary, as a teacher educator, valued the collegial Community of Practice she had developed with her students, but she also valued open and honest confrontation of racism. Mary wanted to challenge the deficit-oriented positions related to race and language that surfaced in some student remarks about Unesha, but Mary was also aware that merely telling her students that such remarks were racist or biased would not likely lead to critical self-examination or change.

Similarly, Karen wanted to do what was best for Josh, her student, but also questioned her own pre-positioning of him as a particular student who had behavior issues, read and wrote at a very low level, and struggled. She did not want to fall in to the trap of "being nice" which often leads to low expectations for achievement (Delpit, 2006). Karen also questioned her own positioning: Should she send Josh to the dean of students for not doing what he was asked to do? Did she not send him because she was concerned that it would appear racist? What should she do about Josh's reading and writing development, given his behavior and how far he lagged behind his peers in his literacy achievement? Karen identified a dilemma.

What a Video Recording May Not Always Capture

These dilemmas also point to some of the limitations of video as a tool for reflection. When we record our classrooms or our teaching, we are collecting data about the teaching context, students, student–teacher interactions, student–student interactions, as well as the practices and events of literacy instruction. When we meet with others to view and discuss videos of teaching or even when we view video of teaching alone, we are analyzing video as a type of data. Video captures a view of a classroom but cannot capture all of the classroom or all of the context. In addition, feelings, values, attitudes, beliefs, and emotions are deep currents that flow through classrooms but are often hidden from view. Literacy researchers Green and Bloome (2012) remind us that "video documentation is not a transparent means of data collection and analysis" (p. 6092). Teachers or others who are recording video must decide "what to record and what to overlook, how to compose the visual frame in the camera, what counts as a beginning, middle, and end of an event, and how to contextualize a captured event" (p. 6092). As such, educators need to keep in mind that:

- Videos are partial representations of events; not everything in a classroom context is captured by video.
- Video records require interpretation; they do not speak for themselves. The act of interpretation begins even before the start of any teaching event when a teacher chooses what to record, where to place a recording device, and what to exclude from recording.
- The context beyond the camera matters.
  - Context may include actions (e.g., teacher or student behavior), but this context also includes those characteristics not readily captured on cameras such as teacher beliefs, values, and dispositions. It also includes broader sociopolitical contexts (e.g., pressures around teacher evaluation or testing).
  - Context also includes the lenses that peers in a Community of Practice may bring to their interpretations or lenses that may be missing.

Dilemmas often confront us in the moment, and they also are not always easy to capture on camera. Think of the example of Chad (Chapter 5) where, when teased by male African–American high school students about his name (Mr. White), Chad decided on the spot to respond with humor rather than **role-based positioning** (McVee et al., 2011) as an authority who had power. This event was not captured on video. The interaction between Chad and the students is one of those brief interactions that happen day-to-day but that may not appear to be integrally linked to literacy instruction. Even if this event had been captured on video, it is quite likely that given an assignment to choose a classroom literacy event or practice to reflect upon, this interaction would not be chosen. Yet, we posit that Chad's brief story is one of the most important events we have described in this book because it begins to chip away at a pre-positioning of Black male youth that has become a hardened metanarrative: that even in schools, adolescent Black males are to be feared and are generally up to no good. Through his response, Chad was able to create a counter-narrative, one that positioned young adolescent males as humorous adolescents engaged in wordplay.

The counter-narrative is important because the negative metanarrative runs through the lives of young Black men. Black boys are more likely to be disciplined and suspended from preschool through high school (Gilliam, Maupin, Reyes, Accaviti, & Shic, 2016). They are labeled "at risk" and disproportionately placed in special education (Blanchett, 2006; Codrington & Halford, 2012). Often during adolescence, this repeated storyline leads to a shift for Black youth that can result in separation from school, feelings of invisibility, and a disconnection from literacy experiences and achievement (Tatum, 2005). This type of positioning is a stance that Sabat (2008) has labeled *malignant positioning*. Malignant positioning is talk, action, gesture, or other forms of communication that position people negatively in terms of their perceived deficits (McVee & Carse, 2016). Malignant positioning locates students in terms of the qualities and attributes that they do not possess. This, in turn, limits students' access to particular discourse repertoires. Discourse repertoires are particular ways of talking, writing, representing, acting, and communicating (Gee, 1991). These discourses are also linked to rules regarding who has access to power and how that power is obtained (Delpit, 1988, 1995/2006). These rules of power are worth repeating here:

1. Issues of power are enacted in classrooms.
2. There are codes or rules for participating in power; that is, there is a "culture of power."
3. The rules of the culture of power are a reflection of the rules of the culture of those who have power.
4. If you are not already a participant in the culture of power, being told explicitly the rules of that culture makes acquiring power easier.
5. Those with power are frequently least aware of—or least willing to acknowledge—its existence. Those with less power are often most aware of its existence (1988, p. 282).

When students such as Josh or Unesha are repeatedly positioned by the qualities they do not possess or what they cannot do, it affects their literacy development. While Unesha and Josh are Black students, it has also been shown that teachers sometimes respond to and treat children of different social classes in different ways, repeating societal stratifications within school walls (Rist, 1970; 2000). Over time, different opportunities to learn through different discourses lead to different outcomes (e.g., different reading levels) for students, which affect children's school success and opportunities to learn (Brock, Boyd, & Pennington, 2011; Carger, 1996; Finn, 2009; Heath, 1983; Hicks, 2013).

 Stop and Think

1. Where and how have you seen issues of power enacted in classrooms? This could be in relation to your role as student, teacher, parent, or school leader. This could also be in relation to gender, race, ethnicity, social class, nationality, religion, or language use.

2. What codes of power have you or others you know (e.g., students, parents, teachers, newcomers in your community) been unaware of? How did you or others become aware of issues of power?
3. Can you give an example of a time when you observed a person with power who seemed unaware of the power she or he possessed? What happened?

Video, Diverse Learners, and a Social Justice Stance

Nearly two decades ago, Wallace wrote that "in order to teach for social justice, [teachers] need 'comprehensive professional preparation that requires transformation in their own thinking and in their lives'..." (Wallace, 2000, p. 1090). What is needed here is not compliant literacy or "doing school" but rather what Finn (2009) calls "literacy with an attitude." This is literacy for reading the word (i.e., learning how to decode and comprehend text) and reading the world (i.e., thinking critically about how sociopolitical systems work) (Freire, 1970) in order to raise teacher consciousness about injustice.

Rosaen (2015) has conducted one of few research reviews of video reflection that explicitly examined the connection between video reflection and social justice stances. Rosaen reviewed research studies that investigated the use of video by preservice teachers who reflected upon their own teaching. She concluded that overall, "the tasks preservice teachers completed did not explicitly guide them to focus on the relationship between characteristics of diverse learners featured in the videos and issues of teaching and learning" (p. 4). While Rosaen's review was limited to preservice teachers, her comments are just as applicable to inservice teachers. There are even fewer studies of inservice teachers and their use of video reflection (Shanahan, Tochelli, & Rinker, 2015).

In her review, Rosaen (2015) is careful not to fault teachers for the lack of attention to diversity and social justice. In the context of teacher education, preservice teachers are novices who need direction and scaffolding from more knowledgeable others, and even inservice teachers need support in addressing diversity. Just as a novice might need scaffolding to learn how to conduct a guided reading lesson, a novice may also need scaffolding in how to attend to the many needs of diverse learners. Meeting the needs of diverse learners is particularly challenging because diversity can be tied to language, socioeconomic background, cultural practices, gender, ethnicity, race, religion, and other social, cultural, and cognitive needs. As we noted in Chapter 2, teaching is complex! Teachers and teacher educators must focus on multiple diversities, rather than one monolithic and generic notion of diversity.

We use the term *diversities* here intentionally. Educational philosopher Maxine Greene once noted that we live in a time of "unimaginable diversities" (1993, p. 13). She went on to say:

We do not know the person in the front row of our classroom, or the one sharing the raft, or the one drinking next to us at the bar by her/his cultural or ethnic affiliation. Cultural background surely plays a part in shaping identity, but it does not determine identity. It may well create differences that must be honored; it may occasion styles and orientations that must be understood; it may give rise to tastes, values, even prejudices that must be taken into account (p. 16).

Teacher educators, educational consultants, and video study group leaders must be willing and prepared to lead exploration and discussion about what diversity/ies means. Often times in educational discussions "diversity" is a substitute for a visible racial marker (e.g., Native American), an economic indicator (e.g., poor), or label for language use (e.g., Arabic speaker). Ladson-Billings (2006) discusses how many preservice teachers use the "diverse" to apply to school settings with students of color:

If they are in schools whose population is primarily students of color, they [preservice teachers] describe it as a "diverse" setting. I once had a student who was working in a school with a 100 percent African American population. She described it as a "diverse" school setting. I corrected her and said, "No, you're in an all-black school." (p. 105).

Interpretations based on visible markers such as race can influence video analysis because, as in the introductory vignette with Unesha and Nancy, these markers can lead to pre-positioning and assumptions from viewers.

Learners do bring many different types of diversities to the classroom. Even in a classroom where all racial markers may appear to indicate a homogenous classroom (i.e., all children appear to be White; all children appear to be Black), diversity will be present in socioeconomic status, linguistic background and varieties of speech, as well as literacy development. Children who appear to be outwardly Black, White, Asian, Native American, brown, or from other racial or ethnic groups may, in fact, be multiracial or multiethnic, an increasing common circumstance in the United States (Funderburg, 2013).

As we wrote this book, one of our students shared how as a fair-skinned, biracial (Black–White) woman living in a predominantly White suburban area, people often feel free to make derogatory racial comments in front of her because they do not realize that she is biracial. Her own children who are multiracial have experienced similar positioning based on their appearance and language use since they speak Arabic and English. Similarly, the hip-hop artist and rapper Logic has talked about, and been criticized for, attempting to explore what it feels like to grow up biracial with a Black father and White mother who both struggled with drug addiction (Greene, 2017). Logic has seven brothers and sisters who looked, in his words, "prominently Black" while he looked "white as white can be, I guess." Logic has described how his White appearance has led people to ask, "Oh, what's it like being a White rapper?" In trying to navigate two racial identities, Logic has been called racial slurs on both sides of the color line. This challenge of between-ness is a common experience of biracial and multiracial youth (McVee & Zhang, 2016; Obama, 1995/2004) as well as many immigrants and refugees (Gross, 2017; Roof, 2016; Sarroub, 2005).

Around all of these many forms of diversities (including the many other types of diversities we have not referred to), a key point is, **what you value, you talk about.** Teacher educators, the more knowledgeable others who help guide preservice and inservice teachers, must be ready to tackle these issues, even if they see these issues as hot lava. Furthermore, Rosaen (2015) determined that teachers need explicit guidance in making observations as well as scaffolding in "more focused discussion regarding their developing knowledge and beliefs about student diversity" (p. 4). Video reflection also needs to include culturally responsive instruction. Ultimately, more knowledgeable others (i.e., teacher educators, professional development consultants) must support preservice teachers in taking "a critical stance to question power, inequality, and the status quo in order to teach for social justice" (p. 5). But how is that to be done?

Building a Social Justice Stance: "What You Value, You Talk About"

"What you value, you talk about" are words spoken by Mrs. Hawkins, a Black parent to Vivian Paley, a teacher who explored her own identities as a White Jewish woman and her relationships with children (1979/2000, p. 131). Paley shared these words as she realized that she was avoiding topics, not only related to race, but also to other uncomfortable topics. In addition to engaging with topics she previously avoided, Paley had multiple strengths as a teacher. She listened closely to others and listened to children (1986, 1995), and she valued the role of stories (1995). (For more on listening see Lake, 2016; McVee & Boyd, 2016; Parker, 2010; Schultz, 2003.)

The role of stories brings us back to the beginning of this chapter and the example of personal narrative. We introduced a personal narrative early in this chapter because we believe that even as teachers view themselves or others on video, they must also reflexively engage with their own identities and positions. This work is challenging. Numerous studies of teacher education have documented how difficult it is for teachers, especially White teachers, to have open dialogue about differences (Rogers & Mosley, 2008; Santoro, Kamler, & Reid, 2001) while Van Galen (2010) also reminds us that these identity issues are grounded in class as well as race.

Although most research has followed teachers within a teacher-education context, usually one course or one teaching placement, some research has been conducted over longer periods. Using an ethnographic approach, educational anthropologist Susan Florio-Ruane (2001) and colleagues (Florio-Ruane & de

Tar, 1995) followed several groups of White, female teachers as they discussed autobiographies and personal narratives to surface discussions of racial, linguistic, and socioeconomic difference. In one of these studies, she found that it took two years before participants could fully "break their silence and create for themselves a 'new curriculum' for thinking and speaking about what, for White and middle-class Americans, are historically difficult topics" (p. 139). Likewise, Shanahan and Tochelli (2012; Chapter 3) followed one group of inservice teachers through two years of a study group and found that it took time to time to build relationships and trust. One obvious take away from both sets of studies is that reflection at any deep and challenging level, whether that be related to video or diversities, takes time. Here, we are suggesting that preservice and inservice teachers need to use video to reflect upon their own teaching but also on diversities. At the same time, most study groups or classes don't have two years to stay together and reflect.

Because time is limited, teacher educators and teachers need to risk the conversations that will take them into deeper discussions and explorations of perplexity and the dilemmas they face in education. Given this time constraint, it may not be possible to rely upon luck or happenstance to provide the most optimal means for surfacing discussion of social justice issues in video analysis. Indeed, it may be that other powerful tools such as narrative need to be included to help provide additional perspectives and voices. In addition, other powerful means of exploration exist in video clips from popular media and news stories, teacher ethnographies and writing, personal memoir and autobiography, poetry, and the arts. We have also included a short list of print resources for raising critical consciousness at the end of this chapter. Drawing upon many and varied sources as a springboard can help build conversations around beliefs, values, and dispositions that may not be readily apparent on video recordings.

Research on Narrative and Positioning: Creating Displacement Spaces

Researchers have found that exploration of positions through discussion, personal narrative, and reflective writing can be a powerful tool to uncover much of what is

> usually unexamined in the tightly braided relationships of language, culture, and power in schools and schooling. This kind of examination inevitably begins with our own histories as human beings and as educators; our own experiences as members of particular races, classes, and genders; and as children, parents, and teachers in the world.
>
> (Cochran-Smith, 1995, p. 500)

This means we need to start exploring our own beliefs alongside those of others, and it is possible to make progress. For example, in the context of using narrative to explore language, literacy, and culture in a graduate literacy course, McVee (McVee et al., 2004; McVee, 2014) found that students who had deeper engagement and reflection with course topics (e.g., Eve, Karen, and Bridget, White females) made more connections across multiple types of texts (*intertextual positionings*) and had more *reflexive positions* (connections back to the self) across various texts. These same participants also revealed shifts in perceptions around language, literacy, and sociocultural issues, such as race, through written artifacts by taking up multiple positions, analyzing their positions, and shifting their perspective-taking from a self-oriented perspective toward a perspective of *self-aligned-with-others*. In contrast, other students (e.g., Krissy, a White female; Ted, a White male; Janice, a multiracial Black/White female) took up very few **reflexive positions** and rarely used **intertextual positions** to explore challenging topics.

Glazier (2005) examined the ways that teachers positioned themselves in relation to texts they had chosen to read, in conversations about those texts, and in conversations with students about the same texts. The teachers were participants in a professional development group and also examined their own discourse, their students' discourse, as well as their own teaching practice through discourse analysis to enact change. Likewise, Sonu, Oppenheim, Epstein, and Agarwal (2012) examined the teaching and learning of three justice-oriented teachers and suggest that "teachers and teacher educators might use the explanatory power of positioning theory to understand, reflect, and move forward from rigid notions of social responsibility" (p. 187). The hypothesis put forward by Sonu et al. (2012) is demonstrated in practice by Vetter and Schieble (2016), who draw upon positioning theory to introduce their students' reflective processes in relation to video and teaching. In one compelling example, they describe how Tammy, an African–American middle-class female, acknowledges her discomfort. Tammy states that she had

> a really hard time answering the question about race, class, gender. I told Emma in the beginning that I don't even pay attention to all of that when I'm teaching. I thought it was about respect and about love and teaching and all that, but listening to her response made me think more about it and I'm like hmmm, how does it really affect me in the classroom and my kids and their interactions.
>
> *(p. 94)*

While most studies of narrative as a reflective tool have focused on White teachers, it should be noted that it is not only White teachers or women who can benefit from these studies. Glazier (2009) studied the positioning of five English teachers in an out-of-school multicultural book discussion group for a year and found that Daniel, an African–American male, was positioned and positioned himself as an authority across the year. In the end, Glazier concludes that Daniel's own learning was limited because of this *role-based position*. While the discussion group contained a mix of genders and races (Black/

White), participants were able to take up multiple perspectives and positions allowing them a greater range of exploration and learning while Daniel's positions remained fixed or constant.

Brock and colleagues (Brock et al., 2006; Brock, Nikoli, & Wallace 2011) found that combining personal narrative, teacher reflections, and experiences abroad led to positions they labeled **displacement spaces** that were lived by six experienced teachers who engaged in a course exploring literacy across languages and cultures. These displacement spaces are defined as

> places we move into (either by force or choice) whereby we see aspects of our lives and experiences in new, different, and unique ways. Thus, displacement spaces offer potentially fertile ground for growth. Of course, pain also can be associated with growth.
>
> *(Brock et al., 2011, p. 135)*

In Brock's study, some displacement was physical (i.e., students completed some coursework while in Costa Rica), but other displacement was emotional, cognitive, social, and cultural resulting in deeper understandings of self and others.

Video contains a similar possibility for displacement. In viewing and reviewing video, we may be positioned in ways that we had not expected to be or that make us feel uncomfortable. Also, if teacher educators or video group leaders (the more knowledgeable others) observe that members in a Community of Practice are not engaging in displacement spaces or have become too comfortable with the status quo, more knowledgeable others should be prepared to help introduce dissonance and perplexity to encourage video group members to take up a critical inquiry stance. This requires more knowledgeable others or teacher leaders to step in and scaffold video group members at the point of need and attempt to intentionally introduce displacement spaces. Group leaders or teacher educators should be mindful that there are times when even a safe, trusting, and collegial atmosphere in a group can be a detriment.

> In a tight community a lot of implicit assumptions can go unquestioned, and there may be few opportunities or little willingness inside the community to challenge them. The intimacy communities develop can create a barrier to newcomers, a blinder to new ideas, or a reluctance to critique each other.... The very qualities that make a community an ideal structure for learning—a shared perspective on a domain, trust, a communal identity, long-standing relationships, an established practice—are the same qualities that can hold it hostage to its history and its achievements. The community can become an ideal structure for avoiding learning.
>
> *(Wenger, McDermott, & Snyder, 2002, p. 141)*

If we want to profoundly affect the lives of teachers in relation to topics that some of those same teachers wish to avoid, we need to treat teachers with the same respect and developmental concerns that we apply to children. This means providing targeted, scaffolded guidance at the point of need and helping teachers work toward greater responsibility and independence. Recently, in a blind review of a manuscript, one of our co-authors was discussing the limitations of inservice teacher learning in relation to discussions of diversities. In response to comments made by teachers a reviewer had written, "These teachers should know better." This is a bit like saying to a struggling reader, "You should read better." It is easy to agree that teachers *should* be more clued in to social justice teaching, race literacies, and other intersectionalities, just as it is the case that a struggling reader *should* read better. But, neither teachers nor children are likely to learn if they are merely told to "just do better." We must find means of scaffolding teachers to think about diversities just as we are committed to scaffolding children's literacy learning.

 Stop and Think

1. Go back through the chapter and identify the various types of positioning that were described.
2. Which of these types of positioning do you feel you have observed in action?
3. Think for a moment about education-related stories that might be linked to these positions. These stories could be your own experience, a student's experience, or even something you have seen enacted in video stories online or in films.
4. Write up one of these stories. What positions can you identify within the story?
5. Create or name positions that you may identify that have not yet been named in this chapter.

Conclusion

It is up to teacher educators, consultants, video study group leaders, or more knowledgeable video group members to introduce and maintain critical inquiry related to diversities and to help learners look beyond the single story. If video provided by study group members does not explore these issues, these issues can be introduced through literature, film, poetry, popular and social media, film, comedy, or other texts and activities. These additional texts and storylines can help to provide a backdrop for exploring positions and positionality. Teacher educators and other leaders are not exempt from explorations; instead, they must lead by example. In addition, the more knowledgeable others or facilitators must take an active role in providing guidance and scaffolding learners in order to "look beyond what they see." We invite you to continue this challenging task by working through the **Ethnographic Video Viewing Activity** at the end of this chapter.

Additional Resources to Assist Educators in Developing a Critical Inquiry Stance

Articles

Beech, J. (2004). Redneck and hillbilly discourse in the writing classroom: Classifying critical pedagogies of whiteness. *College English, 67*(2), 172–186.

Gay, G., & Kirkland, K. (2003). Developing cultural critical consciousness and self-reflection in preservice teacher education. *Theory into Practice, 42*(3), 181–187.

Gutierrez, K. D. (2008). Developing a sociocritical literacy in the third space. *Reading Research Quarterly, 43*(2), 148–164.

Gutierrez, K. D., & Rogoff, B. (2003). Cultural ways of learning: Individual traits or repertoires of practice. *Educational Researcher, 32*(5), 19–25.

Haddix, M. (2008). Beyond sociolinguistics: Towards a critical approach to cultural and linguistic diversity in teacher education. *Language and Education, 22*(5), 254–270.

Ladson-Billings, G. (1995). But that's just good teaching! The case for culturally relevant pedagogy. *Theory into Practice, 34*(3), 159–165.

Lin, X., & Kinzer, C. K. (2003). The importance of technology for making cultural values visible. *Theory into Practice, 42*(3), 234–242.

McInnes, B. D. (2017). Preparing teachers as allies in Indigenous education: Benefits of an American Indian content and pedagogy course. *Teaching Education, 28*(2), 145–161.

Milner, H. R. (2010). What does teacher education have to do with teaching? Implications for diversity studies. *Journal of Teacher Education, 61*(1–2), 118–131.

Rumenapp, J. C. (2016). (Re)Positioning the "Chinatown" default: Constructing hybrid identities in elementary classrooms. In W. Ma & G. Li (Eds.), *Chinese-heritage students in North American schools* (pp. 137–152). New York, NY: Taylor and Francis.

Scherff, L. (2012). "This project has personally affected me": Developing a critical stance in preservice English teachers. *Journal of Literacy Research, 44*(2), 200–236.

Skerrett, A. (2010). Teaching critical literacy for social justice. *Action in Teacher Education, 31*(4), 54–65.

Books

Bell, L. A. (2010). *Storytelling for social justice: Connecting narrative and the arts in antiracist teaching*. New York, NY: Routledge.

Cochran-Smith, M. (2004). *Walking the road: Race, diversity, and social justice*. New York, NY: Teachers College Press.

Frank, C. (1999). *Ethnographic eyes: A teacher's guide to classroom observation*. Portsmouth, NH: Heinemann.

Gay, G. (2000). *Culturally responsive teaching: Theory, research, and practice*. New York, NY: Teachers College Press.

McVee, M. B., & Boyd, F. B. (2016). *Exploring diversity through multimodality, narrative, and dialogue: A framework for teacher reflection.* New York, NY: Routledge.

Milner IV, H. R. (2015). *Rac(e)ing to class: Confronting poverty and race in schools.* Cambridge, MA: Harvard Education Review.

Paris, D., & Alim, H. S. (Eds.). (2017). *Culturally sustaining pedagogies: Teaching and learning for justice in a changing world.* New York, NY: Teachers College Press.

Rex, L., & Juzwik, M. (2011). *Narrative discourse analysis for teacher educators: Managing cultural differences in classrooms.* Cresskill, NJ: Hampton Press.

Schultz, K. (2003). *Listening: A framework for teaching across differences.* New York, NY: Teachers College Press.

References

Adichie, C. N. (July 2009). *The Danger of a Single Story.* Retrieved May 14, 2017, from http://www.ted.com/talks/chimamanda_adichie_the_danger_of_a_single_story.

Blanchett, W. (2006). Disproportionate representation of African American students in special education: Acknowledging the role of White privilege and racism. *Educational Researcher, 35*(6), 24–28.

Brock, C. H., Boyd, F. B., & Pennington, J. L. (2011). Variation in language and the use of language across contexts: Implications for literacy teaching and learning. In D. Lapp & D. Fisher (Eds.), *Research on teaching the English Language Arts* (pp. 83–89). New York, NY: Routledge with International Reading Association & National Council of Teachers of English.

Brock, C. H., Nikoli, M., & Wallace, J. (2011). Shifting positions: One teacher's journey exploring literacy and diversity. In M. B. McVee, C. H. Brock, & J. A. Glazier (Eds.), *Sociocultural positioning in literacy: Exploring culture, discourse, narrative, and power in diverse educational contexts* (pp. 119–138). Cresskill, NJ: Hampton Press.

Brock, C., Wallace, J., Herschbach, M., Johnson, C., Raikes, B., Warren, K., Nikoli, M. & Poulsen, H. (2006). Negotiating displacement spaces: Exploring teachers' stories about learning and diversity. *Curriculum Inquiry, 36*(1), 35–62.

Bruner, J. S. (1986). *Actual minds, possible worlds.* Cambridge, MA: Harvard University Press.

Bruner, J. S. (1990). *Acts of meaning.* Cambridge. MA: Harvard University Press.

Carger, C. (1996). *Of borders and dreams: Beginnings.* New York, NY: Teachers College Press.

Codrington, J., & Halford, H. F. (2012). *Special education and the mis-education of African American children: A call to action.* Position paper published by the Association of Black Psychologists. Retrieved online http://www.abpsi.org/pdf/specialedpositionpaper021312.pdf.

Cuban, L. (1992). Managing dilemas while building learning communities. *Educational Researcher, 21*(1), 4–11.

Davies, B., & Harré, R. (1990). Positioning: The discursive production of selves. *Journal for the Theory of Social Behaviour, 20*(1), 43–63.

Deeney, T., & Dozier, C. (2015). Constructing successful video reflection experiences in practicum settings. In E. Ortlieb, M. B. McVee, & L. E. Shanahan (Eds.), *Video reflection in literacy teacher education and development: Lessons from research and practice* (pp. 41–57). Bingley, UK: Emerald Group Publishing.

Delpit, L. (1988). The silenced dialogue: Power and pedagogy in educating other people's children. *Harvard Educational Review, 58*(3), 280–298.

Delpit, L. (2006). Lessons from teachers. *Journal of Teacher Education, 57*(3), 220–231.

Delpit, L. (1995/2006). *Other people's children: Cultural conflict in the classroom.* New York, NY: The New Press.

Finn, P. J. (2009). *Literacy with an attitude* (2nd ed.). Albany, NY: SUNY Press.

Florio-Ruane, S. (2001). *Teacher education and the cultural imagination.* Mahwah, NJ: Lawrence Erlbaum.

Florio-Ruane, S., & de Tar, J. (1995). Conflict and consensus in teacher candidates' discussion of ethnic autobiography. *English Education, 27*(1), 11–39.

Freire, P. (1970). *Pedagogy of the oppressed* (M. B. Ramos, Trans.). New York, NY: Continuum.

Funderburg, L. (2013, Oct). The changing face of America. *National Geographic.* (Retrieved online May 21, 2017). http://ngm.nationalgeographic.com/2013/10/changing-faces/funderburg-text.

Gee, J. P. (1991). What is literacy? In C. M. Mitchell & K. Weiler (Eds.), *Rewriting literacy: Culture and the discourse of the other* (pp. 3–11). New York, NY: Bergin & Garvey.

Geertz, C. (1973). *The interpretation of cultures.* New York, NY: Basic Books.

Gilliam, W. S., Maupin, A. N., Reyes, C. R., Accavitti, M., & Shic, F. (2016). *Do early educators' implicit Biases regarding sex and race relate to behavior and expectations and recommendations of preschool expulsions and suspensions?* Yale University Child Study Center: Yale University.

Glazier, J. A. (2005). Talking and teaching through a positional lens: Recognizing what and who we privilege in our practice. *Teaching Education, 16*(3), 231–243.

Glazier, J. A. (2009). The challenge of repositioning: Teacher learning in the company of others. *Teaching and Teacher Education, 25*(6), 826–834.

Green, J., & Bloome, D. (2012). Video documentation and analysis in literacy research. In C. A. Chapelle (Ed.), *The Encyclopedia of Applied Linguistics* (pp. 6089–6096). Chichester, SXW, UK: Wiley-Blackwell.

Greene, M. (1993). The passions of pluralism. *Educational Researcher, 22*(1), 13–18.

Greene, D. (Host) (2017, May 15). *Logic Is Ready to Tell the World Who He Is.* National Public Radio. [Radio Broadcast Episode]. Retrieved May 21, 2017 http://www.npr.org/2017/05/15/528159035/logic-is-ready-to-tell-the-world-who-he-is.

Gross, T. (Host) (2017, May 20). *Comic Hasan Minhaj.* National Public Radio. [Radio Broadcast Episode]. Retrieved May 21, 2017 http://www.npr.org/2017/05/20/529133156/fresh-air-weekend-comic-hasan-minhaj-cape-verdean-dance-music-jill-soloway.

Hardy, B. (1968). Toward a poetics of fiction: (3) An approach through narrative. *NOVEL: A Forum on Fiction, 2*(1), 5–14.

Harré, R., & van Langenhove, L. (1991). Varieties of positioning. *Journal for the Theory of Social Behaviour, 21*(4), 393–407.

Harry, B., & Klingner, J. (2014). *Why are so many minority students in special education?: Understanding race and disability in schools* (2nd ed.). New York: Teachers College Press.

Hayden, H. E., & Chiu, M. M. (2013). Lessons learned: Supporting the development of reflective practice and adaptive expertise. In P. J. Dunston, S. K. Fullerton, C. C. Bates, P. M. Stecker, M. W. Cole, A. H. Hall, D. Herro, K. Headley, (Eds.) *62nd Literacy Research Association Yearbook*, pp. 279–296. Oak Creek, WI: Literacy Research Association, Incorporated.

Heath, S. B. (1983). *Ways with words.* New York, NY: Cambridge University Press.

Hicks, D. (2013). *The road out: A teacher's odyssey in poor America.* Berkeley, CA: University of California Press.

Ladson-Billings, G. (2006). It's not the culture of poverty, it's the poverty of culture: The problem with teacher education. *Anthropology & Education Quarterly, 37*(2), 104–109.

Lake, R. (2016). Radical love in teacher education praxis: Imagining the real through listening to diverse student voices. *International Journal of Critical Pedagogy, 7*(3), 79–97.

Lee, S. J. (2009). *Unraveling the "model minority" stereotype: Listening to Asian American youth* (2nd ed.). New York, NY: Teachers College Press.

Lyotard, J.-F. (1984). *The postmodern condition: A report on knowledge*. Minneapolis, MN: University of Minnesota.

McIntyre, A. (1997). *Making meaning of whiteness*. Albany, New York, NY: SUNY Press.

McLaren, P. (1993). Border disputes: Multicultural narrative, identity formation, and critical pedagogy in postmodern America. In D. McLaughlin & W. G. Tierney (Eds.), *Naming silenced lives: Personal narratives and the process of educational change* (pp. 201–235). New York, NY: Routledge.

McVee, M. B. (2014). "Some are way left, like this guy, Gloria Ladson Billings": Resistance, conflict, and perspective taking in teachers' discussions of multicultural education. *Peace and Conflict: Journal of Peace Psychology, 20*(4), 536–551.

McVee, M. B., Baldassarre, M., & Bailey, N. M. (2004). Positioning theory as lens to explore teachers' beliefs about literacy and culture. In C. M. Fairbanks, J. Worthy, B. Maloch, J. V. Hoffman, & D. L. Schallert (Eds.), *53rd National Reading Conference Yearbook* (pp. 281–295). Oak Creek, WI: National Reading Conference.

McVee, M. B., & Boyd, F. B. (2016). *Exploring diversity through multimodality, narrative, and dialogue: A framework for teacher reflection*. New York: Routledge.

McVee, M. B., Brock, C. H., & Glazier, J. A. (Eds.). (2011). *Sociocultural positioning in literacy: Exploring culture, discourse, narrative, and power in diverse educational contexts*. Cresskill, NJ: Hampton Press.

McVee, M. B., & Carse, C. (2016). A multimodal analysis of storyline in the "Chinese Professor": Narrative construction and positioning in economic hard times. *Visual Communication, 15*(4), 403–427.

McVee, M. B., & Zhang, Z. C. M. (2016). Of cowboys and communists: A phenomenological narrative case study of a biracial Chinese-White adolescent. In W. Ma & G. Li (Eds.), *Beyond test scores: Understanding the hearts and minds of Chinese-heritage students in North American schools* (pp. 180–194). New York, NY: Routledge.

Obama, B. (1995/2004). *Dreams from my father: A story of race and inheritance*. New York, NY: Random House.

Paley, V. (1979/2000). *White teacher*. Cambridge, MA: Harvard University Press.

Paley, V. (1986). On listening to what the children say. *Harvard Educational Review, 56*(2), 122–131.

Paley, V. (1995). *Kwanzaa and me: A teacher's story*. Cambridge, MA: Harvard University Press.

Parker, W. (2010). Listening to strangers: Classroom discussion in democratic education. *Teachers College Record, 112*(11), 2815–2832.

Rist, R. C. (1970). Student social class and teacher expectations: The self-fulfilling prophecy in ghetto education. *Harvard Educational Review, 40*, 411–451.

Rist, R. C. (2000). The enduring dilemmas of class and color in American education. *Harvard Educational Review, 70*(3), 257–301.

Rodgers, C. (2002). Seeing student learning: Teacher change and the role of reflection. *Harvard Educational Review, 72*(2), 230–253.

Rogers, R., & Mosley, M. (2008). A critical discourse analysis of racial literacy in education. *Linguistics and Education, 19*, 107–131.

Roof, L. M. (2016). *"But I am still strong"*: *The schooling experiences and identities of three refugees from Burma.* Unpublished doctoral dissertation. University at Buffalo, SUNY. Buffalo, NY.

Rosaen, C. (2015). The potential of video to help literacy pre-service teachers learn to teach for social justice and develop culturally responsive instruction. In E. Ortlieb, M. B. McVee, & L. E. Shanahan (Eds.), *Video reflection in literacy teacher education and development: Lessons from research and practice* (pp. 3–19). Bingley, UK: Emerald Group Publishing.

Sabat, S. (2008). Positioning and conflict involving a person with dementia: A case study. In F. M. Moghaddam, R. Harré, & N. Lee (Eds.), *Global conflict resolution through positioning analysis* (pp. 81–94). New York, NY: Springer.

Santoro, N., Kamler, B., & Reid, J. (2001). Teachers talking difference: Teacher education and the poetics of anti-racism. *Teaching Education, 12*(2), 191–200.

Sarroub, L. (2005). *All American Yemeni girls: Being muslim in a public school.* Philadelphia, PA: University of Pennsylvania Press.

Schultz, K. (2003). *Listening: A framework for teaching across differences.* New York, NY: Teachers College Press.

Shanahan, L. E., & Tochelli, A. L. (2012). Video-Study Group: A context to cultivate professional relationships. In P. J. Dunston, S. K. Fullerton, C. C. Bates, K. Headley, & P. M. Stecker (Eds.), *61st Literacy Research Association Conference Yearbook* (pp. 196–211). Oak Creek, WI: Literacy Research Association.

Shanahan, L. E., Tochelli, A. L., & Rinker, T. W. (2015). Insights into inservice teachers' video-facilitated reflection of literacy practices. In E. Ortlieb, M. B. McVee, & L. E. Shanahan (Eds.), *Video reflection in literacy teacher education and development: Lessons from research and practice* (pp. 21–40). Bingley, UK: Emerald Group Publishing.

Sonu, D., Oppenheim, R., Epstein, S. E., & Agarwal, R. (2012). Taking responsibility: The multiple and shifting positions of social justice educators. *Education, Citizenship and Social Justice, 7*(2), 175–189.

Spradley, J. P. (1980). *Participant observation*: Belmont, CA: Wadsworth.

Tatum, A. W. (2005). *Teaching reading to black adolescent males: Closing the achievement gap.* Portland, ME: Stenhouse Publishers.

Van Galen, J. (2010). Class, identity, and teacher education. *Urban Review, 42*(4), 253–270.

Vetter, A., & Schieble, M. (2016). *Observing teacher identities through video analysis.* New York, NY: Routledge.

Wallace, B. (2000). A call for change in multicultural training at graduate schools of education: Educating to end oppression and for social justice. *Teachers College Record, 102*(6), 1086–1111.

Wenger, E., McDermott, R. & Snyder, W. M. (2002). *Cultivating communities of practice: A guide to managing knowledge.* Boston, MA: Harvard Business School Press.

Wetzel, M. M., Hoffman, J. V., & Maloch, B. (2015). Video-based mentoring tool for cooperating teachers coaching preservice teachers: Supporting reflection around literacy practice. In E. Ortlieb, M. B. McVee, & L. E. Shanahan (Eds.), *Video reflection in literacy teacher education and development: Lessons from research and practice* (pp. 81–103). Bingley, UK: Emerald Group Publishing.

Wetzel, M. M., Maloch, B., & Hoffman, J. V. (2016). Retrospective video analysis: A reflective tool for teachers and teacher educators. *The Reading Teacher, 70*(5), 533–542.

APPENDIX 8.1

ETHNOGRAPHIC VIDEO VIEWING ACTIVITY

You will need:

1. Paper and highlighters or colored pens, or digital device to take notes and highlight electronically.
2. Digital device to view video. (NOTE: You will need to view the video and take notes at the same time so you may want to use paper for your notes or use a device with a large enough screen to view and take notes simultaneously.)
3. Access to a video about 5–15 minutes in length of a classroom teaching interaction. It will be easier to do this activity if you choose a video where a teacher is interacting with students. This could be a video shared by a group leader, a course instructor, or a video of your own teaching. While this activity is probably best with a video provided with some guidance from a more knowledgeable other, you can find videos of teaching in many online sites such as:

   a. https://www.teachingchannel.org
   b. http://www.teachertube.com
   c. https://www.edutopia.org/videos

This activity extends the Critical Incident Description from Chapter 5. There are three parts to this activity. Parts I and II provide opportunities to make more detailed observations and examinations of a teaching event. Part III scaffolds reflection on this event through sharing with a peer who can provide feedback and other ways of thinking about what is noticed and examined.

Teacher educators or professional development leaders may want to introduce and work through these aspects of noticing and observing, and examining positions in a group or class context before learners try these independently. It will take several sessions to work through the various parts of the activity.

Part I: Noticing and Observing

1. Watch the video: What do you notice? Write down as many ideas as you can. Watch the video again and add to your list.
2. Now go through your list. Using one color highlight or circle all *descriptions*. *Descriptions* are observable actions, words, spaces, materials, gestures, movement, and so on.
3. Using another color go through and highlight or circle all *inferences*. *Inferences* are your judgments, interpretations, analyses, evaluations, and so on.
4. Look across your descriptions and inferences. Do you have more *descriptions* or *inferences*? Which did you find more challenging, *description* or *inference*? Why?
5. Look carefully through your list of *inferences*.

   a. Which *inferences* can be supported by the *descriptions* of actions, words, spaces, materials, gestures, movements, etc. that you saw take place in the video?
   b. Use another color to draw connecting lines between the evidence (*descriptions*) that support your *inferences*.
   c. Are there any *inferences* that cannot be supported by observed behaviors?
   d. What other evidence, if any, can you use to support these *inferences*? Is your evidence grounded primarily in the observable behavior (*descriptions*), your own experience, assumptions, etc.?

6. How confident are you in the *inferences* you have made? What other types of information would be helpful to you to support your *inferences*?

Part II: Explaining and Examining Positions

7. What positions can you identify in the *inferences* and *descriptions* you made? How did your *descriptions* and *inferences* position student(s) or teacher(s)?
8. Consider how your own dialect, language use, race, ethnicity, gender, or age are different or similar to those in your video. What role did positions based on dialect, language use, race, ethnicity, gender, or age (e.g., teacher/ student) play in your *descriptions* or *inferences*?
9. What pre-positions, bias, or assumptions, if any, do you feel you may have brought to your video viewing experience?

10. Whenever we view a video of teaching, some context may be lost. How might this absence of context around a video (your own or one you found online) pre-position viewers?

11. How might contextual aspects of the video that are visible (e.g., students'/teacher's age, race, language/dialect, gender) or tags or descriptors linked to the video (e.g., Learning Disabled, English Second Language, bilingual, immigrant) pre-position viewers toward the teacher and student(s)?

12. Are there any **inferences** or **observations** you made that you are/were uncomfortable writing down or sharing? If so, what were these? Why did they make you uncomfortable?

Part III: Sharing with a Partner

13. Share your video and your insights with a partner or small group in your learning community.

Extensions

1. Repeat Steps 1–12 while analyzing a video of your own teaching. (If you are not in a classroom, you can analyze a video found online at one of the resources listed above, and adapt the questions to analyze another teacher's teaching.)

2. Examine the various positions you take up in your own teaching. Consider:

   a. Where do you position yourself physically within the classroom space? What message does your body position and posture send to students?

   b. What do you say during the video? What is the content you are talking about? And, how do you say this? (Consider elements of *prosody*: tone of voice, pitch, inflection, rhythm, and stress, as well as elements of *structure*: questions, statements, commands, requests, etc.)

   c. Who does most of the talking in your lesson? Who does most of the listening?

   d. Many times, classroom interactions emphasize talk, but listening can be just as important. What types of listening are required in the lesson you chose?

   e. There are many tools that provide opportunities for teachers to communicate ideas. Common classroom tools for teachers include talk, gesture, reading, writing, and multimedia presentations (e.g., Power-Point, online websites, web apps, YouTube videos, images). What are the tools that you use for teaching in the video you have chosen?

   f. There are many tools that provide opportunities for students to communicate ideas. Common classroom tools for students include talk,

gesture, writing, reading, etc. What are the tools the students are using in the video?

g. How might the tools you use as a teacher link to a Gradual Release of
Responsibility Model for literacy?

h. How might the students' tools link to a Gradual Release of Responsibility Model for literacy?

i. How do the tools you used scaffold student learning?

3. Share your analysis with a partner or a Community of Practice.

4. Visit other frameworks for sharing and analyzing video (e.g., Deeney &
Dozier, 2015; Reichenberg (Chapter 7); Vetter & Schieble, 2016; Wetzel,
Hoffman, & Maloch, 2015; Wetzel, Maloch, & Hoffman, 2016). How
do various frameworks help you gain new perspectives into teaching and
learning? Into reflection?

9

THE GRADUAL RELEASE OF RESPONSIBILITY MODEL AND A PEDAGOGY OF VIDEO REFLECTION

Where To from Here?

Have you ever watched an Olympic athlete like gymnast Gabrielle Douglas or swimmer Michael Phelps? They make what they do appear effortless, but their so-called effortless moves are grounded in many hours of practice, training, and critique from coaches—these are examples of the GRR Model in action.

In the beginning of this text (Chapter 2), we used the example of learning to swim as a metaphor for the GRR. Novice swimmers come in all ages, and no matter the age when learning to swim, there are devices that help novice swimmers stay afloat (e.g., a kickboard), but having a more knowledgeable other (i.e., a coach, a sibling, a parent, a friend) who helps provide guidance is also critical. Learners may move in fits and starts in the beginning. Beginning swimmers may even have episodes where they accidentally inhale water and have a coughing fit or where they panic in the deep end. Novices may originally have a technique that looks more like a two-legged water bug than an Olympian. In other words, it is not easy to learn something well enough to make it appear effortless, and the process can be awkward and even anxiety inducing. As Michael Phelps said, "I think goals should never be easy, they should force you to work, even if they are uncomfortable at the time" (Park, 2012, p. 10). With encouragement from a coach, the support of teammates, and goals in mind, novices who have difficulty managing multiple tasks (e.g., breathing while swimming, turning in a lane, keeping a smooth stroke) can become swimmers who develop a strong, confident stroke and who navigate turns to complete the race. Similarly, as you have engaged in video reflection, you may have felt there were moments where you lost your breath or couldn't find the right stroke. In that discomfort, however, we hope you have also been able to reach out to a more knowledgeable other as well as peers or colleagues in a Community of Practice for support and guidance while practicing the techniques and activities of video reflection using the GRR Model.

Stop and Think

1. Look back at the various representations of the GRR Model in Chapters 1, 2, 3 and 7. Now that you have spent some time learning about, thinking about, and applying the GRR, which model is the one that most resonated with you? Why?
2. Do a Google Image search for "gradual release of responsibility model." Look through the different models that appear as images. Choose one model or adaptation that you find particularly useful. Why do you find this useful? How or where might you use this version of the model?

Reflecting on the Gradual Release of Responsibility Model

> I would like to propose a new model…a model in which the teacher assumes a more central and active role in providing instruction, a model in which practice is augmented by teacher modeling, a guided practice and substantive feedback, a model in which the teacher and child move along that continuum of task responsibility [the Gradual Release of Responsibility], a model that says just because we want students to end up taking total responsibility for task completion does not mean that we should begin by giving them total responsibility.
>
> *(Pearson, 1985, p. 736)*

Although David, a co-author on this book, wrote these words about reading teachers working with students using the GRR, the ideas are just as applicable today as they were in 1985. In the intervening decades, it has become clear that the GRR is a useful model not only for teachers working with children but for teacher educators, coaches, or other educational professionals who help teachers—novices, veterans, and those in between—to learn new ideas. In this book, we have introduced the GRR Model and a pedagogy of video reflection for critical inquiry. Our goal has been to represent the GRR through metaphors, research, anecdotes, examples, guiding questions, and activities so that readers can better understand the GRR Model and implement it in video-based reflections. Video reflection appears deceptively simple because video appears to be a straightforward record of classroom events, but the use of video is not straightforward. Those wishing to use video to change or improve teaching must be thoughtful about the pedagogical practices they use. Using video as a reflective tool takes time, practice, and support. There are key aspects of the GRR that educators need to keep in mind as they apply the model to video reflection.

The GRR Is a Dynamic Model and Process

Figure 9.1 (also in Chapter 2) represents the GRR Model. While working on this book, one of the things David shared with his co-authors was that over the years, he has noticed there is sometimes a perception that the GRR is about sliding down the continuum toward Utopia, where kids can do anything and everything on their own, which just isn't true. Rather than a smooth, linear "slide toward Utopia," movement along the diagonal often moves in fits and starts, jumping backward and forward. For example, a teacher may introduce a skill like summarizing and work on it for two or three days. As the students apply this skill, the teacher will observe that the students are getting better, and it may appear that students have nearly mastered the skill. Then after a weekend break, Monday comes, and when the teacher returns to the same skill, it may seem that the students no longer remember what summarizing is about. Here, the teacher must step in again, reintroducing some more support and taking on more responsibility until learners once again grasp the skill of summarizing. A part of the GRR Model is making continual adjustments as learners move forward.

Likewise, as preservice and inservice teachers learn particular skills related to video reflection, they will need support from more knowledgeable others and while that support will change over time, the line is also jagged and the process is non-linear in many cases. This is particularly true when teachers are attempting to wrestle with dilemmas rather than technical problems (e.g., Chapters 5 and 8). In sum, educators should keep in mind that whether working with young children or adult teachers, the GRR is a dynamic model that articulates a dynamic process.

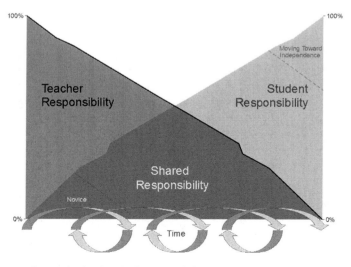

FIGURE 9.1 The gradual release of responsibility.

A More Knowledgeable Other Is Integral to the GRR Model

A prominent part of the GRR Model has always been the teacher as more knowledgeable other. When working with children, it is the teacher who helps provide guidance and scaffolding to assist students, gradually releasing them to work toward independence. Given the model's roots in reading processes and how widespread the GRR Model has become (see Chapter 1), it is not surprising that educators and researchers alike have focused on teachers as more knowledgeable other, even though peer-to-peer scaffolding is also very effective. The GRR Model has added value as well because there are few models that are applicable directly to adult learners (i.e., teachers) reflecting on their own learning, even as they consider how the model might also be applied to understanding children and youth (i.e., students in classrooms).

While there is a great deal of focus on the more knowledgeable other in teaching reading to children, there is relatively little attention to the specific role of the more knowledgeable other or facilitator in relation to video reflection. For example, when the GRR has been applied to preservice and inservice teachers learning how to teach, improve their teaching, or reflect through video, most attention has focused on the learners (i.e., the preservice and inservice teachers) with comparatively little attention focused on facilitators (e.g., teacher educators) and how they guide the use of reflection as more knowledgeable others. Furthermore, in relation to video reflection, there are more published articles and chapters that pertain to preservice teachers than inservice teachers. This is important because the role of more knowledgeable others (e.g., teacher educators, coaches, professional consultants) will vary in some important ways, depending upon whether they are working with teacher candidates, novice teachers, or veteran teachers. A more knowledgeable other is an integral element in the GRR Model.

Scaffolding Is Crucial in the GRR

Scaffolding underpins the GRR. It is the thread that runs throughout, and it is absolutely essential for effective use of the GRR. Without effective scaffolding, which is used and removed at key times, the GRR frays away, just as removing a cross thread on a piece of woven fabric loosens and ultimately frays the remaining fabric. The importance of effective scaffolding holds true for teachers, and for teacher educators. Recall in Chapter 6 how Lori, a teacher in a reading clinic, used video to reflect on her practice (specifically her use of wait time), develop scaffolds for herself (the use of a hashtag symbol to remind herself to wait), and develop scaffolds for her student Junie. Recall Caitlyn, a graduate student in the final practicum of her literacy specialist program, and how the teacher educators working with Caitlyn adapted the reflection process to release more responsibility to her. These teacher educators then moved in flexibly to provide more direction and support when Caitlyn needed guidance to adjust her guided reading format in order to address both learning objectives and classroom management challenges. Knowing how and when to build scaffolds for instruction as well as how and when to remove them is the art of using the GRR. As little scaffolding should be used as needed, but there should always be enough to ensure learning.

The previous diagram (Figure 9.1) illustrates the back-and-forth process between teacher support and student input during the process of scaffolding in the GRR. When students can't complete a learning task or are able to complete only part of a learning task, the teacher must provide more support. Likewise, when students are able to take on more of a learning task, teachers can pull back their support. When Caitlyn's teacher educator perceived that part of Caitlyn's trouble with classroom management might stem from a lack of pacing in her guided reading lessons, the teacher educator moved in to provide more scaffolding and guidance in this specific area of instruction.

In our discussions around the GRR Model, another insight David provided was that researchers and teachers alike often want to know: How much support needs to be provided within the GRR? David acknowledges that knowing how much to scaffold a learner of any age is an art. There is no easy one-size-fits-all approach. Recognizing when to provide more scaffolding support and when students can go ahead on their own requires close observation, reflection, and adaptive expertise. Like all human interactions, teacher-student interactions are dynamic. Knowledge is also dynamic. One day, a group of students may seem to have mastered a learning task, and the next day they may be unable to apply that learning in a new setting. Transfer doesn't always happen smoothly, and sometimes learning breaks down. Even in the moment of teaching, scaffolding can be added or adjusted, and teachers as well as teacher educators can draw on the GRR Model to adapt their approach, sliding up or down the GRR. Providing the right type of scaffolding, and the right amount of support, is key to success in learning.

Reflecting on Video Reflection

> Being able to 'go beyond the information' given to 'figure things out' is one of the few untarnishable joys of life. One of the great triumphs of learning (and of teaching) is to get things organised in your head in a way that permits you to know more than you 'ought' to. And this takes reflection, brooding about what it is that you know. The enemy of reflection is the breakneck pace—the thousand pictures.
>
> *(Bruner, 1996, p. 129)*

When Bruner wrote these words in 1996, video was becoming broadly available through analog 8mm video cameras, which cost around $1,000. VHS tapes were widely available, and literacy researchers were experimenting with interactive interfaces housing video, such as the *Reading Classroom Explorer* (Hughes, Packard, & Pearson, 1997). Now, two decades later, video is digital and can be uploaded to the web or even streamed in real time. The cameras in cell phones that people carry in their pocket have the ability to capture high quality video and audio. In this quick-changing landscape, it seems odd to think that there was a time without YouTube, which was created in 2005, or any of the sites for sharing photos and videos that have seamlessly meshed with our lives (e.g., Vimeo, Instagram, Snapchat, TeacherTube). It is unlikely that Bruner imagined just how many thousands of pictures would be at our fingertips in only two decades! Similar to life-loggers who record every moment of their lived experience, teachers have the ability to record their entire teaching lives. But, Bruner's words also remind us of a few truisms around video and provide some cautions.

More Video Is Not Necessarily Better Video

Capturing video of one's teaching should never be the end goal of a video record. Video records are merely a tool that produces particular affordances and constraints. Teachers and those requiring teachers to reflect on video (e.g., teacher educators, state departments of education, school administrators) must be mindful that it is not the video that makes the difference; it is the practice of reflective inquiry and engagement with the video record by the practitioner that should be the end-goal. In addition, teachers, school leaders, teacher educators, and professional consultants must recognize that some fundamentally critical issues are not easily captured by video records. Among these are the subtle positionings, pre-positionings, and even bias that occur around the intersectionalities of race, class, poverty, language use, and gender (see Chapter 8). Even when captured on video, those guiding video analysis should be aware that such intersectionalities may often be excluded from scrutiny within a Community of Practice due to fear and anxiety. As such, more knowledgeable others should intentionally introduce discussions of these "hot lava" topics (McVee & Boyd, 2016, p. 85).

Slowing Down Teaching Is One of the Best Affordances of Video

Anyone who has spent even a short while teaching or working full time in a school can speak to the breakneck pace of the school day. Schools must serve to carry out many mandates and goals, often within a tight timeframe. Modern schools were influenced by factory models of education which were predicated upon allegiance to the clock through a tight down-to-the minute schedule designed to bring efficiency to nineteenth- and early twentieth-century schools (Robinson, 2006, 2010; www.youtube.com/watch?v=zDZFcDGpL4U). The challenge is that such models seldom leave room within or even after the school day for teachers to engage in reflective practice. Memory is a useful device and can be very helpful in reflecting upon one's teaching, but across a busy school day, teachers engage with many students and face many demands. A video record is one way of lowering the cognitive and reflective load for teachers in the moment—so they can come back later at a slower pace with a relaxed mindset and thoughtful manner to analyze their teaching based on a video.

Both a Pedagogy of Video Reflection and the GRR Model Focus on Assisting Learners at the Point of Need

The GRR and a pedagogy of video reflection are both effective tools in addressing learners at the point where they need assistance. The GRR encourages teachers to seek out and assist a child at the place where the child needs help in the moment (i.e., working to master the strategy of visualization while reading). Teachers who are seeking to improve their practice in order to obtain an advanced degree or certification, meet state certification requirements, or address national standards, may also benefit from the GRR at the point of need (i.e., when an instructor views a video and helps identify an alternative strategy for teaching argumentation in academic writing). Children and youth are assisted by classroom teachers as well as their peers who can both function as more knowledgeable others. In video-study groups, participants are assisted by teacher educators, professional development consultants, teacher leaders, and also by their peers. Peers (i.e., classmates, colleagues) can also serve as more knowledgeable others, so that all responsibility is distributed across the Community of Practice.

Dynamic Assessment Is Essential in the GRR Model

With the increased focus on assessment linked to reform initiatives and the implementation of standards, it may seem odd to introduce assessment here. Many teachers and teacher candidates may feel they are already being over-assessed through increased requirements for state certifications and increased scrutiny in classroom-based teaching performance. In many schools and even colleges of education, there is heightened focus on accountability. Often, this translates into narrow interpretation of following rules, regulations, parameters, procedures, and testing. In those scenarios, the meaning of *assess* is closely aligned with its original meaning: **an assessment** was a tax levied and meant to be paid. In the current era of high-stakes testing for teachers and children, it is not unrealistic to think of a test as a tax that must be paid.

On the other hand, **to assess** also means to make a judgment or an evaluation. Another way to think of this is to evaluate growth and progress toward a goal over time. In the GRR Model, evaluating growth and progress is dynamic and ongoing. In traditional forms of assessment, a common belief is that equity is achieved when everyone is given the same task, and the goal is to get every learner to do the same task. However, true equity is created when all the support needed is given to the learner (i.e., preservice or inservice teacher) to reflect so that the learner can accomplish the task (i.e., reflection on teaching practice). Dynamic assessment focuses not so much on whether a learner "got it right" but how much support a learner needed to accomplish a task. In a pedagogy of video reflection, it is critical that those most responsible for learning in a video study group (e.g., teacher educator, literacy coach) engage in dynamic assessment for and with learners to provide targeted scaffolding for video reflection.

Work to Be Done Related to the GRR Model in Video Reflection

While our primary goal in this book has been to provide a useful guide for those wishing to apply the GRR Model to the analysis and application of videos of teaching, there is still much more that could be said on the topic. In particular, there are some areas that we feel merit the attention of literacy teachers and teacher educators as well as educational leaders, researchers, and policy makers.

Research and practice work is needed that foregrounds critical literacy and social justice alongside and in relation to video reflection. Cochran-Smith (2004) has argued that "teacher education needs to be conceptualized as both a learning problem and a political problem aimed at social justice" (pp. 1–2). As we noted in Chapter 8, there is very little work examining reflective video and justice-oriented pedagogy or social justice stances in teaching and learning based on teachers reflecting on their own teaching. (This contrasts with the expanding portraits of teachers using video as a tool to engage and help students learn content and reflect [e.g., Bruce & Chiu, 2015; Miller & McVee, 2012].) The socioeconomic, ethnic, racial, linguistic, religious, and gender diversities of classroom and society require that teachers attend specifically to these diversities by using video as a tool to reflect on their own teaching stance. Additionally, as teachers reflect on their work, they can draw upon research-based practices, learning to read and understand research visually with or without video (Bailey & Van Harken, 2014).

Cases of Video Reflection Need to Draw Upon a More Diverse Representation of Teachers and Teacher Candidates

Similar to other published work related to teaching and teacher education, cases of video reflection tend to focus on White women. This is not surprising given that approximately 84 percent of teachers in the United States are women, and this percentage continues to rise over time (Feistritzer, 2011). While there has been a slight increase in teachers of color in the United States, there is still a need to recruit and retain minority teachers of color and teachers who are multilingual. Retaining teachers can be problematic if they do not see themselves portrayed in class readings or discussions. Creating a cohort of teachers who are more representative of the children they teach has been a long-standing challenge in the United States (Haddix, 2017). In addition, although it is seldom mentioned, researchers and practitioners need to include portraits of male teachers, especially in subjects or grade levels where male teachers are not typically represented (e.g., elementary or early childhood education).

Examinations of Video Reflection in Research and Practice Are Needed that Address Inservice Teachers

The majority of studies on using video reflection in teaching focus on pre-service teachers or teachers still working toward certification. Few studies have used video reflection with experienced teachers. Shanahan, Tochelli, and Rinker (2015) completed a review of inservice teachers using video reflection and concluded that in the field of literacy, far less is known about the use of video as a reflective tool for inservice teachers; on the other hand, much more is known about how, when, and why video is used with teachers in preservice settings. When studies are carried out with experienced teachers, these are often in the context of graduate work or clinical settings (e.g., Collet, 2013). There are very few examples of experienced teachers reflecting in a professional development setting situated within their school teaching context (Shanahan & Tochelli, 2012).

Portraits of practice, analysis, and research are needed on the outcomes of requiring video reflection in new teacher assessment models such as the Education Teaching Performance Assessment (edTPA) and the Praxis Performance Assessment for Teachers (PPAT). While both the edTPA and the PPAT supply information and frameworks for video self-reflection in their practice materials and manuals, it remains to be seen how well these assessment models actually capture the complexities of teaching and reflection on teaching. This book is one attempt to provide support in this area by providing guidance to those who need to complete video reflection as part of teaching performance evaluations or frameworks. In addition, analysis of edTPA and PPAT outcomes could potentially provide more support for reflecting individually, or conversely, analysis might reveal that these assessment frameworks are not as useful as they could be. Either way, research and portraits of practice related to edTPA and PPAT are needed, particularly since these approaches do not necessarily include a focus on a Community of Practice or more knowledgeable other.

More explicit attention needs to focus on the facilitator of the video study group or more knowledgeable other within a Community of Practice. Throughout this book, we have tried to highlight the role played directly by a more knowledgeable other. We have attempted to demonstrate how the more knowledgeable other scaffolds, supports, and then, ultimately, releases responsibility to students. Within the GRR Model, the more knowledgeable other is a key position, but many portraits of video reflection minimize or fail to address this critically important role. While we consider best practices of video reflection to include the support of a more knowledgeable other and a Community of Practice, this book was written, in part, out of growing concern that individual teachers may be required to complete video reflection tasks (e.g., for certification or local or state requirements) but may not have ready access to a guide or more knowledgeable other. Providing detailed portraits of how facilitators work with learners as they engage in video reflection will help educational leaders and policy makers recognize this key role and, we hope, build in spaces, time, as well as supports for a more knowledgeable other to build and sustain a Community of Practice around video reflection.

Conclusion

There is an old saying that "You know an idea has taken hold when no one remembers where it came from." The GRR Model has shown remarkable staying power over the decades, wending its way through multiple published works by scholars and researchers. But, perhaps more importantly are the ways that the GRR has been adopted by those on the front lines of teaching. The GRR Model and various adaptations of it proliferate on the web. Multiple schools, teachers, districts, states, departments of education, and individuals have adopted the GRR Model or adapted it to fit their own needs. The various iterations of the GRR and the ways it has been adopted demonstrate a sense of shared ownership that goes far beyond what Pearson and Gallagher (1983) envisioned in their initial articulation of the GRR. The use of the GRR with video reflection is only one more iteration in the multitude of works representing the practical, influential, and dynamic nature of the GRR.

In the initial introduction of the GRR Model, Pearson and Gallagher (1983) wrote about a child's reading and a teacher's guidance:

> The hope is that every student gets to the point where she is able to accept total responsibility for the task, including the responsibility for determining whether or not she is applying the strategy appropriately (i.e., self-monitoring). But the model assumes that she will need some guidance in reaching that stage of independence and that it is precisely the teacher's role to provide such guidance. Only partly in jest we like to refer to the model as a model of "planned obsolescence" on the part of the teacher; but just because you want to end up being obsolete doesn't mean you have to start out by being obsolete! (p. 35)

These words remind us that one objective of this book is to enable teachers to become independent learners who are capable of accepting responsibility for the task of reflectively examining and interpreting video of their own teaching as well as others' teaching. The GRR Model does involve some "planned obsolescence," where as time goes by and learners learn, a teacher or guide *does* become obsolete or unnecessary when learners reach the point they can work independently. Although as Pearson and Gallagher (1983) pointed out, the teacher as guide is essential in the beginning. As for the GRR Model itself as a tool for reflection and teaching, it seems to be an example of "unplanned sustained evolution" as variations and adaptations continue to proliferate on the web in images, posters, videos, graphic representation, and throughout scholarly publications. We suspect that the GRR will continue to be a useful construct to educators for many years to come.

References

Bailey, N. M., & Van Harken, E. M. (2014). Visual images as tools of teacher inquiry. *Journal of Teacher Education, 65*(3), 241–260.

Bruce, D., & Chiu, M. M. (2015). Composing with new technology: Teacher reflections on learning digital video. *Journal of Teacher Education, 66*(3), 272–287.

Bruner, J. S. (1996). *The culture of education.* Cambridge, MA: Harvard University Press.

Cochran-Smith, M. (2004). *Walking the road: Race, diversity, and social justice.* New York, NY: Teachers College Press.

Collet, V. (2013). The gradual increase of responsibility model: Mentoring for improved intervention. In E. Ortlieb & E. H. Cheek Jr. (Eds.), *Advanced literacy practices: From the clinic to the classroom* (pp. 327–351). Bingley, UK: Emerald Group Publishing.

Feistritzer, C. E. (2011). *Profile of teachers in the U.S. 2011.* Retrieved from Washington, DC: National Center for Education Information.

Haddix, M. (2017). Diversifying teaching and teacher education: Beyond rhetoric and toward real change. *Journal of Literacy Research, 49*(1), 141–149.

Hughes, J. E., Packard, B. W.-L., & Pearson, P. D. (1997). Reading classroom explorer: Visiting classrooms via hypermedia. In C. K. Kinzer, K. A. Hinchman, & D. J. Leu (Eds.), *46 Yearbook of the National Reading Conference* (pp. 494–506). Chicago: National Reading Conference.

McVee, M. B., & Boyd, F. B. (2016). *Exploring diversity through multimodality, narrative, and dialogue: A framework for teacher reflection.* New York, NY: Routledge.

Miller, S. M., & McVee, M. B. (2012). *Multimodal composing: Learning and teaching for the digital world.* New York, NY: Routledge.

Park, A. (2012, May 15). He's baaack: Inside the mind of Michael Phelps. *Time.com.* Retrieved from http://keepingscore.blogs.time.com/2012/05/15/hes-baaack-michael-phelps-readies-to-make-more-olympic-history/.

Pearson, P. D. (1985). Changing the face of reading comprehension instruction. *The Reading Teacher, 38*(8), 724–738.

Pearson, P. D., & Gallagher, M. C. (1983). The instruction of reading comprehension. *Contemporary Educational Psychology, 8*(3), 317–344.

Robinson, K. (2006, February). *Do Schools Kill Creativity?* [Video file]. Retrieved from https://www.ted.com/talks/ken_robinson_says_schools_kill_creativity#t-698850.

Robinson, K (2010, October 14). *Changing Education Paradigms* [Video file]. Retrieved from https://www.youtube.com/watch?v=zDZFcDGpL4U).

Shanahan, L. E., & Tochelli, A. L. (2012). Video-Study Group: A context to cultivate professional relationships. In P. J. Dunston, S. K. Fullerton, C. C. Bates, K. Headley, & P. M Stecker (Eds.), *61st Literacy Research Association Conference Yearbook* (pp. 196–211). Oak Creek, WI: Literacy Research Association.

Shanahan, L. E., Tochelli, A. L., & Rinker, T. W. (2015). Insights into inservice teachers' video-facilitated reflection of literacy practices. In E. Ortlieb, M. B. McVee, & L. E. Shanahan (Eds.), *Video reflection in literacy teacher education and development: Lessons from research and practice.* (pp. 21–40). Bingley, UK: Emerald Group Publishing.

INDEX